LATINO URBAN ETHNOGRAPHY AND
THE WORK OF ELENA PADILLA

LATINOS IN CHICAGO AND THE MIDWEST

Series Editors
Frances R. Aparicio, University of Illinois at Chicago
Pedro Cabán, State University of New York
Juan Mora-Torres, De Paul University
Maria de los Angeles Torres, University of Illinois at Chicago

A list of books in the series appears at the end of this book.

Latino Urban Ethnography and the Work of Elena Padilla

EDITED BY
MÉRIDA M. RÚA

UNIVERSITY OF ILLINOIS PRESS
Urbana, Chicago, and Springfield

© 2010 by the Board of Trustees
of the University of Illinois
All rights reserved
Manufactured in the United States of America
1 2 3 4 5 C P 5 4 3 2 1
∞ This book is printed on acid-free paper.

Library of Congress Cataloging-in-Publication Data
Latino urban ethnography and the work of Elena Padilla /
edited by Mérida M. Rúa.
    p.   cm.—(Latinos in Chicago and the Midwest)
Includes bibliographical references and index.
ISBN-13: 978-0-252-03576-0 (hardcover : alk. paper)
ISBN-10: 0-252-03576-3 (hardcover : alk. paper)
ISBN-13: 978-0-252-07763-0 (pbk. : alk. paper)
ISBN-10: 0-252-07763-6 (pbk. : alk. paper)
    1. Puerto Ricans—Cultural assimilation—New York (State)—New York.
    2. Puerto Ricans—Cultural assimilation—Illinois—Chicago.
    3. Puerto Ricans—New York (State)—New York—Social conditions.
    4. Puerto Ricans—Illinois—Chicago—Social conditions.
    5. New York (N.Y.)—Social conditions.
    6. Chicago (Ill.)—Social conditions.
    7. Padilla, Elena, 1923– I. Rúa, Mérida M.
F128.9.P8L37   2010
305.868'7295—dc22   2010043115

CONTENTS

ACKNOWLEDGMENTS

First and foremost, my thanks go to Elena Padilla, whose willingness to publish her master's thesis and contribute to the project made editing this collection possible and an incredibly rewarding experience. Since 2002, when we first met at the Puerto Rican Studies Conference in Chicago, Dr. Padilla has supported this endeavor and welcomed the opportunity to engage with scholars reclaiming her work. For their part in making this volume possible, I am deeply indebted to its contributors, Zaire Z. Dinzey-Flores, Ana Yolanda Ramos Zayas, Nick De Genova, Arlene Torres, and Elena Padilla. Thank you for many rich discussions and your unfailing enthusiasm for the project.

Words of appreciation must be extended to the undergraduate students at Williams College who provided invaluable assistance at different stages of this work: Angelica Rodríguez, Christine Rodríguez, and, most especially, Taisha Rodríguez.

I would like to thank Alford A. Young Jr. and the anonymous reader who reviewed the manuscript for the University of Illinois Press. The comments, suggestions, and insights they offered made this a better book. Joan Catapano, the acquisitions editor at the press, was helpful at many turns in the book-making process, and thanks, too, to Jane Curran for superb help with copyediting and to Laurie Prendergast for putting together a top-notch index. To Frances Aparicio for her vision and championing of a series that would produce critical editions of previously unpublished manuscripts documenting the histories, struggles, and contributions of Latinos in the Midwest. She has encouraged and guided this collection from the earliest conception.

And finally, to the many who have inspired ideas, asked difficult questions, and offered good cheer when it was most needed, I am profoundly grateful.

Mérida M. Rúa

At the Crossroads of Urban Ethnography and Puerto Rican Latinidad

Mérida M. Rúa and Arlene Torres

Elena Padilla was at the crossroads as a scholar undertaking community studies in order to develop theories about social change in a rapidly changing urban landscape in the mid-twentieth century. She was asking questions about the utility of ethnographic method to address these very concerns experimenting with grounded theories and anthropological approaches—evinced in the Chicago- and New York–based studies. In her 1958 ethnography, *Up from Puerto Rico*, Padilla questioned if a positivistic approach, which entailed participant observation, would allow her to understand the Puerto Rican experience in East Harlem. *Up from Puerto Rico* was a community study that dealt with the sociocultural landscape from the perspective of the ethnographer and her interlocutors. Therein, she experimented with a grounded theoretical model, albeit unevenly throughout the work, that included perspectives of people to critically present and analyze culture and social change.[1] Her legacy is reflected in the scholarship of the contributors to this volume.

Each chapter in *Latino Urban Ethnography and the Work of Elena Padilla* addresses the contradiction embedded in the "objective" theoretical lens of urban sociology and ecological studies that do yield data about structural relations but limit our understanding of how social processes inform day-to-day social interaction in a particular social milieu in Chicago and New York.[2]

While Padilla was known, then and even now, for the work *Up from Puerto Rico* and her contribution to Julian Steward et al.'s *The People of Puerto Rico*, little is known about the work that ensued prior to these publications.[3] Padilla's 1947 master's thesis, "Puerto Rican Immigrants in New York and Chicago: A Study in Comparative Assimilation," has been more recently incorporated in the scholarship of individuals seeking to understand the

Puerto Rican and broader Latina/o experience in Chicago and the Midwest.[4] This volume seeks to focus on the thesis and to bridge the theoretical and methodological concerns represented in the larger corpus of her scholarly endeavors via the historical and contemporary analysis of the Puerto Rican experience in Chicago, New York, and Puerto Rico.

The Making of an Urban Ethnographer

At the tender age of nineteen, Elena Padilla was already a graduate student at the University of Chicago and the youngest member of a cadre of University of Puerto Rico graduates sponsored by the chancellor of the University of Puerto Rico (UPR), Jamie Benitez, in 1944. Benitez's objective was to prime the future faculty of the University of Puerto Rico as part of the nation-building project to establish a system of higher education with a largely autochthonous faculty and administration trained at elite institutions abroad. Ricardo Alegría, the first director of the Institute of Puerto Rican Culture and the founding director of the Museum of the Americas in Old San Juan, and Muna "Munita" Muñoz Lee, daughter of Puerto Rico's first popularly elected governor, Luis Muñoz Marin, and the poet, feminist, and Pan-American activist Muna Lee, were other members of the Chicago group.[5] UPR graduates were also enrolled in programs at Harvard and Michigan. Initially Padilla was selected to attend the University of Michigan medical school but she was too young for admission.[6] Benitez's vision was not only to have these individuals assume positions in academic institutions but also to develop a corps of government officials in health and human and cultural services that would participate in a nation-building project. Some of these individuals went on to become the leading figures who continued to question Puerto Rico's colonial relationship to the United States.[7] Unlike her peers, Padilla remained based in the continental United States, where she has pursued long-term research among diasporic Puerto Ricans.[8]

As a graduate student in the anthropology program at the University of Chicago from 1944 to 1947, Padilla worked with leading scholars in the discipline. She enrolled in courses with Sol Tax, Robert Redfield, Lloyd Warner, Faye Copper Cole, and John V. Murra. Famed Chicago School sociologist Louis Wirth, for whom she served as a research assistant on the Committee on Interracial Relations (1946–1947), was another central figure in her preparation at Chicago.[9] The Chicago tradition of empirical research underscores the ethnographic case study as a means to discern the sociocultural and spatial dynamics of city dwellers. Ethnographers carry out intimate and systematic investigations of urban social life and culture whereby the researcher compiles detailed accounts of direct observation, conducts formal and informal interviews with willing participants, and consults accessible documentation (i.e., institutional archives or personal collections of papers and photographs). Early studies dealt with the prevailing social questions of immigration, race relations, community structures, and a host of other social issues of the time. These scholars were interested in developing theories about how sociocultural transformations take place, on the one hand, and how individuals assimilate and are integrated in new settings, on the other hand. In short, their primary concern was how individuals or ethnic groups adapt in environments constituted by rapid social change (see the chapter by Nicholas De Genova).

Aside from the Chicago intelligentsia, Padilla consulted periodically with New York Puerto Rican labor activist and intellectual Jesús Colón and made use of his extensive personal archive for the New York portion of her research. Of Colón and his collection, Padilla wrote: "The documentary material belonged to and formed part of the personal library of a Puerto Rican labor leader in New York City who has been collecting data on the Puerto Ricans in New York for over twenty-seven years of his residency in that city."[10] Self-taught, Colón penned four hundred essays and was a regular contributor to many New York City newspapers, including the *Daily Worker* and *Daily World*. He collected books and other written materials (pamphlets, newsletters, leaflets, and periodicals) documenting Puerto Rican daily life in New York City and other parts of the country. He dedicated his life to developing grassroots leadership, unionizing workers, and bringing to the fore the plight of Puerto Rican and Latino communities as he argued for sociopolitical change. Today, the Jesús Colón collection, comprising his personal archive, correspondence, and essays, is a centerpiece of the Center for Puerto Rican Studies archive on early Puerto Rican and Latino life in the United States.

Under the direction of Tax, Redfield, and Wirth, Padilla submitted her thesis, titled "Puerto Rican Immigrants in New York and Chicago," wherein she took a comparative approach to the interplay of labor, residence, and social networks on identity and community formation. The study situates her as a pioneering scholar of Puerto Rican racial identities and inter-ethnic relations, as well as what we presently examine as latinidad (a common sense of a Latina/o identity). Padilla qualified her master's thesis as "an attempt to depict in general terms *processes* by means of which ethnic groups become integrated into the social and cultural life of the larger communities where they settle, with particular reference to what has happened to some of the ethnics in American industrial communities."[11]

Jesús Colón in personal archive, Brooklyn, New York. Source: Jesús Colón Papers, 1901–1974, Box 30, Folder 2, Archives of the Puerto Rican Diaspora, Centro de Estudios Puertorriqueños, Hunter College, CUNY.

The theoretical and methodological approaches applied by Padilla make evident the influence of Warner's style of community study where the importance of a "way of life" and variations of public interaction at the individual and collective level were prime gauges of the social adaptation of individuals to place and space.[12] Drawing on the work of William I. Thomas and Florian Znaniecki, Padilla used personal documents and life history as data and modes of analysis of the dilemmas of personal life adjustment, changing family relations, neighborhood formations, deviance, and cultural assimilation of immigrants to U.S. urban life. Moreover, her conceptual and analytic focus on "size of ethnic group" and "ecological distribution" as two factors influencing, adjusting, and shaping the acculturation and assimilation of ethnic groups in U.S. society cues Wirth's interest in density and intensity of interaction among immigrant groups as another central imprint in the study.[13]

Departing from the conventional research on urban communities, Padilla's study signals the important dimension of gender in migration studies. She focused on the recruitment and settlement of Puerto Rican women in Chicago. Moreover, Padilla earnestly deliberated on the meaning and function of the researcher in gathering, interpreting, and disseminating data. Indeed, her thesis demonstrates her affinities to a Chicago ethnographic tradition and simultaneously suggests a problematization, wittingly and unwittingly, of some of the prevailing conventions, as can be noted in her experiments with reflexivity in ethnography at a time when the social sciences almost exclusively endorsed positivism (see the chapter by Ana Y. Ramos-Zayas). Consonant with postwar African American social scientists' concerns with rural to urban migration and the effect of this transition on the mores and structural character of African Americans, Padilla explored the adjustment of Puerto Ricans (and to some extent Mexicans) to the complex urban context and the socioeconomic industrial order of U.S. society as a means to evaluate their investment in modernity.[14]

This project derives from an appreciation of this embrace of and transgression from an urban ethnographic tradition. Her work provides unique insight into the social theories that came to understand, and in some cases misunderstand and misconstrue, these formations. While unable to be as forthcoming in the thesis regarding these concerns, in her subsequent works she posed more direct questions about the cultural competency of researchers, and later, medical professionals, who "othered" the subjects of study (see Padilla, *Up from Puerto Rico*). Via her attention to the politics of representation, comparative research, and identity and community formation in relation to space, Padilla opens up our comprehension of a Latino metropolis (see the chapter by Zaire Zenit Dinzey-Flores).

The special issue of *Centro: Journal of the Center for Puerto Rican Studies* (2001) dedicated to the Puerto Rican community in Chicago underscores the intellectual debt owed to Padilla for her groundbreaking comparative research where place, both regionally and locally, is considered central in the construction of identities. Likewise, the ways in which Padilla's theoretical and methodological forays into the study of latinidad informed her analyses of a Puerto Rican experience is critically examined. Edited by Gina M. Pérez, the special issue positions Puerto Rican studies in Chicago within the sociocultural history of the city and within the emerging intellectual domains of Latina/o studies, ethnic studies, and Puerto Rican studies. In addition, the issue locates the study of Puerto Ricans in Chicago within the specialty defined in many ways by "the City"—urban ethnography.

Similar to other projects that revisit Padilla's groundbreaking scholarship, *Latino Urban Ethnography and the Work of Elena Padilla* locates Padilla in the tradition of urban ethnographers, especially those who critically tested notions of race and space. However, in this volume, a more explicit connection is presented between Padilla and the urban community studies perspective made famous by the University of Chicago and its relationship to the cultural ecology approach developed at Columbia University and the University of Illinois by Julian Steward and his colleagues. Unlike previous scholarship, this project precisely engages Padilla's earliest work in relation to her subsequent work in New York, which led to the publication of C. Wright Mills, Clarence Senior, and Rose Kohn Goldsen's *The Puerto Rican Journey* (1950).[15] Our aim here is to demonstrate not only the continuities in her work but also the shift toward an applied anthropology. In our estimation, one cannot fully grasp the significance of prior projects reclaiming her work without considering Padilla's first study, which indexes her as the innovator of a Puerto Rican and, more broadly, Latino urban ethnography that posed theoretical and methodological challenges in the discipline of anthropology, and the social sciences more broadly, as well as interdisciplinary modes of analysis.

Padilla's thesis raised questions about the use of migration as a strategy to help alleviate the economic situation of the island at the expense of migrant workers. In the footnotes to the thesis she made mention of migration policies and practices that mitigated against the well-being of Puerto Ricans on the island and in urban enclaves on the U.S. mainland. In her description and analysis of the "recent migration," she included a report authored by Puerto Rican and non–Puerto Rican graduate students from the University of Chicago, including Muñoz Lee and herself, exposing the fraudulent practices of a Chicago-based private employment agency sanctioned by the Insular Department of Labor to contract Puerto Rican women for domestic labor and men for foundry work.[16] The "Puerto Rican maids" captured headlines early in their arrival because they expressed displeasure with their working conditions. Moreover, disgruntled employers and the employment agency depicted the workers as shiftless, wanton, and diseased.[17] "Puerto Rican students at the University of Chicago," Clarence Senior noted, "took the lead in giving publicity to the complaints of some of the girls and an official investigation was made."[18] The island Senate suspended the private recruitment of labor migration from Puerto Rico until the Puerto Rican legislature adopted a new policy regulating the labor contracts of migrants.

On the heels of the Chicago contract labor controversy came the discovery in the New York City press of a "Puerto Rican problem" in the Northeast. Sensationalist articles sounded the alarm of invading islanders—promiscuous, criminal, uncivilized, and lazy in nature—overcrowding slums and overwhelming welfare department offices in the summer of 1947. Much of the commotion had to do with the fact Puerto Ricans were "the only substantial influx of colored migrants from a non-English speaking culture" entering the city.[19] Social services workers and administrators lacked the experience to deal with the new arrivals since the implementation of immigration laws restricting Southern and Eastern Europeans and excluding Asians in 1924. At the height of the pandemonium Jesús T. Piñero, the first Puerto Rican appointed governor of the island, took measures to mitigate the news reports with a $35,000 grant to Columbia University's Bureau of Applied Social Sciences to study Puerto Rican migration to New York.[20] The findings of the 1950 study were published in Mills, Senior, and Goldsen's *The Puerto Rican Journey*, primarily a report statistically documenting the "normative" experience of Puerto Rican migrants in New York City.

The Puerto Rican Journey attempted to address the question: Will Puerto Ricans follow the "classic" pattern of assimilation? The study concluded that avenues for upward mobility were narrowing, thereby encumbering Puerto Rican prospects and possibilities for assimilation. Little consideration was given to the possibility that Puerto Ricans might not want to assimilate; nor was the very model of assimilation questioned. The study also identified Puerto Rican migration to New York as distinctively different from earlier migrations because women predominated the numbers of sojourners joining the U.S. workforce. Women, the authors argued, were less able to adjust to life in the continental United States because of their limited exposure to mainstream society. Given Mills, Senior, and Goldsen's statistical findings, the profile of the Puerto Rican migrant ought to have been female; however, conceding to the conventions of the era, rather than actual findings, the image of the Puerto Rican migrant as male was cemented. Men were largely characterized as "deciders" while women were limited to the role of "followers" in the migration process. The Puerto Rican case profoundly complicated this model. In short, the data reveals that women were, in fact, forging a distinct path to ensure their economic prosperity via their migration and labor patterns.[21]

Clarence Senior in the preface to *The Puerto Rican Journey* acknowledges the research assistance and expertise of Padilla and Carmen Isales, "whose intensive interviews and close-up memoranda from the field were indispensable to the design and execution of the work."[22] Isales, a Puerto Rican social worker appointed by the YWCA to work with the migrants in Chicago, wrote reports for U.S. officials and for Puerto Rican policymakers and politicians concerning the circumstances of contract workers. Given the expertise that Padilla and Isales developed in Chicago and applied elsewhere, we gain new insight about the place of Chicago as a pivotal site in the study and scholarship of the Puerto Rican diaspora.

The thesis was also Padilla's first attempt to influence policy via grounded research and activism (see the chapter by Mérida M. Rúa). Her later work *Up from Puerto Rico* is also illustrative of the potential of ethnographic work to more directly shape social policy.[23] Working for two and a half years with a team of anthropologists, Padilla investigated the health beliefs, routines and habits, and medical care among diasporic Puerto Ricans in East Harlem.[24] Padilla described the study as "both an invention and an exploration in applying anthropology both to an urban area and to medicine."[25] In the preface to *Up from Puerto Rico*, Padilla pens: "I have written this book for the people interested in the quiet dramas of anonymous lives. It is neither an apology nor a condemnation. Rather, I hope that it will serve the cause of offering the general public access to the findings of the scientific study of society, with the additional hope that this kind of knowledge may be applicable to more skillful living and human understanding."[26] Here, she signaled the necessity for the development of a "social contract" to promote skillful living.

Consistent topics in her work include her emphasis on the internal heterogeneity of Puerto Ricans and interracial/inter-ethnic relations, housing, health and life stresses, and how they correlate with labor conditions. For example, in her "Health and Life Stress" chapter in *Up from Puerto Rico*, Padilla quoted her interlocutors—Carmen Gomez, Julio Dante, Miguelina Mendez, and Jose Gontan, among others—verbatim to provide the reader with concrete examples about Puerto Rican perspectives regarding the etiology of disease. She believed that in order to garner trust researchers had to enter a milieu that the "omniscient observer" rarely traversed.[27] In this context she also comments on the relationship between fieldwork and cultural and linguistic proficiency. Padilla begins to map out her interest in and concern for the mental health and well-being of Puerto Ricans in an urban sphere. An ethnographic turn toward applied anthropology is made more explicit here even though the seeds of this endeavor formed part of her thesis. She asks readers to question how as scholars we collude with the state and agencies that purport to improve the well-being of its citizenry. She then argues for grounded research that will provide for better health services for Puerto Ricans in New York.[28] Her scholarship predates contemporary work on the psychological effects of race and racism. Padilla sought to understand the affects of poverty, race, and racism on mental health. Day-to-day racial micro-aggressions that can become emotionally debilitating or destructive were examined to further develop our understanding about the lasting effects of racism and poverty. Notably, although Padilla was concerned with the mental health and well-being of Puerto Ricans in the community of study, her subjects were not viewed as pathological. Simply put, she portrayed the complexities of community life and the trials and tribulations of her interlocutors.

As such, she sought to challenge the paradigm of Puerto Rican pathology at the time in the popular press and academic scholarship by demonstrating the ways by which the socioeconomic environment and concomitant structures of power, informed by race, profoundly affected the lowest socioeconomic and marginalized sector of the Puerto Rican community in New York. Or as Padilla put it, "The book tells about Puerto Ricans who live in the slums and who with their other American neighbors experience the lives of the underprivileged. It has to do with living in poverty, coming to New York, with what happens to the uprooted family, the children, the health, and friends, and with the changing traditions and values of Puerto Ricans."[29]

Consistent with this point of view, Padilla's assessment of Oscar Lewis's 1966 ethnography *La Vida* is instructive. She concluded of *La Vida*:

> One might speculate from some of the data provided by Lewis himself that the Rioses are an ironical example of progress and its corollary effects of human uprootedness and alienation. Yet, Lewis is a gifted writer and *La Vida* is a well-written book; the translation of field data is so faithful that it has retained the colorful vivacity of the Spanish language; and the respondents have been verbal to the point of exhibitionism. *La Vida*, however, is neither a contribution to science nor to humanistic scholarship. Lewis has failed to provide the concept of the culture of poverty with analytical dimension, has failed to use unbiased sampling procedures in the selection of his respondents and has neglected to use historical methods to place the Rioses in their proper historical and social perspectives.[30]

Upon the completion of her studies at the University of Chicago, and on the recommendation of John V. Murra, Padilla joined Julian Steward, then on the faculty of Columbia University, in Puerto Rico on a research project, which took on a distinct ecological approach (cultural ecology). The edited volume, *The People of Puerto Rico* (1956), was the first anthropological attempt to study the culture of an entire region, taking into account political, economic, and ecological relationships. The project established the Caribbean as an important site of anthropological inquiry. Among the five senior researchers were Robert A. Manners, Sidney W. Mintz, Elena Padilla Seda, Raymond L. Scheele, and Eric R. Wolf; Padilla was the only Puerto Rican holding such a position. She had completed all of her coursework for the dissertation. Sidney Mintz and Eric Wolf, by contrast, had yet to obtain their master's degrees. While Mintz and Wolf gained international prominence for their contributions to the discipline of anthropology, Elena Padilla's contributions have remained at the far fringes of the discipline.[31]

Murra was reunited with Elena Padilla in Puerto Rico, where he was part of the Social Science Research Center at the University of Puerto

Rico and was Julian Steward's only contact in Puerto Rico at the time.[32] Steward was looking for Puerto Rican research assistants, and Murra recommended Padilla, among other Puerto Rican researchers. However, he lobbied for Padilla to be promoted to senior researcher. Through a variety of circumstances, Murra, who was an instructor in anthropology at the University of Chicago during Padilla's time there (1944–1947), was a visiting professor at UPR from 1947 to 1950.[33] He taught the first ethnology course Padilla took at Chicago. In his teaching, mainly to undergraduates, Murra stressed "ethnographic detail and human diversity." His colleagues tended to believe he "exaggerated the potential range of cultural variability," and Murra admitted he found "the diversity of human solutions more intriguing than the narrow classificatory range perceived by others." Opportunities to teach graduate students were limited to the African ethnology courses at the University of Chicago, where "the presence of colleagues like Mark Hanna Watkins or St. Clair Drake made an important difference in the classroom."[34]

The Chicago-Columbia competition regarding the development of theoretical paradigms and methodological approaches in anthropology is highlighted in the *People of Puerto* project but was foreshadowed as scholars attempted to carry out research on the Puerto Rican diaspora.[35] For example, Sol Tax and C. Everett Hughes proposed a study based on Padilla's master's thesis and the attention given to Puerto Rican contract workers because of her extra-anthropological interventions (along with Muñoz Lee and Isales). The correspondence between Ruth Senior and Sol Tax, as well as the newspaper articles from the Fundación Luis Muñoz Marín archive, indicate that Clarence Senior made it difficult for Sol Tax to get the necessary information from the Puerto Rican government to pursue his project. Senior claimed that the names of contract workers were withheld because of the public scrutiny placed on the Puerto Rican government with the intervention of Padilla and her fellow classmates. No mention was made of the prospect of a Puerto Rican migration study in New York through Columbia University's Bureau of Applied Social Sciences.[36] Tensions that ensued as a result of theoretical and methodological divides contributed to Murra's departure as field director; however, Steward argued the following in the preface to *The People of Puerto Rico*: "The project was assisted, though not closely directed, by an Advisory Committee consisting of Julian H. Steward, Clarence Senior, and John Murra. During the initial months of field work, John Murra, then visiting professor of anthropology at the University of Puerto Rico, was the field director, but subsequently his teaching duties prevented his continuing the task and Julian Steward assumed direction of all phases of the research during the remainder of the study and the preparation of the materials for publication."[37]

Padilla acknowledges Murra's contribution to the study and his insistence that she be included as a senior researcher in the project. As a mentor, Murra had a profound influence on the direction of Padilla's scholarship: "To Professor John V. Murra, who directed the community study in the field, I also owe much. He taught me my first ethnology course, and through his initiative I had the privilege of joining the Columbia University group which did the field study in Puerto Rico."[38] Her participation in the project and in the discipline nonetheless was riddled with ambivalences given the ways by which the team sought to gather data to understand social processes. On January 3, 1948, she wrote to Sol Tax of the University of Chicago's Anthropology Department:

> By ordinary mail I have sent you a couple of papers, one, a short history of the migration of Puerto Ricans to Chicago during 1946–47, and another one, sort of a "report" on the project on the Puerto Ricans. The file with all the stuff, I asked somebody to hand it in to you. In case this was not done I left it for that person on the table next to the door that is not supposed to be used in the study room. It was the last desk of that table. The file is a cardboard box that has written with pencil for Dr. Tax, Social Sc. Research Project #2. (I hope this is not too complicated). It was impossible for me to see you before I left Chicago on the 21st to work with Dr[.] C. Wright Mills in the Bureau of Applied Social Science Research at Columbia on his "Puerto Rican Migration Study". I am doing intensive interviews in East Harlem, but learning very little. The only fascinating thing I see on this migration stuff and ethnic life in American cities is that it strengthens a lot the prediction angle in sociology, which at the same time makes the investigator bored.
>
> By the 23rd I'll be leaving for Puerto Rico and join the Steward-Murra research on Puerto Rican communities. The five Columbia people, Murra and I have been having seminars in order to coordinate the project. My own opinion is that the Columbia people speak another language, specially when I am told such things as "we want to do process", etc. and one wonders how that is done in the field[,] and it is amazing how words can be given more useless content for research purposes. Murra's abilities have shown very strikingly and if he continues with us the project will probably be saved, and instead of more histories of communities, we get useful sociology.
>
> If there is anything regarding the Migration stuff you want me to clear out, please do let me know. On the other hand I hope I will have the opportunity of your advice on my fieldwork and as soon as I write down what I'll be doing, I send you a copy for criticism.
>
> I calculated an expense account of $26. on the Puerto Rican project. Those expenses were on transportation, phone calls, paper, and nothing else.

As to the follow-up of the informants I suggest the cards be mailed to them and not located in the addresses we have, then be sent to the CYO, Palmer House Hotel, Stevens Hotel, Hotpoint, etc., the main employers of Puerto Ricans in the city. It might be useful to have the cards as if signed by me, in so far as the familiarity with the name may encourage them to cooperate. Please let me know if I can be useful in anything regarding this project.

Elena Padilla articulated the need for a paradigmatic shift if social processes and cultural practices in a rapidly changing urban milieu were to be understood. We argue here that the scholarship of Elena Padilla is invaluable and fundamental to comprehensions of Latinos in the urban sphere. She is a pioneer Latina social scientist who has dedicated her career to trying to rethink the relationship of theory, method, and practice. The objective of the book is to portray some of the tensions involved in Padilla's efforts to enrich the Chicago School tradition in ethnography while also confronting some of the same challenges concerning studies of ethnic relations, the politics of scholarly production on marginalized people, and the personal and intellectual politics of a scholar.

Despite earning a Ph.D. in anthropology, Padilla has never held an academic position in an anthropology department.[39] She was offered a position at University of Illinois, where Julian Steward and Oscar Lewis were located, but she opted to remain in New York and returned an unsigned contract. She noted in an interview that there was no way she was going to the cornfields.[40] However, she did take an academic appointment for a short period of time at Michigan State University, where she once again demonstrated a turn toward applied work.[41] Faye V. Harrison and Ira Harrison cogently characterized the overriding impediment to Padilla's admittance to the "fraternity of anthropologists": the "ideologically constructed assumption concerning the necessary distinction and distance between the 'purity' of science and the 'pollution' of the partisan advocacy often embodied in subjugated knowledges."[42] Reflecting on the goals of her own scholarship, Padilla draws a clear distinction between disclosing the theoretical grounds and results of a research experiment and "doing research to confirm rather than question one's political views" (see the prologue of Padilla, "Puerto Rican Immigrants in New York and Chicago).

While the times required Padilla to bracket her deeds, these activities should not remain parenthetical, for they were, and are, central to her research interests and political commitments and mark her entry into public intellectualism. A dialectic relationship between research and activism that can also be located within an anthropolitics (borrowing from Ana Celia Zentella's call for an anthropolitical linguistics) that unravels the processes by which racist and unjust policies that categorize stigmatized groups with static and disparaged labels and hopeless outcomes stand in as representative of their real lives.[43]

While Elena Padilla may not have been formally accepted in anthropology, she remains engaged in anthropology, considering herself and her expertise as an anthropologist. And as we argue, she should be viewed as an anthropologist with community-engaged activist scholarship—her anthropolitics.[44]

Elena Padilla and the Study of U.S. Latinos

This collection of essays that reflect on the merits of "Puerto Rican Immigrants in New York and Chicago" first developed at a session of the International Congress of the Puerto Rican Studies Association in Chicago in October 2002. The association took the occasion of the meeting location to honor Padilla for her for her pioneering work in Puerto Rican studies, particularly her research on Puerto Rican Chicago. The session, entitled "Retrospective Constructions of *latinidad*: Elena Padilla, Puerto Rican Studies, and the Politics of Space," included presentations by Nicholas De Genova, Zaire Zenit Dinzey-Flores, Ana Y. Ramos-Zayas, and Mérida M. Rúa, with Arlene Torres serving as the discussant for the panel. Panelists were fortunate to have Elena Padilla present at the conference and willing to meet with us. This meeting prompted discussions about developing the essays for a larger project, with Elena Padilla providing her contemporary observations and a re-examination of her groundbreaking study in a prologue. Toward this end, Dinzey-Flores, Ramos-Zayas, and Rúa came together to present revised versions of their essays at the American Anthropological Association Annual Meeting in November 2003, also held in Chicago. This was further viewed as an opportunity to expand the audience for this work to those in the discipline of her training.

Latino Urban Ethnography and the Work of Elena Padilla begins with Padilla's prologue, followed by a complete reproduction of Padilla's 1947 University of Chicago master's thesis. The second half of the volume contains four original essays in which contributors examine how Padilla's work allows us to rethink the relationship of theory, method, and practice in urban design, working-class activism, identity politics, and the politics and purpose of knowledge production.

Zaire Zenit Dinzey-Flores, in a comparative study of segregation, tunes into what she calls Padilla's "urban Latino ecology"—the ecological exploration of Puerto Rican everyday ethnic and racial associations—to examine the cadence of routine sociospatial interactions in Chicago, New York, and Puerto Rico. Highlighting the geographic, physical, and social locations in "Puerto Rican Immigrants in New York and Chicago," Dinzey-Flores pursues Padilla's contingent interest in home and work life to uncover housing design vis-à-vis industry in the production of racially segregated Puerto Rican urban spaces. Reading Padilla's footnotes as a semi-public transcript of her scholarly activism, Mérida M. Rúa presents a historical account and contemporary ethnographic analysis of the ways in which the footnotes in scholarship and everyday life need to be recuperated and examined for what they can reveal about the political commitments of scholars, individuals, and collectives in an urban environment.

Nicholas De Genova provides a textual analysis of Padilla's account of the racialization and re-racialization of Puerto Ricans in Chicago as a "moment of possibility" (following Walter Benjamin). He suggests that the emergence of a Puerto Rican migrant social formation found in Padilla's investigation of acculturation and assimilation in fact intimates a budding sense of latinidad, and one that is profoundly gendered in form and content. Taking on questions of Latinos' absence from discussions of U.S. pubic intellectualism, Ana Y. Ramos-Zayas gleans from Padilla's academic career and the "personal narrative" she adopts in her work as a means to interrogate the rigid distinction between public and private in the manifestation of the public intellectual. The life and work of Padilla offers a unique opportunity to consider the ways in which the crude compartmentalization "public/private" actually assists in decoding racial and gender disparity in academic and public life.

In short, *Latino Urban Ethnography and the Work of Elena Padilla* will serve as a critical introduction, for many, to the work of Elena Padilla. It is not an exhaustive study but rather one that encourages provocative dialogues concerning the remarkable work of Padilla's engagement with race, space, and sociospatial configurations. This edited volume is, more importantly, our attempt to recuperate those theoretical and methodological interventions, thus continuing Padilla's project to produce knowledge that "may be applicable to more skillful living and human understanding."

NOTES

1. Elena Padilla, *Up from Puerto Rico* (New York: Columbia University Press, 1958).
2. Mindful of Padilla's objection of the rubric of "Latino" to describe and interpret the lives of diverse populations of Spanish-speaking descent, because of the potential of such categories to distort and obliterate critical historical, political,

social, and economic distinctions among populations, the title *Latino Urban Ethnography and the Work of Elena Padilla* was nonetheless selected because it best captures the unique analytic lens she provides to the study of a Latino metropolis. Padilla's thesis is clearly about Puerto Ricans, yet it is also an early Latino studies project using a relational Puerto Rican studies framework. See Elena Padilla, "Retrospect of Ethnomedical Research among Puerto Ricans: Living at the Margin of East Harlem," in *The Anthropology of Lower Income Urban Enclaves: The Case of East Harlem*, edited by J. Friedenberg (New York: New York Academy of Sciences, 1995).

3. Julian Steward, Robert A. Manners, Eric R. Wolf, Elena Padilla Seda, Sidney W. Mintz, and Robert L. Scheele, *The People of Puerto Rico: A Study in Social Anthropology* (Urbana: University of Illinois Press, 1956).

4. Elena Padilla, "Puerto Rican Immigrants in New York and Chicago: A Study in Comparative Assimilation" (master's thesis, University of Chicago, 1947). The thesis is reprinted in part 1 of this volume; all citations are to the reprint.

5. Muñoz Marin was president of the Puerto Rican Senate during the years his daughter attended the University of Chicago.

6. Personal communication with Elena Padilla, October 20, 2005.

7. The University of Puerto Rico (UPR) at Rio Piedras, instituted as a teacher-training school in the beginning of the nineteenth century, has always served as a tool to regulate Puerto Rican culture and society. Teachers were trained with the objective of grooming an "Americanized" workforce. Decades later, the university became the locus of Pan-Americanization efforts, where Puerto Rico served as the arch linking U.S. and Latin American culture. During this formation period, UPR developed as a center of Hispanic studies, where notably in the 1950s the public university system secured the right to offer its courses in Spanish and likewise became a hub of anti-imperialist activity. John Howland Rowe, "An Interview with John V. Murra," *Hispanic American Historical Review* 64, 4 (1984): 633–653; Antonio Lauria-Perricelli, "A Study in Historical and Critical Anthropology: The Making of 'The People of Puerto Rico'" (Ph.D. diss., New School for Social Research, 1989), p. 29.

8. Other members of the Chicago cohort included Angel Quintero and Milton Pabón; both men held faculty positions at the University of Puerto Rico. In both cases, their offspring have also become prominent figures in Puerto Rican studies and the University of Puerto Rico. Angel G. Quintero Rivera is a professor at the Center for Social Research at the University of Puerto Rico and is known for his work on salsa music; Carlos Pabon is known for his work as part of the postmodern radical statehood sector of Puerto Rican studies.

9. Louis Wirth, Sol Tax, and E. C. Hughes supervised the Committee on Interracial Relations, Division of Social Sciences at the University of Chicago. Padilla was at Chicago about a decade after the departmental split between anthropology and sociology; however, there still remained ties between the disciplines as noted in the lineup of scholars with whom she worked, and more notably within her master's thesis itself.

10. Padilla, "Puerto Rican Immigrants," p. 49; letter from Elena Padilla to Jesús Colón, December 26, 1945, Box 3, Folder 2; letter from Elena Padilla to Jesús Colón, October 3, 1946, Box 3, Folder 5; letter from Elena Padilla to Jesús Colón, December 9, 1946, Box 3, Folder 5, all in the Jesús Colón Papers, 1901–1974, Archives of the Puerto Rican Diaspora, Centro de estudios puertorriqueños, Hunter College, CUNY.

11. Padilla, "Puerto Rican Immigrants," p. 31; emphasis added.

12. Faye V. Harrison, "Introduction: An African Diaspora Perspective for Urban Anthropology," *Urban Anthropology: Studies in Cultural Systems and World Economic Development* 17, 2–3 (1988): 111–141; Alford A. Young Jr. and Donald Deskins Jr., "Early Traditions of African-American Sociological Thought," *Annual Review of Sociology* 27, 1 (2001): 445–477.

13. Padilla remarked that her use of an ecological perspective was limited to demographic distribution, lacking a specific link to social class (personal communication, October 20, 2005).

14. See Young and Deskins, "Early Traditions."

15. Gina M. Pérez, ed., *Centro: Journal of the Center for Puerto Rican Studies* 13, 2 (2001), Special Issue on Puerto Rican Community; Judith Friedenberg, ed., *The Anthropology of Lower Income Urban Enclaves: The Case of East Harlem.* New York: New York Academy of Science, 1995.

16. Héctor Alvarez, Anne Duvendeek, Henry Goodman, Muna Muñoz, Milton Pabón, Elena Padilla, Albert Rees, and Manuel Zambrana, "Preliminary Report on Puerto Rican Workers in Chicago," Welfare Council of Metropolitan Chicago Papers, Chicago Historical Society (now Chicago History Museum) Archives, November 25, 1946.

17. "Maid Problem," *New Republic,* April 28, 1947, p. 7.

18. Clarence Senior, *Puerto Rican Emigration* (Rio Piedras: Social Science Research Center, University of Puerto Rico, 1947), p. 38.

19. C. Wright Mills, Clarence Senior, and Rose Kohn Goldsen, *The Puerto Rican Journey: New York's Newest Migrants* (New York: Harper and Row, 1950), p. 87.

20. John V. Murra, "Review of *The Puerto Rican Journey: New York's Newest Migrants,*" *Hispanic American Historical Review* 31, 4 (1951): 680–681. The following articles were compiled for the president of the Puerto Rican Senate: Luis Muñoz Marin, "Puerto Rican Drift to Mainland Gains," *New York Times,* July 31, 1947; Albert J. Gordon, "Officials Worried by Influx of Migrant Puerto Ricans," *New York Times,* August 2, 1947; Albert J. Gordon, "Crime Increasing in 'Little Spain,'" *New York Times,* August 3, 1947; "Puerto Rican Progress," *New York Times,* August 7, 1947; "Economy of Puerto Rico," *New York Times,* August 7, 1947; "Governor of Puerto Rico Planning Study by Columbia of Migration," *New York Times,* August 8, 1947; "Columbia Accepts Puerto Rico Study," *New York Times,* August 10, 1947; "Puerto Rican Governor Calls Influx a Trifle," *New York Herald Tribune,* August 10, 1947; "Sugar-Bowl Migrants," *Time,* August 11, 1947; "Columbia Is Ready for

Migrant Study," *New York Times,* October 14, 1947 (section IV, subsection 1, series 2, subseries 1C, Fundación Luis Muñoz Marin).

21. Women made up 63 percent of Puerto Rican migrants; men made up 37 percent. According to Mills, Senior, and Goldsen, the preponderance of women was a defining characteristic of Puerto Rican migration to New York City (*Puerto Rican Journey,* pp. 23–26).

22. Clarence Senior, preface to ibid., p. x.

23. See Friedenberg, *Anthropology of Lower Income Urban Enclaves.* After earning her doctorate from Columbia University, Padilla secured a clerkship at the medical school of Cornell University, where she directed the cultural component of a mental health project concerned with Puerto Ricans in a New York City barrio, out of which emerged the study *Up from Puerto Rico.*

24. According to sociologist Clarence Senior, *Up from Puerto Rico* was the first major study about Puerto Ricans in the United States carried out under the direction of a Puerto Rican (Senior, "Review of *Up from Puerto Rico* by Elena Padilla," *American Sociological Review* 24, 2 [1959], p. 287). The study has been ignored in historical overviews and attempts to construct intellectual lineages of urban anthropology. See Ulf Hannerz, *Exploring the City: Inquires toward an Urban Anthropology* (New York: Columbia University Press, 1980); Roger Sanjeck, "Urban Anthropology in the 1980s: A World View," *Annual Review of Anthropology* 19 (1990): 151–186.

25. Elena Padilla, "Retrospect of Ethnomedical Research among Puerto Ricans: Living at the Margin of East Harlem," in *The Anthropology of Lower Income Urban Enclaves: The Case of East Harlem," edited by J. Friedenberg (New York: New York Academy of Sciences, 1995).*

26. Padilla, *Up from Puerto Rico,* p. xiii.

27. Renato Rosaldo, *Culture and Truth: The Remaking of Social Analysis* (Boston: Beacon Press, 1993).

28. Public Image of Mental Health Services, Jack Elinson, Elena Padilla, and Marvin E. Perkins (1967); Mental Training and Public Health Manpower; Master Plan for Comprehensive Mental Health and Mental Retardation Services in New York City, Marvin E. Perkins and Elena Padilla (1967); Stephen E. Goldston and Elena Padilla (report produced for NIMH 1971).

29. Padilla, *Up from Puerto Rico,* p. viii.

30. Padilla, "Review of *La Vida: A Puerto Rican Family in the Culture of Poverty—San Juan and New York* by Oscar Lewis," *Political Science Quarterly* 82, 4 (December 1967): 651–652. Muna Muñoz Lee served as a translator for Lewis so Padilla may actually be complimenting Muñoz Lee in the review. Oscar Lewis's acknowledgments in *La Vida* state: "To Muna Muñoz Lee I am deeply grateful for her excellent translation of the field data upon which this volume is based."

31. Refer to Antonio Lauria-Perricelli and Robert Duncan for a more extensive discussion of *The People of Puerto Rico* project. In her effort to re-historicize the discipline of anthropology, Arlene Torres has reviewed and critically assessed the work

and contributions of Elena Padilla to the field. Lauria-Perricelli, "Study in Historical and Critical Anthropology"; Torres, "Re-Articulating Hidden Histories: Puerto Rican Ethnography in the Late Twentieth Century," paper presented at *New Perspectives in Latino/Latina Studies Lecture Series,* University of Michigan, 1999; Ronald Duncan, ed., *The Anthropology of the People of Puerto Rico* (Puerto Rico: Inter American University of Puerto Rico, 1979); Joan Vincent, *Anthropology and Politics: Visions, Traditions, and Trends* (Tucson: University of Arizona Press, 1990).

32. Clarence Senior was the director of the Social Science Research Center of the University of Puerto Rico, 1945–1948. From 1948 to 1949 he was director of fieldwork for the study of Puerto Rican migrants in New York City based out of Columbia University.

33. After the Second World War, the Social Science Research Council awarded Murra a fellowship to return to the Andes to continue fieldwork. Upon trying to secure his travel documents, Murra discovered that the U.S. government would not allow him to travel. Moreover, the Justice Department was holding up his naturalization (he had to sue to become a citizen). From 1937 to 1939 he had served in the Spanish Republican Army, Fifteenth International Brigade. His return to the Andes was postponed; however, this led to an interlude in the Caribbean. (Rowe, "Interview with John V. Murra").

34. Ibid., pp. 645–646.

35. Pérez notes: "The nexus of University of Chicago researchers and Puerto Rican government officials has important historical precedents. Rexford Tugwell, governor of Puerto Rico from 1941 to 1946, was also a professor at the University of Chicago, and Jaime Benítez, one of the founders of the Social Science Research Center at the University of Puerto Rico in 1945, was a University of Chicago student." Clarence Senior was then director of the center and the one who proposed the project to Steward when both men were at Columbia University (Steward et al., *People of Puerto Rico*). Gina M. Pérez, *The Near Northwest Side Story: Migration, Displacement, and Puerto Rican Families* (Berkeley: University of California Press, 2005), p. 216, fn. 28.

36. Letter from Sol Tax to Clarence Senior, July 15, 1947; letter from Ruth M. Senior to Sol Tax, July 22, 1947; letter from Sol Tax to Ruth M. Senior, August 5, 1947; and letter from Ruth M. Senior to Sol Tax, August 8, 1947, all in Box 256, Folder 4, Sol Tax Papers, Special Collections Research Center, University of Chicago Library.

37. Steward et al., *People of Puerto Rico,* p. vi.

38. Elena Padilla, "Nocorá: An Agrarian Reform Sugar Community in Puerto Rico" (Ph.D. diss., Columbia University, 1951), p. ii.

39. Padilla has held academic positions in various departments of administrative medicine, politics, public health, public service, and psychiatry and preventative medicine. She was a scholar in residence at Saint Barnabas Hospital in the Bronx and currently is a fellow at the New York Academy of Medicine.

40. Personal communication with Elena Padilla at the 5th International Congress of the Puerto Rican Studies Association, Chicago, October 5, 2002.

41. Padilla served as acting director of the Comprehensive State Health Planning Agency in Michigan and professor of psychiatry at Michigan State University from 1970 to 1972.

42. Faye V. Harrison and Ira E. Harrison, "Introduction: Anthropology, African Americans, and the Emancipation of a Subjugated Knowledge," in *African-American Pioneers in Anthropology,* edited by Ira E. Harrison and Faye V. Harrison (Urbana: University of Illinois Press, 1999), p. 11.

43. Zentella proposes an anthropolitical linguistics with the purpose of comprehending and facilitating "a stigmatized group's attempts to construct a positive self within an economic and political context that relegates its members to static and disparaged ethnic, racial, [gender] and class identities, and that identifies them with static and disparaged linguistic codes." Ana Celia Zentella, *Growing Up Bilingual: Puerto Rican Children in New York* (Malden, Mass.: Blackwell, 1997), p. 13.

44. See Faye V. Harrison, *Outsider Within: Reworking Anthropology in the Global Age* (Urbana: University of Illinois Press, 2008); Roslado, *Culture and Truth*. In recovery efforts of the works and lives of accomplished, yet unjustly neglected, scholars, as we draw attention to their work, we also tend to give prominence to the hierarchical adviser/advisee relationships; that is, the intellectual imprint of advisers as mentors on their students—for example, the focus on Padilla's affiliations with Tax, Wirth, and Steward. While this was important, arguably deserving of our critical attention are the significance of the more horizontal, or at least less hierarchical, intellectual and activist community engagements of which Elena Padilla was a part, in particular her relationship to Muna Muñoz Lee, Jesús Colón, and John V. Murra. The fellowship Padilla experienced with these individuals left a profound impression in her first academic work and extended throughout the rest of her career. More explicitly, it is a legacy of socially conscious, rigorous academic work that challenges how academia understands aggrieved populations, but that also, and more to the point, seeks to actually affect some positive change in the immediate circumstances in which people found themselves.

WORKS CITED

Alvarez, Héctor, Anne Duvendeek, Henry Goodman, Muna Muñoz, Milton Pabón, Elena Padilla, Albert Rees, and Manuel Zambrana. "Preliminary Report on Puerto Rican Workers in Chicago." Welfare Council of Metropolitan Chicago Papers, Chicago Historical Society (now Chicago History Museum) Archives, November 25, 1946.

Duncan, Ronald, ed. *The Anthropology of the People of Puerto Rico.* Puerto Rico: Inter American University of Puerto Rico, 1979.

Friedenberg, Judith, ed. *The Anthropology of Lower Income Urban Enclaves: The Case of East Harlem.* New York: New York Academy of Sciences, 1995.

Hannerz, Ulf. *Exploring the City: Inquires toward an Urban Anthropology.* New York: Columbia University Press, 1980.

Harrison, Faye V. "An Africa Diaspora Perspective for Urban Anthropology." *Urban Anthropology: Studies in Cultural Systems and World Economic Development* 17, 2–3 (1988): 111–141.

———. *Outsider Within: Reworking Anthropology in the Global Age.* Urbana: University of Illinois Press, 2008.

Harrison, Faye V., and Ira E. Harrison. "Introduction: Anthropology, African Americans, and the Emancipation of a Subjugated Knowledge." In *African-American Pioneers in Anthropology,* edited by Ira E. Harrison and Faye V. Harrison. Urbana: University of Illinois Press, 1999.

Lauria-Perricelli, Antonio. "A Study in Historical and Critical Anthropology: The Making of 'The People of Puerto Rico.'" Ph.D. diss., political and social science, New School for Social Research, 1989.

Mills, C. Wright, Clarence Senior, and Rose Kohn Goldsen. *The Puerto Rican Journey: New York's Newest Migrants.* New York: Harper and Row, 1950. Murra, John V. "Review of *The Puerto Rican Journey: New York's Newest Migrants.*" *Hispanic American Historical Review* 31, 4 (1951): 680–681.

Padilla, Elena. "Nocora: An Agrarian Reform Sugar Community in Puerto Rico." Ph.D. dissertation, Anthropology, Columbia University, 1951.

———. "Puerto Rican Immigrants in New York and Chicago: A Study in Comparative Assimilation." Master's thesis, Anthropology, University of Chicago, 1947.

———. "Retrospect of Ethnomedical Research among Puerto Ricans: Living at the Margin of East Harlem." In *The Anthropology of Lower Income Urban Enclaves: The Case of East Harlem,* edited by J. Friedenberg. New York: New York Academy of Sciences, 1995.

———. "Review of *La Vida: A Puerto Rican Family in the Culture of Poverty—San Juan and New York* by Oscar Lewis." *Political Science Quarterly* 82, 4 (December 1967): 651–652.

———. *Up from Puerto Rico.* New York: Columbia University Press, 1958.

Pérez, Gina M., ed. *Centro: Journal of the Center for Puerto Rican Studies* 13, 2 (2001), Special Issue on Puerto Rican Community in Chicago.

———. *The Near Northwest Side Story: Migration, Displacement, and Puerto Rican Families.* Berkeley: University of California Press, 2005.

Rosaldo, Renato. *Culture and Truth: The Remaking of Social Analysis.* Boston: Beacon Press, 1993.

Rowe, John Howland. "Interview with John V. Murra." *Hispanic American Historical Review* 64, 4 (1984): 633–653.

Sanjeck, Roger. "Urban Anthropology in the 1980s: A World View." *Annual Review of Anthropology* 19 (1990): 151–186.

Senior, Clarence. *Puerto Rican Emigration.* Rio Piedras: Social Science Research Center, University of Puerto Rico, 1947.

———. "Review of *Up from Puerto Rico.*" *American Sociological Review* 24, 2 (1959): 287–288.

Steward, Julian, Robert A. Manners, Eric R. Wolf, Elena Padilla Seda, Sidney W.

Mintz, and Robert L. Scheele. *The People of Puerto Rico: A Study in Social Anthropology.* Urbana: University of Illinois Press, 1956.

Torres, Arlene. "Re-Articulating Hidden Histories: Puerto Rican Ethnography in the Late Twentieth Century." Paper presented at *New Perspectives in Latino/Latina Studies Lecture Series,* University of Michigan, 1999.

Vincent, Joan. *Anthropology and Politics: Visions, Traditions, and Trends.* Tucson: University of Arizona Press, 1990.

Young, Alford A., Jr., and Donald Deskins Jr. "Early Traditions in African American Social Thought." *Annual Review of Sociology* 27, 1 (2001): 445–477.

Zentella, Ana Celia. *Growing Up Bilingual: Puerto Rican Children in New York.* Malden, Mass.: Blackwell, 1997.

PART ONE

Puerto Rican Immigrants in New York and Chicago

A Study in Comparative Assimilation

Elena Padilla

Looking Back and Thinking Forward

The study comparing Puerto Ricans in Chicago with Puerto Ricans in New York was, in effect, an effort by a then young graduate student to find out if anthropological methods and techniques could be applied to learn how a population of migrants of common backgrounds (who for all practical socioeconomic and cultural purposes were immigrants) living in two different American cities differed or were similar to each other. The study was largely provoked by the works of William I. Thomas and Florian Znaniecki on Polish peasants in Europe and in the United States as well as by the Yankee City studies of Lloyd Warner and by studies on urbanization by C. Everett Hughes, Robert E. Park, Robert Redfield, and Louis Wirth—who at that time were the social science brain trust of the University of Chicago. The study was done to meet requirements for the master's degree in the Anthropology Department. It was the very first scholarly effort by someone trying to be but not yet born as an anthropologist.

The Chicago–New York investigation was guided by the following questions:

—What happens to the social arrangements and social beliefs of an immigrant population when its members move from their homeland to live in two different American cities?

—Does living in proximity with people of the same social class and cultural background make a difference, and if so, what kind of difference for them in the new society?

—If that happens to be the case, how applicable are the concepts of human ecology, adaptation, acculturation, and assimilation to understanding their accommodation to living in an American city?

These questions were also stimulated by the personal experiences of observing and participating in protest activities of these two Puerto Rican migrant subgroups in the 1940s.

> —Can a study such as this be conducted today among Puerto Rican migrants and Mexican immigrants in the current sociopolitical and economic contexts?
> —Has the status of knowledge changed, and if so, how?

Following is an exploration of these questions in a forward mode.

Population Composition

In spite of their status as major American cities, Chicago and New York were different in their sociopolitical and economic contexts and demography and have continued to be so in spite of the growth of their suburbs and in the composition of newcomers. Furthermore, not only did New York have more than an additional one-third the population of Chicago, but their socioeconomic and ethnic compositions differed.[1]

Segregation and Integration

The two largest minorities in New York were the Blacks and the Puerto Ricans, both living in segregated communities. They depended largely on the sewing industry and, increasingly, on services, especially in health care, which was heavily unionized. Eventually this was to lead to massive unionization and to leadership roles of national and international significance as in the case of labor leader Dennis Rivera. Unionization also led to the election of Herman Badillo as congressman (Bronx) and later on to the elections of Jose Serrano (Bronx) and Nydia Velazquez (Brooklyn). In Chicago, the largest minorities were Blacks and Mexicans, who largely depended on food services and heavy industries for employment. The increase of Puerto Ricans in turn led to politicalization and to the election of such congressmen as Luis Gutierrez.

In both Chicago and New York City, Puerto Ricans lived in their own "colonies" or settlements, in delimited geographic areas in the cities—or, in the larger American politicolegal context, they were segregated, ghettoized. Yet, these communities were largely integrated in spite of their segregation from the larger American society. Whites, especially those with middle and higher incomes, had moved to co-ops and higher-rent areas in the cities and the suburbs in the peripheries of the cities. The minority populations of both cities depended heavily on welfare aid due to high unemployment and lower wages. That reliance on welfare has been and is still changing.

Also, access within the cities and from the cities to the suburbs depended on mass transit, as the geographic space and its usage kept changing, as zoning and urban planning had become dominant factors in their development. As the whites abandoned their own ethnic base neighborhoods, immigration of minorities into both cities replaced the neighborhoods that had been previously occupied by whites.

Changing Societal Contexts

The Puerto Rican migration to New York City had started before the American occupation of the island, with massive increases after the two world wars. Puerto Ricans occupied areas abandoned by white ethnics and neighboring Blacks. In those areas, they lived in apartments, houses, rooming houses, hotels, and, later on, in shelters. In time, also, the population composition of the city had continued to change with large outflows (about 1.4 million or 8 percent of the total population) moving to the suburbs and to the Sun Belt, including Puerto Ricans. These population movements were paralleled by massive inflows of newcomers (1.0 million or 6 percent of the population) to the point that in balance between 2000 and 2006 the New York City population had increased by 205,750, while increasing immigration from the Dominican Republic and Mexico had become dominant.[2] Still, Puerto Ricans comprised the largest Hispanic group, making up almost one half of those populations.

In Chicago, the situation was different from that of New York. Among Puerto Ricans, coming first from the island as "contract workers" for agricultural and manufacturing companies, the tendency was to leave (*escaparse*) those jobs, move to areas occupied by Mexican immigrants, and rent rooms and apartments within those neighborhoods. Their commonality was largely based on sharing the same socioeconomic status, speaking Spanish, and not knowing English, yet the social identity and loyalty remained Puerto Rican while "Hispanic" was used with reference to other Spanish-speaking people or to their own network of interpersonal social relations. Yet, over time, Puerto Ricans in Chicago as in New York were to continue to affirm their national identity in the city.

Latino/Hispanic Solidarity

In a cultural/historical perspective, the Hispanic solidarity in the United States has its roots in the Spanish conquest of the New World. This led to distinct national and regional cultural and ecological adaptations and political solidarity strengthened by their liberation from Spain in Latin

America. Yet, the structural relation between and among Spanish-speaking populations in the United States as Latinos/Hispanics, first initiated by the White House, became more a product of American educational, political, and economic institutions formalized by the U.S. census, which presumably used these designations for simplification. Such definitions had been developed by the Office of Management and Budget and standardized in 2003. These designations simplified statistical compilations and analyses but were not based on a process of linguistic and cultural integration or assimilation within those populations. Hispanics or Latinos came to be a national classification for persons identified as "Cuban, Mexican, Puerto Rican, South or Central American, or other Spanish culture or origin regardless of race." To be noted here is that immigrants from the Dominican Republic, in spite of their numbers, are not identified as a distinct population group. Nonetheless, as had been observed by Bosworth, "Hispanics are not a monolithic group," and the official extension of a national classification to small, local areas and districts leads to confusion and intergroup tensions. As Juan Flores put it, "It is that core of resistance and self affirmation that makes the Puerto Rican case so deeply revealing."[3] Thus, the sense of national identity of Puerto Ricans qua Puerto Ricans in New York and in Chicago has continued as self-reference based on social and cultural values, and standards of behavior, continue, especially those that are linked to family relations.[4]

As rapid changes have occurred in the processes of social, economic, and political urbanization in Chicago and New York and in their surrounding suburbs, the question emerges about what has happened to minorities in such contexts. When so-called urban slums have been "Trumped" and have given way to large and expensive condos, how do minorities cope? Research is needed to understand better the contemporary conceptualizations of urban living and of the opportunities and limitations that minorities face. Anything else is political commentary.[5]

What follows is the original text of the master's thesis as approved by the Anthropology Department of the University of Chicago in June 1947. Further research on social and cultural transformation in Chicago is needed in order to access change appropriately.

Elena Padilla
May 29, 2010
New York City

NOTES

1. The study of Puerto Ricans in Chicago and in New York was not connected at all with that undertaken as part of Julian H. Steward's research project to apply anthropological methods to the study of a nation, in this case, Puerto Rico. The Steward project was sponsored by the Rockefeller Foundation. My own association with Steward started with an introduction by John V. Murra, a University of Chicago instructor in ethnology who was then a visiting professor at the University of Puerto Rico and whom Steward, a professor at Columbia University, had designated as field director of the Puerto Rico social anthropology project. This was also an opportunity to do predoctoral field research in one of the local communities on the island with a team that included four other social anthropologists in addition to myself: Robert A. Manners, Sidney W. Mintz, and Eric R. Wolf. Raymond L. Scheele, who had already finished his Ph.D., was assigned to study the San Juan upper class. We all had the opportunity to hire University of Puerto Rico graduates as research assistants. As a team exploring what was a new approach in anthropology, moving from small social units to complex national and international sociopolitical and market processes, the Steward team met regularly for lengthy discussions and clarification of what were altogether new directions for social and cultural anthropology. The study that led to *Up from Puerto Rico* was a product of interdisciplinary research by anthropologists and physicians in an urban area in the Puerto Rican barrio of East Harlem in New York City. This was an intrusion into medical anthropology since it linked ways of life and belief systems to health, illness, and medical care practices in that community. The anthropological component of this research was a modification of Steward's cultural ecology theoretical model since the social arrangements and ways of life of this neighborhood, its problems, and approaches to solutions called for more specialized political economy approaches of an urban area.

Up from Puerto Rico required the participation of anthropology graduate students as team workers who carried out special studies designed to link ways of life and cultural belief systems of a neighborhood in New York City to concepts and practices around health and disease and medical care in the contexts of their economic and sociocultural adaptations in this city. These ranged from health studies in relation to family organization, the role of schools in the socialization of children, to work and dependence on social welfare, small businesses and illegal practices like distribution of illegal drugs, selling stolen goods, recreation and gambling, to institutional forms of social control such as magic, spiritualism, to formal religious beliefs and practices and church going. The examination of these problems centered on cultural factors in definitions of health and disease and their management throughout the life cycle—from birth to death—and experiences with physical and emotional conditions, treatments, recovery, rehabilitation, and chronicity.

2. See "Overview of Race and Hispanic Origin," *Census Brief,* March 2001; Michael Barone, "Demography Is Destiny: The Realignment of America," *Wall Street Journal,* May 8, 2007, http://www.opinionjournal.com/editorial/feature

.html?id=110010045 (accessed April 30, 2010); Dennis Cauchon and Paul Over-berg, "Big Apple, Southern Cities Tops in Growth," *USA Today,* June 28,2007; B. Sanderson, "NY Crowds In," *New York Post,* April 5, 2007; William Bosworth, "Key Changes in the Bronx over the Past Decades," http://www.lehman.edu/deannss/bronxdatactr/discover/bxtime.htm (accessed April 30, 2010).

3. Juan Flores, *Divided Borders: Essays on Puerto Rican Identity* (Houston: Arte Publico Press, 1993), p. 14.

4. Ibid.

5. There is a difference between reporting the theoretical basis and findings of a research activity and doing research to confirm rather than to question one's personal political views. Still, one can be an anthropologist by training and go for additional training in other fields, depending on one's professional interests, (e.g., studying economics of development or community mental health and bringing them into anthropological frameworks). One still is an anthropologist, but one who goes beyond the traditional boundaries of the field. One still can investigate the pros and cons of one's theoretical assumptions rather than confirming one's political perspectives. Although social and political research has become a public, market-oriented enterprise, not all scholars are oriented to or even can reach large markets of audiences, even if they try. Others can exercise such outreach outside the confines of strict theories and methods while still following rigorous analytical principles.

*   *   *

Editor's note:
The remainder of part 1 reproduces Elena Padilla's "Puerto Rican Immigrants in New York and Chicago: A Study in Comparative Assimilation." The thesis is reproduced in its original format, with occasional minor changes in punctuation and correction of grammatical errors and inconsistencies.

Preface

This study is about comparative acculturation and assimilation. It is an attempt to depict in general terms processes by means of which ethnic[1] groups become integrated into the social and cultural life of the larger communities where they settle, with particular reference to what has happened to some of the ethnics in American industrial communities. The basic problems of this study are, however, limited to the analyses of the main observable similarities and differences found between immigrants and ethnics who settle in "colonies," in comparison to those who settle scattered along the larger American communities. The two-fold factors of "size of the ethnic group" and "ecological distribution" are analyzed as basic axes influencing, modifying, and, to a large extent, shaping the acculturation and assimilation of ethnics in American society.

The Puerto Rican immigrants in the city of Chicago, who compose a relatively small number of individuals, were selected as type-immigrants for the analysis of that aspect of the problem dealing with immigrants living in relative isolation from each other. The Puerto Ricans in New York City, who compose comparatively a much larger population than the Puerto Ricans in Chicago, and who are ecologically distributed in the city of New York in "colonies" or districts of major concentration of Puerto Ricans, were selected for comparative purposes. Differentials between Puerto Rican immigrants in both Chicago and New York to Puerto Ricans in the homeland are identified and analyzed with reference to a discussion on the backgrounds of the Puerto Rican immigrants.

Summaries of data on the Mexican immigrants in South Chicago and the Italian immigrants in New York City are presented to provide further comparisons on ethnic acculturation and assimilation in urban America.

Note

1. "Ethnic" is a classificatory term applied to members of a cultural or racial group within a larger society. In this thesis the term "ethnic" is used with special reference to the cultural and racial groups deviant from the dominant American society.

CHAPTER ONE

Acculturation and Assimilation

Present sociological knowledge on the phenomena and the implied processes undergone by ethnic groups in American communities has received a momentum through intensive accomplished research. The onset of scientific production along these lines was marked by the appearance of such classical works as W. I. Thomas and F. Znaniecki's *The Polish Peasant in Europe and in America*[1] and R. E. Park and H. A. Miller's *Old World Traits Transplanted,*[2] among others. More recently the application of modern anthropological methods and techniques as used by W. L. Warner and his associates in the study of ethnic groups in a New England industrial community have propounded new and useful knowledge on the dynamics of the social transferences that operate to condition ethnic groups to American life.[3]

The concepts of acculturation and assimilation are at present sharp enough to be of methodological precision in the analysis of certain situational observations of social life. A Sub-Committee for the Study of Acculturation of the Social Science Research Council provided a basic outline for future research on the problems of acculturation by defining both the contextual and the limiting factors of the process involved.

> Acculturation comprehends those phenomena which result when groups of individuals having different cultures come into continuous first hand contacts, with subsequent changes in the original cultural patterns of either or both groups.[4]

The said sub-committee distinguished "culture change," of which acculturation is but one aspect, and "assimilation," which may be an aspect of acculturation, as well as "diffusion," which as a process does not necessarily imply contacts between the members of the societies involved in the modification of their original cultures.[5]

The process of adapting the established ways of social life of a community or of individuals to other types and kinds of social life is a gradual process. The very nature of culture claims for such a gradation. The culture of a people or the standardized social behavior of the members of a given society tends to be consistent with each of its aspects, the ideal possibility being that of total integration. The tendency towards maintaining an equilibrium among the adapted new ways of behavior and the use of new tools in a culture imply by themselves the existence of a total system composed of parts. The conception of a systematic entity implies that a change of any of the parts of the total whole will produce a change in the total whole itself. Because a culture has a time persistence and changes within that context, and its implicit function is to provide man with suitable adaptations to social life, it is "regenerative," to use Redfield's term. The regeneration or modification of a culture through direct human contact between two different societies implies, therefore, that either or both of the cultures of the societies are to be modified in a direction suitable for both or either of the groups in order to avoid the destruction of both through the destruction of the standardized ways of doing things prevailing in both societies.

The implication that culture is selective[6]—that is, that matters of choice operate in the process of acculturation—is self-evident. The phenomenon of cultural selection, nevertheless, does not necessarily mean that conflict is avoided. What seems to happen is that the choice of a different aspect of culture tends towards a greater integration, and that if the result is conflict, the peoples involved in such a situation either compromise in some way so as to articulate the adopted way to their own, or substitute the old with the new completely, or resist the acquisition of the new element by stressing their own element and reacting against the conflictual element. Conflict is at least symptomatic of integration and ultimately a form of integration.[7]

The end products of acculturation, therefore, may take the forms of acceptance, some compromise in adaptation, or reaction.[8] Acceptance ultimately may be equated with assimilation.[9] Srole[10] described assimilation as a phenomenon to be distinguished from acculturation in a contentual level. His dichotomy is of undoubted methodological value.

> Acculturation may be described as the transformation in the culture of one group or society in the direction of conformity with the culture of another group or society with which the first group is in contact. Social assimilation, on the other hand, has reference to the absorption or incorporation into a society's social organization of an intrusive or neighboring, and originally differentiated, group to a point in which the latter's differentiated character and identity are lost.[11]

acc. vs. ass.

Field research under the direction of W.L. Warner in a situation where both acculturation and assimilation were at work in a highly integrated American community was the empirical test of that dichotomy. The results brought forth several scientific generalizations on the acculturation and assimilation of ethnic groups in American society.[12]

Ethnic Groups in American Society

Ethnics, *per se,* occupy minimal status in the American society with the exception of prominent refugees and their descendants. American society with its tendency towards uniformity—which means conformity to its prevailing standards—sanctions diversity in a negative form. The more different from the dominant society the social background of an immigrant, the more difficult is his acceptance by the dominant society, and the more difficult for him to learn to articulate socially with America. It takes, therefore, less time for an Englishman than for an Italian to become American. The explanation for such a statement is to be found in analyses of both factors that hinder and factors that foster a more rapid acculturation and assimilation of foreign groups into the American population.

The Ethnic Community

The social histories of particular immigrant groups in American society have followed to a large extent a more or less uniform pattern. Twentieth century migrations from Europe and other parts of the world to the United States responded to such factors as political, religious, economic, or general social conditions prevailing in the nation of emigration. The first migrants to arrive usually settled by and probably mixed with an already established ethnic neighborhood that was close to the factories where they worked. The increase in the number of immigrants would tend, on the other hand, to produce a concentration of the members of the same nationality or social group in residential nuclei or colonies. This has been one of the characteristic results of the arrival and establishment of large numbers of immigrants with a common background in American industrial communities. The situation is known throughout American cities under such names as "Little Italy," "Little Warsaw," "Little Greece," et cetera. Correlated with this stage of ecological concentration is found the appearance of an immigrant community organization with a semi-autonomous social sub-system operating as a satellite structure of the dominant American community. Immigrants and their descendants with a social personality at variance with the American type of orientation will channelize their relationships with the American community through the ethnic community and both its formal and informal organizations. They will learn about American social values and attitudes while their contacts are more intimately with the members of their own group. The disorganizing effect, so to speak, of the larger American society on the social sub-system of an immigrant colony necessarily occurs insofar as such factors as communication, propaganda, economic organization, and the realization of many basic social needs of the ethnics have to be obtained in dependency from the larger American society. In other words, although the personal contacts among the members of an immigrant group living in a colony are greater than the personal contacts between the members of the host society and the immigrants, there are countless impersonal ways of channelizing processes of contact between the larger society and the immigrants. Ethnics living in colonies in American cities may learn, after a certain period of residence in an American community, the "culture" or proper social conventions, rituals, and values of American society, but while they remain being a group with an identity of their own, namely, that which characterizes the members of the group in one way or another at variance with the larger society, they will not be as fully accepted by the larger society as if they were natives. Assimilation, then, does not occur in the organized immigrant colonies. The fact that colonies are usually renovated by new migrations explains the above statement to a great extent.[13] Assimilation occurs when the colony starts a process of breaking down, and social solidarity increases with the larger society, whereas it is diminishing within the colony. This usually happens to members of the second or third generation of immigrants in this country.

The third stage in the ecological aspect of the immigrant social life is characterized by a disintegration of the consolidated residential area and a new orientation in the configuration of formal organizations. It is in this stage where presumably the crystallization of a broader perspective takes place as represented by the partial acceptance of the social orientation as provided by American life. This is a stage where at least overtly the dominant ways of behavior of the host societies are accepted by the immigrants, and probably in a compromise with the dominant traits of the original society. In terms of process, the results of this situation of adjustment eventually will yield the total assimilation of the ethnic into the inner rituals of American social life. Gardner summarizes the social history of the immigrant communities in the cities of the United States as follows:

In the industrial areas each of the newcomers followed a similar pattern. Each new group tended to move in at the bottom of the community structure. The latest comers always had the lowest status; they moved into the poorest districts; they were looked down upon by all the older groups and were considered the poorest, dirtiest, least intelligent and less desirable group in the community. Each new group formed its own neighborhood, speaking its own language, and living its own culture, and generally formed a little island separated from the groups around it. The passage of time, however, gradually reduced this separation and its barriers. The children learned new ways and moved to new neighborhoods.[14]

children learn & move on

The Colony

The situation in the colony curbs both the processes of acculturation and assimilation insofar as the colony is in some sense a reaction of an ethnic group against its incorporation into the host society. The colony resists contacts by providing a cell of relationships among the ethnics, in many occasions exclusive of other non-ethnic individuals. The ethnic community organization develops associated with the ecological concentration of ethnics. The breaking down or disintegration of the residential base of a colony breaks the ethnic community by building direct contacts between the ethnics as individuals and the larger society.

The colony situation has been widely discussed in the literature.[15] Data on the Mexican ethnics in Chicago and on the Italians in New York City illustrate to a large extent the patterning of ethnic life in American industrial communities.

Mexicans in Chicago

Mexican migration to Chicago is a special aspect of the general migration problem of Mexicans to the United States. The Mexicans compose the largest Spanish-speaking population in this country.[16] Mexican migration obeys to a great extent the need of establishing a balance between the unemployed and low-wage earners on one hand, and the supply of labor and relatively higher-paid jobs in the United States.[17] Besides the economic causes, Mexican migrants to this country have been influenced by other phenomena of crises that were common to Mexico during the twenties, namely among others, the revolutionary period that covered over ten years of the recent history of Mexico.

Background of the Mexican Immigrants

Mexican society is largely of a village type.[18] Mexican migrants belong mostly to the lower classes of wage earners and the middle classes of crafts-men and small business owners.[19] Mexican society has a very strong Span-ish-Catholic component in its social and cultural make-up. Social control in this society is organized mainly around the principles of the Catholic Church. The family of procreation is the temporal power that regulates and organizes the socialization of its members to more extent than any other secular institution. There is a double system of standards operating for the sexes. Society is lax in regard to the overt behavior of men but imposes strong controls over the women. Age institutions operate to subordinate the younger people to the older ones. The family is the supreme authority in the home, and the mother, although powerless and subordinated, is a venerated figure. The social role of women is mostly in the home in devo-tion to their husbands and children. Women are supposed to be virginal before marriage and loyal to their husbands after marriage, but men are not necessarily acting wrong if they carry on an illicit love affair. Women are not supposed to work for a living since men carry the responsibility of being the providers of economic satisfactions for the family. Divorce is seen with contempt, disapproval being greatest against women. Older children work for their aged parents and live in their parents' home even after they marry and have children. Reverence to the parents and the ancestral household increases with the age of the children.[20]

Mexican society, in other words, settles the basic human relations within a family structure that finds a sacred counterpart in the Catholic Church.

In the United States the directions taken by the processes of acculturation and assimilation of the Mexican migrants are in many instances at great variance with the original pattern of Mexican society. In the pages that follow, the main changes operating in Mexican immigrants in this country are to be outlined and analyzed with reference to the main overt patterns of adjustment developed by Mexicans in this country. The settlement of Mexicans in South Chicago was selected for this purpose insofar as it is probably the most representative Mexican nuclei in this city, as well as one of the best known in the literature.

The Mexican Colony in South Chicago

Mexican migration to Chicago became a mass phenomenon in 1923.[21] Before this year, Mexicans in this city formed a very small group. The mass migra-

Mex → Chicago b/c Steel mills labor

tion that started in 1923 was in answer to the labor market in the steel mills. Several hundreds of Mexican laborers were contracted as strike breakers in the Southwest by the Illinois Steel Company during a strike at their plants in Chicago. As strike breakers, the Mexicans gained much antipathy from the community where they settled. The steel mills provided them with shelter in their property areas in South Chicago to prevent increasing antagonisms.

Probably because of the circumstances surrounding the Mexican mass migration to Chicago, it would consist mainly of young unmarried adults. Immigrants already established in the city helped their friends and relatives to come by sending them money for the trip and giving them housing until they could find jobs.[22]

After 1924, when the steel mills were laying off men, the railroad companies and the meatpacking industries became sources of employment for Mexican labor. In 1924 more than one thousand Mexicans appeared on the payroll of the Illinois Steel Company. By this time, the first Catholic Church for Spanish-speaking peoples was established in Chicago.[23] The appearance of this church indicated the presence of a strong institution in the organization of an ethnic sub-system in the Chicago area.

The Mexican colony in South Chicago settled around the steel mill areas and the properties of the railroad companies. Houses tended to be small and in bad condition. Coal stoves were in many instances used as winter heaters. Mexican shops and small businesses appeared soon in the development of the colony. Restaurants, pool halls, barber shops, tailor shops, movies, grocery stores, and express services owned and exploited by Mexicans operated to satisfy the necessities of the Mexican immigrants. Societies, clubs, and other organizations with an exclusive Mexican membership appeared early in the life of the colony. It is to be remarked that the first organized structure that appeared in the Mexican community of South Chicago was the Catholic Church. Bi-national associations like the Woodmen of the World, the *Frente Popular Mexicano*, and the *Cruz Azul* made their appearance in the colony to promote channels of relationships with the original society. Athletic associations and clubs for secular entertainment of the community were organized also.

In 1936 the Mexican workers joined formally the trade union movements in industry. During the 1946 strike at the steel mills in South Chicago, Mexican pickets participated actively. Early in 1946 the International Workers' Order succeeded in organizing a Mexican chapter in Chicago. At present, Mexican workers own a building in South Chicago for the celebration of civic, educational, and general social activities. The South Chicago Community Center is probably a very significant institution in channelizing the social relationships of young Mexicans within the larger American community.

In Chicago most Mexicans have continued to be Catholics. At present there are at least two Catholic churches in the South Chicago area. Baur reports the assistance to these churches of no less than five hundred Mexicans on Sundays. This figure is considerably high if compared to a membership of twelve to fifty individuals in the five Protestant congregations for Mexicans in South Chicago.

The Mexican family structure suffers modifications under the firsthand contacts with American society. The most affected relationships are those between the sexes and those between the generations. The fact that Mexican women in this society are on many occasions forced to leave the home and become economic providers for their family is a most significant factor in changing the types of relationships between the sexes. Together with the economic independence of women, other kinds of control are weakened and the status of Mexican women in the community is changed. The effects, so to speak, have been in many instances demoralizing to the Mexican family. The conflict between the generations is most noted between the parents and the American-born Mexicans who consider themselves Americans and who accept the standards of American society as the "right" ones. The conflict between Mexican and American standards in the home is a partial explanation for the anti-social behavior among the second-generation youths.

Italians in New York City

Italy constitutes what is probably the single country in Europe that furnished the United States with the greatest number of immigrants.[24] Italians are reckoned in this country since early in the history of its colonization. The story of mass immigration of Italians to this country in terms of its arithmetical maximum, however, belongs to the last two decades of the nineteenth century and to the first decade of this century.[25] Italian immigration was to a large extent an escape from political repression and a rural economy based on absentee-ownership, uneven distribution of land, and heavy taxation.[26] Plagues and other demographic factors complete the picture, partially the picture of the crises, which culminated in releasing Italy from masses of small farmers, laborers, and traders. The growth of the Fascist state and its reorientation of the mobility of the Italian population towards the Italians colonies, plus the establishment of a quota system by the United States for the admittance of immigrants, reduced the figures of Italian immigration to this country in considerable numbers.

The native Italian population in the United States in 1940 was 1,623,580 individuals,[27] while there was a total of 2,971,200 individuals of Italian or mixed parentage.[28]

> Railways, highways, subways, skyways, built mostly by Italian gang labor, and associated more closely than anything else, in the American mind, with modern Italian immigration to these shores, roar now through cities and areas in which our fellow Italian Americans today participate in all current vocations, professions, careers, rewards, splendors, and miseries.
>
> The thickest areas, of course, are New York, where Fiorella La Guardia is Mayor and Edward Corsi is a Deputy Commissioner of Public Welfare; New England's textile centers and truck farms; Chicago and other big cities on the Great Lakes; bright spots in Florida where they help grow oranges; another in the Mississippi delta; and out on the Pacific Coast.[29]

The Italian Colony in New York City

There are various Italian settlements in New York. These settlement nuclei comprise the greatest concentration of Italians in this country.[30] The greatest clusters of Italians are located in Brooklyn, Manhattan, and the Bronx. The first Italian neighborhood in New York was in the downtown district of Manhattan in a section of Mulberry Street known to the Italians as the "Mulberry Bend." In New York the Italians have shown the tendency to concentrate residentially following their ecological distribution in the ancestral society. Neighbors in Italy tend to be neighbors in New York.[31] The prevalence of dialectical provinces in Italy and the "nationality feeling" attached to villages, towns, provinces, and regions explain partially this trend.

Occupationally the Italian immigrants are distributed along several lines. Italians usually start at the bottom of the occupational hierarchy, and their upward mobility in this structure usually runs parallel to the increase in useful contacts with the larger society. The bottom occupations of Italians are those of unskilled workers, small traders, sellers of cheap statuary, and organ grinders.[32] Italians were the most important single ethnic element in the construction of the Lexington Avenue subway. This is significant because it was in connection with this occupation that the first organized Italian labor movement in New York City arose.[33]

The increasing acceptance of Italians in the occupational hierarchy of the city is indicated by the participation of Italians in better-paid jobs than those opened for them at the greatest peak of their mass migration. Laborers, chauffeurs, barbers, tailors, shoemakers, clerks, painters, mechanics, salesmen, bakers, plasterers, carpenters, cooks, pressers, butchers, ice-dealers, waiters, printers, bricklayers, drivers, operators, machinists, plumbers, electricians, cabinet makers, upholsterers, grocers, fruit dealers, laundry workers, restaurant workers, auto-mechanics, cutters, masons, needle-workers, etc., are the occupations usually performed by native Italians and native Americans of mixed or Italian parentage.[34] Italians are also prominent in the crafts, the professions, and the industries.[35] This ethnic group—the immigrants and the American descendants—have already invaded the whole structural hierarchy of the occupational and economic activities of the city of New York.

Labor unions have been active in proselytizing Italian membership. The International Ladies' Garment Workers Union claimed that about 100,000 members of its total membership of 250,000 for Greater New York were either Italians or of Italian parentage.[36] Dressmakers of Italian origin have been organized since 1909. The Amalgamated Clothing Workers' Union has about 15,000 Italian workers on its membership lists. About 100,000 Italians are members of the building trade unions. In many instances, the total membership or a considerable majority of the membership of a union is Italian.[37] In connection with organized labor forces, other organizations have been found. The Italian Labor Educational Bureau operates to provide individual orientation on the economic problems of the working classes plus militant labor and educational propaganda through broadcast and written publication.[38]

The Catholic Church is probably the strongest sacred institution maintaining the coaptation of the Italian nuclei in New York and maintaining the structural connections with the homeland society. As sub-structures of the Catholic Churches, parochial schools have been established providing both secular and religious training. The Italian language is taught in these schools, and it is also included in the curricula of schools of the city located in Italian neighborhoods.[39]

There are some thirty Catholic churches, chapels, and missions in the Italian neighborhoods of New York.[40] About 5,000 Italian Protestants belong to the Waldensian, which is of Italian origin. Most of the Italians in New York, nevertheless, have continued to be Catholics.[41]

The Italians have established hospitals and clinics for their sick. The Columbus Hospital, the Italian Medical Center, and the Parkway Hospital, among others, are institutions owned by Italians and served mostly by Italians and for Italian patients.[42]

Political activities of the members of the Italian colony are of two types: interest in American politics, and chiefly in New York local politics, is found among the Italian Americans; interest in Italian politics is diffused among large groups of Italians and in relatively lesser groups of Italo-Americans.[43] Associations with political programs have appeared in New York. Fascist groupings and associations were prominent during the days preceding the last war. Communist, Socialist, and Anarchist organizations had open conflicts with the Fascist press and associations, and with each other. Italian politics had its strongholds in the largest Italian press in New York.

Newspapers and magazines published in Italian have a wide circulation among the New York Italians. News and articles about the homeland and about the host society that would relate to the Italian colony received wide publicity.

Two different tendencies may be noted among the Italians in New York operating to a large extent in relationship to the length of time they have spent in the country: (1) a strong nationalistic feeling towards the homeland as it mainly prevails among native Italians of recent arrival, and (2) a feeling of identification of the homeland with American society, which is commonly found among the native Italians who migrated in their childhood or early adolescence and whose social orientation was shaped by American society, and among the second generation of Italian immigrants, and to a much greater extent among the members of the third generation of Italian immigrants who were born and raised in this country.[44]

Time has been most important and decisive in the conditioning of Italians to American society. The relationships between the larger American society and the ethnic society increase while those between the ethnic society and the homeland decrease. This generality operates for the Italian immigrants as well as for all other ethnics in American society.

Scattered Ethnics

Small numbers of immigrants with a common national or traditional background tend to live in the community in relative isolation from each other, following no pattern of ecological concentration. They may find accommodation within an already established "colony" of ethnics with a similar social or cultural background, but they do not tend to establish their own colony unless they increase numerically to the point where the foundations of a community organization could be crystallized. Scattered ethnics, therefore, have responded to the host society on an individual level.

In the absence of direct control from a community organization of the type of his original society, the scattered ethnic tends to rely more and more on his individual direction than in the traditional institutions that oriented him socially, and looks for his adjustment to the host society as an individual.

The host society, on the other hand, does not have an organized attitude towards an individual in comparison to the mechanisms of resistance it has developed in order to maintain apart from the more divergent groups of ethnics from its prevailing standards. The scattered ethnics living in relative isolation from each other, and lacking the facilities of direct and continuous and almost exclusive contacts with other ethnics of a common traditional background, becomes acculturated and assimilated in a relatively shorter period of time than the larger number of ethnics who concentrate on certain ecological areas forming a community of their own inside the larger American community.

Test Cases

The Puerto Rican immigrants in New York City have been selected as a test group to be compared with the Puerto Rican immigrants in Chicago. The former composed a rather large population of Puerto Ricans who have established their residence in consolidated neighborhoods or a "colony" with a community organization of its own where contacts between the individual ethnics and the host society are less than those among the members of the ethnic community itself. The Puerto Ricans in Chicago, on the other hand, consist of a group of scattered families and individuals established in the city in relative isolation from each other, and of recently arrived contract workers recruited in Puerto Rico by a Chicago employment agency, who have tended to move into the Mexican neighborhoods in Chicago.

The data on both the Puerto Ricans in New York and in Chicago are examined with reference to the double factors of ecology versus relative size of the immigrant group, and its determinants on the processes of acculturation and assimilation.

NOTES

1. W. I. Thomas and F. Znaniecki, *The Polish Peasant in Europe and in America* (2 vols., New York: A.A. Knopf Co., 1927).

2. R. E. Park and H. A. Miller, *Old World Traits Transplanted* (New York: Harper and Brothers, 1921).

3. W. L. Warner and Leo Srole, *The Social Systems of American Ethnic Groups,* Yankee City Series, vol. III (New Haven: Yale University Press, 1945).

4. R. Redfield, R. Linton, and M. J. Herksovitz, "Memorandum for the Study of Acculturation," *American Anthropologist,* XXXVIII (January–March, 1936), p. 149.

5. *Ibid.,* pp. 149–150.

6. R. Linton (ed.), *Acculturation in Seven American Indian Tribes* (New York: D. Appleton-Century Co., 1940), p. 487.

7. R. Redfield, "Cooperation and Conflict as Modes of Social Integration in Cultural Change" (Lecture delivered at the Oriental Institute, University of Chicago, November 30, 1945).

8. Redfield, Linton, and Herskovitz, *op. cit.*, p. 152.

9. *Ibid.*

10. L. Srole, "Ethnic Groups and American Society" (Unpublished Ph.D. dissertation, Dept. of Anthropology, University of Chicago, 1940).

11. *Ibid.*, p. 5.

12. Warner and Srole, *op. cit.*

13. The quota system has changed this condition as being operational in cases of immigrants whose entrance into this country is restricted.

14. B. B. Gardner, *Human Relations in Industry* (Chicago: R. D. Irwin, 1945), p. 256.

15. See bibliography.

16. U.S. Bureau of the Census, *Fifteenth Census of the United States: 1930. Population,* Vol. II (Washington: Government Printing Office, 1933), pp. 27–34.

17. M. Gamio, *Mexican Immigration to the United States* (Chicago: University of Chicago Press, 1930), p. 20.

18. R. Redfield, *Tepoztlan* (Chicago: University of Chicago Press, 1941), p. 18.

19. E. J., "Delinquency among Mexican Boys in South Chicago" (Unpublished Master's Thesis, Dept. of Sociology, University of Chicago, 1938), p. 20.

20. M.O. Winter, *Mexico and Her People Today* (Boston: The Page Company, 1918), p. 164.

21. Baur, *op. cit.*, pp. 1 and 23.

22. *Ibid.*, p. 20.

23. *Ibid.*, p. 1.

24. Federal Writers' Project, *The Italians of New York* (New York: Random House, 1938), p. 218.

25. *Ibid.*, pp. 5–10.

26. *Ibid.*, pp. 36 ff.

27. U.S. Bureau of the Census, *Statistical Abstract of the United States: 1944–1945* (Washington: Government Printing Office, 1945), p. 40.

28. *Ibid.*, p. 46.

29. W. Seabrook, *These Foreigners* (New York: Harcourt, Brace and Company, 1938), p. 85.

30. In 1940 the Federal Census reported a native Italian population of 584,075 individuals in New York.

31. Park and Miller, *op. cit.*, p. 156.

32. *Ibid.*, p. 64 and *passim.*

33. *Ibid.*, p. 61.

34. *Ibid.*, p. 64.

35. *Ibid., passim.*
36. *Ibid.,* p. 64.
37. *Ibid.,* pp. 65 ff.
38. *Ibid.,* p. 67 f.
39. *Ibid.,* p. 115.
40. *Ibid.,* p. 82.
41. *Ibid.,* p. 75 and *passim.*
42. *Ibid.,* p. 112.
43. *Ibid.,* pp. 93 ff.
44. *Ibid.,* p. 224 f.

CHAPTER TWO

Methods

The materials used in this study were obtained by three different methods: (1) field work, (2) consultation of unpublished documents, and (3) consultation of the published literature.

Field Work

The material on the Puerto Rican immigrants in Chicago was obtained in the field through observation, participation, and the recording of verbalizations. Formal and informal interviews were an important aspect of this part of the research. In relation to the field work, a point to be discussed is that of the native investigator. The field material was collected by a native Puerto Rican who had lived in Chicago for about two years. This point seems important insofar as the field worker, since the beginning of the study, was aware of the fact that the rapport established with the informants would be very much influenced by this circumstance, as also would be the data obtained. The field worker knew some of the informants quite intimately for a period of about a year before this research was planned. These individuals were visited and informed about the research, and nevertheless, they did not seem to accept the field worker in this role, but persisted in continuing their relationship with her on a friendly level. This situation seems to have operated in two ways in relation to the data obtained from these individuals: (1) they tried to impress the field worker with their success and socio-economic status in Chicago and in Puerto Rico, and (2) they resisted giving information on subjects they would consider a negation of the above, i.e., actual incomes, unsuccessful relationships with Americans, etc.

It must be pointed out that the above observations are particularly noticeable in light-skinned Puerto Ricans who speak English relatively well and who are engaged either in business or in the professions. Formal interviews with these individuals were highly unsuccessful. It proved better to "exploit" their interest in impressing the field worker, and informal conversations were very useful in this inquiry. The data were checked and more important information obtained from their Puerto Rican acquaintances in the city. Those Puerto Ricans who knew each other gossiped about their countrymen.

A different type of experience occurred with those informants the field worker did not know before the study was planned. These Puerto Rican informants, at the beginning of their relationship with the field worker, took her in this role, although they dropped it very soon, either in the first or second interview.

Conversations and interviews were conducted in Spanish with members of the first generation of Puerto Ricans. Usually words and phrases were said in English whenever it was easier for either the field worker or the informant to express themselves in this language. Words like "subway," "streetcar," "drinks," "nice," "show," etc., were always said in English.

Conversations with members of the second generation of Puerto Ricans or with members of the first generation whose spouses were unable to speak in Spanish were conducted in English most of the time, with the exception of those members of the second generation who were able to speak and understand Spanish.

The fact that the field worker had known or heard about some of their relatives or friends or their home towns, or just said something about Puerto Rico was very helpful in establishing rapport. The use of mixed Spanish and English in the conversations was also of much help insofar as it avoided embarrassments due to a certain inability of expression in using just one of the two languages throughout all of the conversations.

Data on the recent Puerto Rican migration to the Chicago area were obtained during informal conversations and from written statements or verbalizations from the migrants.[1]

To summarize: there are some advantages as well as disadvantages in being taken for a member of a group investigated. The main advantages lie in the fact that the investigator is in a better position than a stranger is to identify in a shorter period of time certain types of attitudes and overt behavior, namely, those that are individualities and those that are to a greater extent common to a larger number of members of the group. The main disadvantage of being a native investigator lies in the fact that biases are very difficult to check, and that the personal equation is probably greater than in the cases when the investigator is quite familiarized with the subject matter of his study but is not sentimentally or emotionally bound to it. The matter of bias is probably one that varies in degree and not necessarily in kind. It is nevertheless unavoidable. In regard to this particular research, an obstacle was found in regard to the type and quality of the data obtained. It has been already stated that informants systematically tried to impress the investigator about their success in the Unites States. The investigator was always under the impression that they felt they had to act in that particular way because they thought it would not be pleasing to have a countrywoman and a friend have certain kinds of information about them. Of course, the possibility that the investigator was not sophisticated enough to handle the interview-situations in more suitable ways should not be forgotten.

Unpublished Documents

Most of the information on the Puerto Rican immigrants in New York City was obtained in a field trip to New York City where documentary material was consulted. The documents were selected and copied on the basis of their relevance to the corpus of the study. The documentary material belonged to and formed part of the personal library of a Puerto Rican labor leader in New York City who has been collecting data on the Puerto Ricans in New York for over twenty-seven years of his residency in that city. The material consists of newspapers, manifestos, invitations, letters, advertisements, articles, and speeches dealing directly with the Puerto Rican immigrants and other Spanish-speaking ethnics in New York City.

Unpublished studies on the Puerto Rican immigrants were also consulted.

Published Data

The literature was consulted and used in this paper in connection with the material on Puerto Rico, on the Puerto Ricans in New York City, and on other ethnics discussed in this paper.[2]

Notes

1. The data collected among the recent Puerto Rican migrants in Chicago were obtained in collaboration with Miss Muna Muñoz-Lee.

2. See bibliography.

CHAPTER THREE

Background of the Puerto Rican Migrants

Puerto Rico: The Country and Its People

The Country

The island of Puerto Rico is the smallest of the Greater Antilles with an area of 3,435 square miles. It lies between the Atlantic Ocean and the Caribbean Sea at a distance of 950 miles from the coast of Florida and 500 miles from the coast of Venezuela. Seismically the island is in the earthquake and hurricane belts. Climatically it is a tropical land. Its summer temperature averages eighty degrees Fahrenheit and its winter temperature averages seventy-six degrees Fahrenheit. Narrow alluvial plains skirt the island, and a range of central mountains runs through it from east to west. The highest peak of the *cordillera* is 4,398 feet above sea level. Rainfall is varied and ranges from 26 to 145 inches in some areas: showers generally last a few minutes and are followed by a bright, warm sunshine.[1]

Economic, Social, and Political Background

SPAIN AND PUERTO RICO   The island was opened to the Spanish Empire after Christopher Columbus landed there in 1493. It was then mainly populated by Indians of the Arawak-Maipure[2] linguistic family, which had probably migrated from South America as linguistic, archeological, and ethnological data point out. The first successful attempt to establish a Spanish outpost in the island actually occurred in 1508 after Ponce de Leon arrived and started friendly relations with the natives.[3] About fifty years after the establishment of the Spanish government in Puerto Rico, the Indian population had almost vanished. Disease, warfare, miscegenation, and general social disorganization seem to have been the main causes for its disappearance.[4] The island became a Spanish frontier where the established Spanish ways of social life crystallized through time into the dominant persistent ways of life of the Puerto Rican people.

Native technology of food gathering and production, as well as the native use of seeds and vegetables, were learned and adopted by the Spanish conquerors. Arawak-Maipure words were incorporated into the Spanish language.[5]

African slavery was introduced in 1511 in response to a demand for agricultural labor. Slavery was prolonged until 1873 when it was legally abolished by the Spanish government. By this time only five per cent of the Negro population was enslaved.[6] Free labor was very much in practice, and both white and Negro men worked together in the same fields.[7] Due to the fact that there were no strong social barriers separating the whites from the Negroes, miscegenation occurred to a very high degree. This phenomenon occurred mainly through the intermarriage or consensual marriage of white men to Negro or mulatto women.

This firsthand and direct contacts between the African and the dominant Spanish population resulted in a continuous exchange of cultural phenomena that operated in such a way as to integrate both by increasing the content of the Spanish culture in the island. Present folk-like social views show to a great extent that state of equilibrium produced by the adjustment of both cultural types. This is especially observed in the relationships between the individuals and the unknown as is indicated by the contiguous existence of Catholicism mixed with the beliefs in witchcraft, ghosts, and magic that usually prevail in the peasantry and to a great extent among the city-dwellers.

The society that developed in the island had characteristics of folk and peasant life.[8] Agriculture substituted for mining since the early years of the conquest, and a subsistence economic organization grew that later expanded into a money economy of exportation with Europe and North America. Coffee, tobacco, sugar, and minor crops from Puerto Rico achieved a secure market in Europe.

During the four hundred years of Spanish domination, the island was living a parallel life with the Mother Country. In 1898, as a part of the military operations of the Spanish-American War, Puerto Rico was invaded by United States troops. The armistice that followed provided for the immediate withdrawal of the Spanish Government from the island.[9]

THE UNITED STATES AND PUERTO RICO   Since the American Occupation, the island is under a treaty status of a temporary character. The island became the only non-incorporated American territory of Spanish background in the Caribbean Area. Consequently new trends due to American influences have been impinging on the social, economic, and political life of its peoples. In 1903 Congress granted a civil form of government to the island. In 1917 the Federal Congress granted the islanders American citizenship. Those who were not willing to accept it were allowed to refrain from doing so.

POLITICAL STATUS   Since 1898, Puerto Rico has shaped the course of its political life following the path traced by the United States through congressional or presidential action. A bicameral legislature elected by the direct vote of the people of Puerto Rico every four years legislates on Puerto Rican internal affairs. The power of veto as well as the final approval of any law rests in the hands of a governor appointed by the President of the United States with the consent of the Federal Senate.[10]

The President of the United States has veto power over the insular Governor, and the Congress has power to annul any legislation approved by the Puerto Rican legislature.

Judicial power is administered by an insular Supreme Court whose members are appointed by the President of the United States with the consent of the Federal Senate. The judgments of this court are appealable to the first Circuit Court of Boston and to the United States Supreme Court. The United States District Court for Puerto Rico, with officers appointed in Washington, D.C., upholds both Federal and insular laws.[11]

ECONOMIC STATUS   Puerto Rico has continued to be an agricultural country. Since the American Occupation of the island, sugar cane production has increased to the point where it is almost a monoculture, and together with its by-products constitutes the main course of income for Puerto Rico.[12] Coffee, tobacco, sugar, and minor crops of Puerto Rico lost the European market. The island became enclosed within the Federal Tariff laws, and its sugar, tobacco, and fruits acquired a profitable advantage over other countries competing for the American market.[13] The demand for tobacco and coffee from the island, however, is not enough to encourage the production to the same level of sugar cane. Tobacco production, however, is next to sugar the most important item of exportation of the island.[14]

Tobacco farming in Puerto Rico is practiced on thirteen per cent of the total land area.[15] Farms are relatively small, and unlike the sugar farming, forty-seven per cent of all the farms devoted to tobacco growing are operated by their owners and thirty-one per cent by tenants or share-croppers. Only fifteen per cent of all the agricultural workers of the island are employed in the tobacco farms. From October to February, the tobacco land is devoted to the growing of subsistence crops such as beans, maize, and rice.[16]

Coffee farms occupy nearly twice the size of land acreage devoted to tobacco.[17] Most coffee plantations are operated by their owners, seventy per cent of which are Puerto Ricans.[18]

The cultivation of tropical citrus fruits is mostly in the hands of American farmers, with permanent residence in the island, who export the crop to the United States.[19]

The relatively low cash profits for coffee, tobacco, and fruits in the American market have contributed to an increase in interest in the cultivation of sugar. Latifundism and absentee-ownership have been characteristic institutions of the sugar economy in Puerto Rico.[20]

> Nearly half of all the sugar produced in Puerto Rico in 1935 came from the plantations of four large companies. In addition to these four corporate holdings in 1935 there were 26 other properties belonging to companies outside of Puerto Rico, there were 41 sugar mills, which owned the lands in their vicinity, and there were 100 landlords who did not own mills. The average size of all these properties was 40,000 acres. Compared with all agricultural enterprises in Puerto Rico, these plantations comprised about 40% of the farm acreage, about 56% of the value of all farm land and buildings, employed about 50% of all agricultural workers, and produced about 60% of all the value of all Puerto Rico's exports. The importance of sugar in the economic life of the island is obvious.[21]

The sugar economy has been a great influence in shaping the destiny of Puerto Rico. Sugar controls farming, imports, shipping, railroads, labor, wealth, income, labor's buying, politics, tariff benefits, and taxes.[22]

The tariff protection, besides fostering a monoculture of sugar, has impinged upon the phenomenon of an unbalanced increase in the cost of living. The island has to import the main food-stuff for the support of its population, as well as shoes, clothes, cement, raw materials, etc., for all of these essential items are protected by the tariff. Puerto Rico, to avoid payment of custom duties, buys from the United States and uses the expensive services of the American merchant marine for the importation of American commodities.[23]

Sugar is a seasonal crop, and the range of wages paid to agricultural workers was relatively low until 1941, when by law standards of minimum wages were approved and enforced. It was found that 648 families employed in the farming season of sugar, 241 were getting an average of $151.93 per year. Fifty-three of the families were paid $72.43 per year, and only 2 were getting an average of $1,695.31 per year.[24]

In 1941 the Puerto Rican legislature approved a land law creating a laden authority with provisions to reorient the land tenure institutions of the island. A Federal provision in the Organic Law of Puerto Rico forbidding private ownership of land over five hundred acres has also been enforced.[25]

Manufacturing has also been a source of income for thousands of the islanders. Needlework, sugar refining, dressmaking, and other small industries for local consumption have been of economic significance for the island.

Government programs to rehabilitate the island economically have sponsored legislation fostering the development of industries and the maximum exploitation of the natural resources of the island. An insular Board of Urbanization, Planning, and Zoning, as well as several other governmental agencies have been created for such purposes. Factories are being established in the island with the aid of the insular government. The availability of labor forces in the island has been very encouraging for the development of industry. The rise of urbanization and industrial ways is at its beginning. Puerto Rico is still basically rural and agricultural, seventy per cent of its total population being distributed along communities of less than twenty-five hundred inhabitants.[26]

POPULATION AND ITS RESOURCES   In 1940 Puerto Rico had 1,869,000 inhabitants and an arithmetical population density of 546[27] individuals per square mile.[28] The distribution of population in the island is to a great extent related to the prevailing land economy.[29] Along the coastal area where sugar cane plantations are found, the population density is perhaps above a thousand per square mile.[30] High population density is also reckoned in the areas where fruit plantations are established, as well as in the truck farming zones.[31] In the tobacco and coffee areas the densities of population range probably between two hundred and three hundred individuals per square mile, and areas devoted to grazing have densities of over fifty individuals per square mile.[32]

The system of tenure and exploitation of land explains to a high degree the so-called population problem of Puerto Rico in its implicit relationships to the factors of wealth, food supply, and labor.[33]

A problem of population pressure exists in Puerto Rico under the present set-up where the exploitation of the natural resources of the island does not satisfy the needs of its peoples. Puerto Rico has a net birth rate increase of thirty thousand individuals per annum,[34] and as a result of the growth of population an absence of balance between the actual population and the inland resources is in existence. In terms of human experiences this condition can be stated as underemployment and unemployment, malnutrition, inadequate housing and sanitary conditions, a high index of diseases and infant mortality, etc.

Industrialization, a greater development of the agricultural resources, migration, birth control, education, and a better distribution of wealth have been suggested as remedies to control the problem of population pressure of the island. The extrapolated figure of a probable population of 2,900,000 inhabitants for 1960, and the impossibility of adjusting that figured population to the actual yields of the resources of the island, has been an added factor in the rapid encouragement of all the probable solutions to this aspect of the Puerto Rican "problem."

The characteristics of the actual population of Puerto Rico in terms of age, race composition, and ecological distribution show significant sociological factors with particular reference to the problems of Puerto Rican emigration. Census data reveal that the island population is predominantly young, white, and rural. The population is growing old, and the labor force of the island is increasing rapidly. To meet the problem of unemployment, migration to the United States has been fostered by the insular government. The racial composition and the ecological distribution of the population of Puerto Rico is particularly significant with reference to the migrant population of the island to the United States insofar as, in spite of the census racial classification, one of the main problems faced by Puerto Rican immigrants to the United States is the one of "color visibility" and the presence of a different pattern of racial relations to those prevailing in the United States. The other is the absence of background in highly industrialized urban communities.[35] These two factors ought to be examined under the general pattern of social relations in Puerto Rico. The differentials in overt social behavior as shown by the Puerto Rican immigrants to the United States are very much related to the sociological factors of "race" and ecology as well as to the factors of sex.

RACIAL RELATIONS   Puerto Rico has been depicted as one center of racial and cultural fusion in the Caribbean area and as a bridge between the Anglo-American tradition of the North and the Latin American tradition of the South.[36] It has been typed as one of the laboratories where three heritages mixed—the Indian, the Spanish, and the African.

Race in Puerto Rico does not have a clear-cut meaning. In many cases it is not necessarily linked to the biological implication of race or even to color visibility. In Puerto Rico a man may be biologically a mulatto, and the people may know about it but still consider him a white man.[37] This statement, nevertheless, does not hold true for any mulatto. What seems to happen is that social superordination and subordination are in a more valid and open relationship to economic status than to the racial affinities of the individual.[38]

Fewkes claims that in the rather isolated rural areas of Puerto Rico, Indian physical traits are discernable in the population.[39] He postulates a movement to the mountains by part of the Indian population that tried to escape from the Spanish conquistadores. The Indian element, nevertheless, does not seem to have been an important genetical constituent of the present population of the island. Early in the conquest, the Indians disappeared,[40] to some extent through miscegenation. Present racial issues in Puerto Rico are distinctly understood if limited to the white-Negro crossing insofar as they are continuous and highly significant in number and their implications are really the axis of racial and class relations in the island.

In the eighteen century, the *criollo* or white Puerto Rican of Spanish ancestry, the *mulato,* the product of a mixed Spanish-Negro parenthood, and the *negros,* the African slaves, were apparently the categories of classification applied to the population of Puerto Rico.[41] At present, the above terms exist, but their meanings have broken down. A *criollo* is anyone who was born in the island regardless of his color or biological race. The term *mulato* is applied frequently to individuals showing striking Negroid features and who have a low economic status. It is seldom applied to individuals showing distinct Negroid features if they enjoy a high socio-economic position, and when it is done it usually occurs as a form of gossip. There are no legal or social sanctions that prevent the participation of these individuals in activities in which white Puerto Ricans can participate.

The term *grifo* is applied to individuals with kinky hair. The term *negro* is usually a word of endearment.[42] The use of the term lacks the connotation of the English "Negro." The Spanish term *negro* is not a contemptuous epithet. In reference to the racial affiliation of an individual, the phrase *de color* meaning "colored" is the one used habitually.[43] The terms *moreno* or *trigueño* are used in reference to an individual whose skin color is lighter than that of someone considered "colored," but neither the terms *moreno, trigueño* nor *de color* have a deprecatory connotation. It seems, nevertheless, that a social value is attached to a light skin color and to Caucasoid features. The subject of race is usually barred from current conversation, especially when someone considered "colored" is present. The light-skinned mulatto is considered white and as such may be fully accepted by the upper classes, but the dark-skinned mulatto is considered "colored" and as such is not fully accepted by the *crema* or top level in the vertical scale of Puerto Rican society.

Santullano[44] remarked that in Puerto Rico,

> although the people are not prejudiced to the degree known for other countries, the "pure" whites, who are descendants of Europeans, usually of Spanish immigrants, look with some disdain upon the colored people who aspire to "alternate socially" with them, and criticize marriages to individuals of known African descent although their skin color should not show it.

The above observation does convey the feeling found in a very small minority of Puerto Ricans, namely, those whose socioeconomic ranking is very high as compared to the rest of the population of the island. Usually it is among individuals whose African ascendancy is unremarkable, where a feeling of racial discrimination is more observable.[45]

Women are more liable than men to show and exert these sanctions.[46] In other words, the pattern of racial relations in Puerto Rico is basically rooted in socio-economic status rather than in "race" or "color." Prejudice, as it is exhibited in some areas of the world and particularly in the United States does not exist.

> From the middle class down, the union of white women to black men is not unusual enough to astonish or enrage anybody, and the union of black or brown women to white men is of course more frequent. Discreet instances of both varieties of intermarriage may be found in the highest social pinnacles. . . . lynching and the humiliation of Negroes by statute are unthinkable. There are no segregated districts. . . . Jim Crow cars would seem as freakish as a man with two thumbs on one hand and eight fingers on the other. . . . A good proportion of the schoolteachers are of Negro and mixed extraction and they give their services to black, brown, and white indiscriminately. White, Negro, and Mulatto lawyers, physicians, journalists, poets, politicians, philosophers, lead a common professional and spiritual life.[47]

Under American influence, the pattern of racial relations in Puerto Rico has not changed very much, although the impact of American civilization in Puerto Rico undoubtedly has modified by intensification a discriminatory feeling on the basis of color, namely among individuals enjoying a high socio-economic status.

The pattern of racial relations in the rural areas seems to show some variation between peasant and city life. It can be hypothecated that because in the peasant society there is not a class structure or any other mechanism by means of which vertical ranking of the society is framed, racial discrimination does not exist. Assuming that it should exist, due to influence of the city and the town over the country, this condition is much less intense than in cities and towns, where social stratification occurs. This hypothesis stems from the notion that race in Puerto Rico is a class phenomenon or that class is a racial phenomenon rather than the color situation, which determines race in the United States.

The Puerto Rican *jíbaro* furnishes the great bulk of the rural population of the island. The *jíbaro* or "mountain folk" have been described as the "poor whites" driven to the mountains by the pressure of African slavery.[48] The *jíbaro* have also been described as a fusion of white and Indian elements.[49] It seems inaccurate, nevertheless, to assign a distinctive physical type to the *jíbaro*, insofar as his admixtures have not been stabilized. Amalgamation in the rural areas as well as in the urban areas in Puerto Rico is not an accomplished process. Racial mixture is, however, probably greater in the rural than in the urban areas.

The social patterns prevailing in the relations between the sexes in Puerto Rico cut across the sociological racial differences in operation. The social status of women seems to be lower than that of men despite the fact that at present it is not unusual for a woman to be an economic provider for her home. The "double standard" for the sexes is related to the Christian ideal of women's virginhood. A woman who loses her virginity outside of marriage is a "lost woman." Sexual taboos are less binding on men, who usually have affairs outside their legal marriage. Illegitimate children from these "consensual marriages" usually have a lower social status than their parents, especially if the children are not legally recognized by their father.

The apparent inconsistency of the relationship between the sexes in Puerto Rico seems to fade when the father assumes the economic responsibility for his children, and also by the legal wife's higher social status than the concubine, who on the other hand is compensated by the more or less permanent attachment of her lover.

The kaleidoscopic view of the general patterns of social relations operating in Puerto Rico reveals a basic difference from those operating in American industrial communities with a dominant Protestant ethics and a heterogeneous racial, ethnic, and ethno-cultural background. The Puerto Ricans who migrate to the United States are overtly at variance with the dominant patterns of behavior associated with the dominant American society. Nevertheless, they migrate to this country since there are no citizenship bars forbidding them to do so, and because they probably have the feeling that in this country they will be able to achieve a better economic and social life than they could in their homeland.

Changing Puerto Rico and the Trends of Urbanization

Elsewhere in this study[50] it has been emphasized that Puerto Rico is predominantly rural in its social and economic make-up. Puerto Rico is also colonial in its political and economic gears. Geographically, it is an American frontier. Politically, and through its position in the world market, the island is in a relationship of dependency upon the United States. Puerto Rican society is, however, basically integrated by the values propounded by the Catholic Church and the Spanish tradition.[51]

> The general outlook of the people is Spanish, not Anglo-Saxon; and the basic elements of culture, history, and law are drawn from Spain and not from England. A change of sovereignty has made them American only in name. They are still Latin, with different ideals, different manners, and customs, and with a different temperament from that of continental Americans.[52]

Pattee[53] has observed that "the sense of Hispanic tradition and background is extremely deep-rooted."[54] The Puerto Ricans, however, have become very much exposed to American values and traditions in the last forty-eight years despite the fact that firsthand contacts between Puerto Ricans and Americans are almost non-existent. The impingement of American influences in Puerto Rico has channelized mostly through the impersonal relationships of politics, commodities, education, and propaganda. The position of the island in the world market is important in describing increases in contacts with the rest of the world as well as with the American mainland. Many symbols of American life have been accepted by Puerto Ricans as expressions of progress. The diffusion of American influences has not been strong enough to create a marginal society in Puerto Rico.[55] Spanish traditions and the Catholic Church ideals are still the strongest forms of control in Puerto Rican society. The Government of the United States through its Department of Interior, or through the Commissioner of Education of the island has instrumented policies for the Americanization of the islanders. The linguistic orientation of the public schools is a case in point.

The teaching of English has been a permanent aspect of the educational policy of the island. Much controversy has arisen in connection with the goal, use, and the extent of the teaching of this language in the public schools. In some instances, English has been the official language of communication employed in the schools, while in other instances, it has shifted its position in the school curricula. The oscillating status of English has been most confusing in the formal education of Puerto Ricans. A permanent policy has never been specified in regard to the official language of the schools. The policy for the teaching of English has varied with the commissioners of education, the presidents of the United States, Congress, etc. The uncertainty of this issue is connected with the uncertain political status of the island.[56]

Pedagogical recommendations, nevertheless, have been in favor of the use of Spanish as the instrument of communicating knowledge in the public schools and in the intensive teaching of English as a subject insofar as the utilitarian value of this language is undeniable.[57]

Spanish is the language of the home in Puerto Rico. English is never used as a means of communication between and among Puerto Ricans except in official communications of the government and in imparting knowledge in the schools. English phrases and words have been incorporated into Puerto Rican–Spanish and are frequently used particularly in the cities.[58] Usually words and phrases taken from English are pronounced with their approximate Spanish sounds and most of the time are written with their approximate phonetic value. Words like "issue," "record," "injunction," "statement," "swimming pool," "junior," "field day," "partner," "speaker," "floor leader," "at large," "couch," "mattress," "Miss," "Mister," etc., are frequently used in current conversation and writing. Certain English words have been borrowed with changes to fit the Spanish structure, like *zafacón* for "safety can" (trash can) and *tofete* for "tough."

The extent of the use of English by the Puerto Rican population in the current activities of its social life is very limited. In 1940, the population of the island above ten years of age that theoretically was able to speak English was 371,132 individuals,[59] an equivalent of 27.8 per cent of the total population of that age range. It has to be pointed out that the average education of Puerto Ricans is equivalent to four years in grammar school[60] and that the knowledge of English acquired during that period is not adequate to the point of being socially useful.[61]

THE PROTESTANT CHURCHES IN PUERTO RICO   Before the American regime there was only one non–Roman Catholic Church in Puerto Rico.[62] This was an Anglican Church established in the city of Ponce in 1873. After the American occupation of the island, Protestant denominations became active in proselytizing the natives. In 1905, the *Federación de Iglesias Evangélicas de Puerto Rico* was established. Protestant journals, schools, hospitals, etc., have been operating in the island. Puerto Ricans have been trained for the ministry in seminaries maintained in the island for that purpose. The great majority of Puerto Ricans, nevertheless, are at least nominal Catholics and as such conform to a large extent to the patterns of social organization embodied in the Catholic traditions. The people participate actively in the festivities of the Catholic Church especially in Holy Week, the Patron Saint's Day, Christmas, the Three Kings' Day, Corpus Christi, and *verbenas* and *novenas* to the Virgin and the saints. In the towns and in the country, Catholic festivities are popular events. In the cities, they tend to be more sophisticated and are sometimes celebrated—especially in their secularized aspects—within the particular social classes. *Rites de passage* revolve around the Catholic beliefs. Spiritualism and magical practices combined with Catholic beliefs are in existence especially among the peasants and to a great extent in the towns and the cities. These beliefs operate especially in times of crisis as the last resource to control the mysterious and the unknown.

Puerto Ricans, even those who are not regular churchgoers, usually claim to be Catholics. Participation in the Catholic festivals is mostly an unquestioned custom and a "right" thing to do. It is in this environment of customary secularized Catholicism that the relatively recent imported Protestant institutions are operating. Such denominations as the Episcopalian, the Presbyterian, Methodist, Baptist, Adventist, and Pentecostal are very active in proselytizing Puerto Ricans. The work of the Protestant churches is done mainly through charity and social service aid. Rogler did not reckon upper-class people in Comerio among the members of the Protestant churches and claims that the great mass of Puerto Ricans is nominally Catholic.[63]

SECULAR ORGANIZATIONS   Under the Spanish regime the *casino*[64] was the formal association operating as a center of entertainment for the upper classes. A *casino* was in existence in every important town of the island. The local upper classes gathered in the *casino* to dance, chat, and play indoor games. The *Casino de Puerto Rico* and the *Casino Español* both operated in San Juan for the insular upper classes. At present, the *casino* is still an exclusive association, but it has been weakened by the social clubs with Greek letters, fraternities, sororities, etc., of American brand that exist independently. The Rotary International, the Afda, the Elks, the Knights of Columbus, Lions' International, the Bankers' Club, the Optimists' Club, etc., are highly evaluated socially, although as yet they have not displaced the *casino*.[65]

The *café*[66] was the meeting place of cliques of men of different social classes who gathered around the tables to drink coffee, talk, smoke, play chess, dominos, etc. Nowadays, the *café* is practically disappearing and being substituted by the American styled bar.[67] A few *cafés* still operate in some cities, but they are not the exclusive centers for the informal gathering of men. The *plazas*, which are usually located in front of the Catholic churches, continue to be the center for strolling. Older and younger peoples of both sexes meet there during the evenings for courtship, promenading, and chatting.

Private and charity parties in the cities, in many instances, are of a mixed Puerto Rican–American flavor. Bingo parties, teas, cocktails, etc. rank among these. In such parties songs, jokes, and games of American extraction are used as means of entertainment, but these activities have not succeeded and have not been accepted by large groups of Puerto Ricans.[68] Parties and dances requiring girls to invite their partners, as well as the so-called Dutch date, occur to some extent among the upper classes in the large cities but are subject to criticism and gossip.[69] Girls are usually accompanied by chaperones when going out with boys; otherwise they are criticized. Latin American, Afro-Antillean, and Puerto Rican music is preferred to American swing by the Puerto Ricans living in the cities. In the towns and in the open country, native music—both popular and folk—played with native instruments is typical.

Cock fights and horse races seem to be the favorite sports of the islanders, together with basketball, volleyball, and baseball, all of which seem to have many enthusiastic followers.

HOLY DAYS AND HOLIDAYS   The holy days celebrated in Puerto Rico are Catholic feasts that since the days of the Spanish domination have been celebrated by the islanders. Holidays are either Spanish, local, or of American extraction. Among the American holidays celebrated in the island are Halloween, Washington's Birthday, Independence Day, Thanksgiving Day, Lincoln's Birthday, Labor Day, and the President's Birthday. Decoration Day is a secular holiday in Puerto Rico, while the Spanish Day of all the dead is a holy day. American holidays are mostly school and government celebrations. The Spanish holy days are those associated with Christmas, Lent, the Three Kings' Day, Patron Saint's Day, etc. all surrounding the Catholic Church. Secular entertainments are celebrated together with religious celebrations by the mass of the people on these holy days except during the period of Lent. Puerto Rican holidays are chiefly associated with local events and anniversaries of prominent Puerto Ricans.

THE AMERICAN COLONY IN PUERTO RICO   First contacts between continental Americans and Puerto Ricans are channelized through a small colony of continental Americans who live in the island. The Americans form a discrete group and seldom interact with Puerto Ricans except on limited occasions. They have their own formal and informal organizations with their proper buildings, and their gatherings are usually of an exclusive nature. Relationships between Puerto Ricans and Americans are chiefly limited to those natives who are members of the local upper classes, who have been educated in the United States, and who are able to speak English fluently.

> The American colony that has grown up is small and cannot expand in terms of settlers. The result is an intensification of the sense of national consciousness through a compact unity that is to be found in none of the other areas subject to American rule.[70]

During the war, direct personal contacts between Puerto Ricans and Americans increased due largely to the great influx of American servicemen and civilian war workers to the island. The extent to which the impact of the war has affected human relationships in Puerto Rico, nevertheless, cannot as yet be described.

Summary

This chapter has attempted to show the social, political, and economic background of the Puerto Rican immigrants as well as the prevailing basic patterns of social relations operating among the islanders with particular emphasis on conditions and situations at variance with American society.

Puerto Rico is geographically speaking a very small country with limited resources to support its present population. Colonialism—both economic and political—has shaped the historical development of the country. Spain laid its foundations there from the fifteenth century to the end of the nineteenth century. Then the island became an American possession as a war trophy. The islanders are basically Spanish in their cultural and social life. American influences have been diffused without creating consistent and balanced standards of behavior with the ones prevailing in the island. Puerto Rican migrants to the United States, therefore, are, culturally speaking, as unaware of American culture and its social system as any other foreign group, and as such face American society as an unknown equation in their lives.

NOTES

1. Puerto Rico Planning, Urbanizing, and Zoning Board, *A Development Plan for Puerto Rico,* Technical Paper No. 1 (Santurce: Office of Information, 1944), p. 1.

2. C. H. de Coeje, "Nouvelle Examen des Langues des Antilles," *Journal de la Société des Américanistes,* XXXI (1939), pp. 1–120.

3. Fray I. Abbad y Lasierra, *Historia Natural, Geográfica y Civil de la Isla de San Juan Bautista de Puerto Rico,* ed. J. J. Acosta (Puerto Rico: 1865), pp. 19 and 21 ff.

4. See H. Spinden, "The Population of Ancient America," *Annual Report of the Smithsonian Institute for the Year Ended June 30, 1929* (Washington: Government Printing Office, 1929).

5. Coeje, *op. cit.*, p. 1 f.

6. T. Blanco, *El Prejudicio Racial en Puerto Rico* (San Juan: Biblioteca de Autores Puertorriqueños, 1924).

7. Colonel G. D. Flinter, *An Account of the Present State of the Island of Puerto Rico* (London: Longman, Rees, Orme, Brown, Green and Longman, 1834), pp. 259 ff.

8. Cf. Robert Redfield, *Tepoztlan* (Chicago: University of Chicago Press, 1931), and *The Folk Culture of Yucatan* (Chicago: University of Chicago Press, 1941) for discussion and analysis of the concepts of "folk," "peasant," and "urban" types of communities.

9. W. H. Calcott, *The Caribbean Policy of the United States, 1890–1920* (Baltimore: Johns Hopkins University Press, 1942), p. 102.

10. U.S. Congress, Senate, *Independence for Puerto Rico,* Hearing before the Committee on Territories and Insular Affairs, U.S. Senate, 79th Congress, 1st Session on S. bill 227, April 23, 24, 25, 26, 27, and May 1 and 8, 1945. (Washington: Government Printing Office, 1945), Part II, p. 364.

11. Resolution adopted by the Bar Association of Puerto Rico in its annual meeting held on September 1, 1944, at San Juan, Puerto Rico, quoted in U.S. Congress, Senate, *Independence for Puerto Rico,* pp. 367–371.

12. B. W. and J. W. Diffie, *Porto Rico: A Broken Pledge* (New York: Viking Press, 1931), p. 45.

13. P. E. James, *Latin America* (New York: Lothrop, Lee, Shephard Company, 1942), p. 781, and Darwin Degolia, *Problemas Parifarios de Puerto Rico,* translated and commented on by A. J. Colorado (San Juan: 1936).

14. F. Mejías, *Condiciones de Vida de las Clases Jornaleras de Puerto Rico,* Monografias de la Universidad de Puerto Rico, Ciencia Social Numo. 2, Serie C, Universidad de Puerto Rico, 1946, p. 23.

15. The range in size of tobacco farms varies between 14 and 60 acres. See James, *op cit.*, p. 784.

16. *Ibid.*

17. United States Congress, *Investigation of Political, Economic, and Social Conditions in Puerto Rico,* App. to Hearings before the subcommittee (Washington: Government Printing Office, 1944), p. 492.

18. James, *op cit.*, p. 784.

19. *Ibid.*, p. 784.

20. *Ibid.*, p. 782.

21. *Ibid.*, p. 781.

22. R. Gándara, *Land and Liberty* (San Juan: Bureau of Supplies, Printing and Transportation, 1943), p. 27.

23. U.S. Congress, Senate, *Independence for Puerto Rico, op cit.*, p. 46 f., and James, *op cit.*, p. 781.

24. Gándara, *op. cit.*, p. 27.

25. V. Géigel Polanco (ed.), *La Legislación Social de Puerto Rico* (San Juan: 1944). See R. G. Tugwell, *The Stricken Land* (Garden City: Doubleday and Co., 1947) for a thorough presentation and analysis of the program for the rehabilitation of the land economy of Puerto Rico.

26. Puerto Rico Planning, Urbanizing, and Zoning Board, *op. cit.*, p. 16.

27. U.S. Bureau of the Census, *Statistical Abstracts of the U.S. 1944–1945,* No. 66 (Washington: Government Printing Office), p. 8.

28. *Ibid.*, p. 64.

29. James, *op. cit.*, p. 776 *et passim.*

30. *Ibid.*, p. 782.

31. *Ibid.*

32. *Ibid.*

33. R. G. Tugwell, *Changing the Colonial Climate*, ed. John Lear (San Juan: Bureau of Supplies, Printing and Transportation, 1942), p. 71, and James, *op. cit.*, p. 788.

34. Puerto Rico Planning, Urbanizing and Zoning Board, *op. cit.*, p. 7.

35. Infra.

36. See Luis de Santullano, *Mirada al Caribe: Fricción de Culturas en Puerto Rico,* "Jornadas" 54 (Mexico: El Colegio de Mexico, Centro de Estudios Sociales, 1945), and A. S. Pedreira, *Insularismo* (San Juan: Biblioteca de Autores Puertorriqueños, 1942), 21–36.

37. See Rogler, *op. cit.*, p. 38., and C. C. Rogler, "The Role of Semantics in the Study of Social Distance in Puerto Rico," *Journal of Social Forces,* May, 1944, pp. 448–453.

38. *Ibid.*, p. 449.

39. J. W. Fewkes, The Aborigines of Porto Rico and Neighboring Islands, *Bureau of American Ethnology Annual Report* (Washington: Government Printing Office, 1907).

40. *Ibid.*

41. Abbad y Lasierra, *op. cit.*, pp. 398 ff.

42. Tomás Blanco, *El Prejucio Racial en Puerto Rico* (San Juan: Biblioteca de Autores Puertorriqueños, 1942), p. 14.

43. *Ibid.*

44. Luis A. de Santullano, *Mirada al Caribe, Fricción de Culturas en Puerto Rico,* "Jornadas" 54 (Mexico: El Colegio de Mexico, Centro de Estudios Sociales, 1945), p. 285.

45. Blanco, *op. cit.*, p. 49.

46. *Ibid.*, p. 64.

47. Carey McWilliams, "Puerto Ricans and Other Islanders," *Brothers Under the Skin* (Boston: Little, Brown and Co., 1942), p. 206, quoting Luis Muñoz Marín in an article published in *Nation*, April 8, 1925. Cf. Blanco, *op. cit.*

48. McWilliams, *op. cit.*, p. 205.

49. Cf. A. Paniagua, "Ethnologic Social Sketch," *The Book of Puerto Rico*, ed. E.F. García (San Juan, 1923), p. 89.

50. *Passim.*

51. R. Picó and W. H. Haas, "Puerto Rico," *The American Empire* (Chicago: University of Chicago Press, 1940), p. 57.

52. *Ibid.*

53. Richard Pattee, a native American who has taught at the University of Puerto Rico for over ten years, has an intimate knowledge of Puerto Rican life acquired during his long stay in the island.

54. Richard Pattee, "The Puerto Ricans," *The Annals: American Academy of Political and Social Science*, CCXXIII (July, 1942), 49.

55. V. Géigel Polanco, *El Despertar de un Pueblo* (San Juan: Biblioteca de Autores Puertorriqueños, 1942), pp. 141–164.

56. Pedro A. Cebollero, *La Lingüística-Política Escolar de Puerto Rico* (San Juan: Consejo Superior de Ensenanza, Publicaciones Pedagogicas, Serie II, numero 1, 1945), p. 28 f.

57. See United States Congress, House of Representatives, Hearings before the Subcommittee of the Committee of Insular Affairs and Territories, *Investigation of the Political, Economic, and Social Conditions in Puerto Rico*, 78th Congress, Part 18, H. Rep. 159, May 11, 1944, p. 1641. See also Cebollero, *op. cit.*, p. 31, *passim*, and Puerto Rico Planning, Urbanizing, and Zoning Board, *op. cit.*, p. 65.

58. Santullano, *op. cit.*, p. 46 f.

59. U.S. Bureau of the Census, *Statistical Abstract of the United States: 1944–1945* (Washington: Government Printing Office, 1945).

60. Cebollero, *op. cit.*, p. 105.

61. Philip Drury, "The Protestant Church in Puerto Rico," *op. cit.*, p. 134.

62. F. Mejías, *op. cit.*, pp. 181 ff.

63. Rogler, *Comerio*, p. 159.

64. This institution is not the equivalent of the American conception of *casino* centering on gambling.

65. Santullano, *op. cit.*, p. 56.

66. The *café* is a restaurant where meals, soft drinks, and coffee are served, in many cases in the open air.

67. Santullano, *op. cit.*, p. 57.

68. *Ibid.*, p. 57.

69. *Ibid.*, p. 58.

70. Pattee, *op. cit.*, p. 49.

CHAPTER FOUR

The Puerto Rican Migrants
in New York City

The picture presented by the Puerto Rican migrants in New York City is similar to that of other ethnic groups who have migrated to American industrial communities in search of better living conditions, as these are generally understood—by the acquisition of higher-paid jobs than in the homeland.

> The migration of the Puerto Rican to New York is another example of the old and never ceasing movement of people who hope to better their condition. It constitutes an important part of the well known and much larger movement of people to New York and other cities which has been taking place in recent years. The Puerto Rican finding himself landless, unemployed, and herded with others into his native towns and cities, has for some time begun to look to the United States as a possible means of escape from economic conditions which almost beggar description. He has. . . . come to New York to earn the high money wages paid in this country and to take the place of European immigrant groups which are now restricted.[1]

Technically, the Puerto Rican immigrants to the United States are internal migrants. They are citizens of the United States and can move freely between the island and the Mainland without passport or visa. The Puerto Rican nevertheless is a foreign ethnic in American society. Differences in the social heritage account for the phenomenon that distinguishes the ethnics from the native or assimilated American population. Cassidy observed:

> The immigrant groups which are most foreign (1) because of differences in political traditions, social life, religion, stage of industrialization, and economic security in country of origin, and (2) because of the comparatively recent date of establishment as nationality communities within the United States, with all that means in terms of economic position, housing, education, political power, and social recognition, are *peasant groups* from the countries that before the

war furnished the so-called "recent migration," and, since the war, unskilled laborers from the countries not subject to quota, such as Mexico. Again, we must add new arrivals from Puerto Rico and the Philippine Islands, who technically are not immigrants at all but who have to encounter as difficult problems of adjustment as those faced by true immigrants.[2]

The Puerto Rican immigrants in New York City share the basic problems of adjustment that are common to the Little Italy, Little Bohemia, Little Greece, etc., living in American industrial cities. There is, however, a stronger similarity between the Puerto Rican in New York and the Mexican in Chicago insofar as there is a great similarity in their background and both share to much extent "color visibility," which is a sociological phenomenon demanding a type of adjustment not required by American society from most European immigrants.

The Puerto Ricans in New York City, unlike the Puerto Rican in Chicago, tend to concentrate in definite areas of residence. This situation definitely contributes to the growth and permanence of an in-group solidarity as is true among other members of ethnic groups in the United States.

> There is a strong tendency of the Puerto Rican to settle in the Harlem section of New York City. About one-half of all the Puerto Ricans living in the United States in 1930 resided in this area. . . . About 95% of the total number of Puerto Ricans in New York City in 1930 lived in the boroughs of Manhattan and Brooklyn.[3]

No census data have been published on the number of Puerto Ricans living in New York City. Because Puerto Ricans are American citizens, they do not appear in the official census reports of the United States nor in the official census of the city as a distinct immigrant group but are merged with the rest of the native American population.

Rice[4] calculated 44,908 Puerto Rican immigrants in New York City grouped racially into 34,756 whites and 10,152 colored and members of other races. It is usually claimed by members of the Puerto Rican colony that there are about 150,000 Puerto Ricans in the city, and this is the approximate figure given in most calculations.[5]

The Puerto Rican legislature gave an impulse to a mass migration of Puerto Ricans to New York in 1919. A group of one hundred and thirty Puerto Ricans came to Brooklyn in that year to work in a cordage factory.[6] The Puerto Ricans, nevertheless, continued migrating to New York in search of work not related to the cordage industry. In this sense, the Puerto Ricans in New York are unlike the Mexican immigrants in Chicago. The mass migration of Mexicans to Chicago was the response to a demand for labor in the steel mills in 1923, and still today they furnish an important part of the labor in that industry.[7]

The occupational background of the great bulk of the Puerto Rican migrants in New York is mostly composed of unskilled agricultural workers, a small minority of them having been trade workers, factory operators, machine repairers, household servants, and needle workers.

Even those Puerto Ricans who were skilled factory workers in the island want training to adjust themselves to the American type of factories and to the proper basic secular rituals of American industrial society. They have an added difficulty inasmuch as they lack a working knowledge of English and of the prevalent behavioral patterns of American city life.

Most positions filled by Puerto Rican men in New York are those of laundry workers, laborers and construction workers, paper and leather factory workers, janitors, handymen, watchmen, carpenters, painters, plumbers, and aides or helpers.[8] Women are usually employed as domestics, needle workers, hand-sewers, garment workers, factory workers, laundry workers, stenographers, typists, office helpers, waitresses and counter girls.[9] It has been claimed that Puerto Rican laborers are not accepted as members of American Labor Unions except for the Spanish branch of the International Ladies' Garment Union, and in one branch of the Cigar Makers' Union.[10] Most Puerto Rican workers, nevertheless, have been organized by the International Workers Order (IWO) and in other labor organizations together with other Spanish speaking ethnics, as well as in local unions affiliated with the C.I.O. and A.F. of L.[11]

A very small class of Puerto Ricans engaged in the professions, and some business owners have migrated to New York City and live and operate in the areas of greater concentration of Puerto Ricans and other Spanish-speaking ethnics. Significant business enterprises, nevertheless, are not owned by Puerto Rican immigrants in the city.

Association of Puerto Ricans and Other Spanish-Speaking Ethnics in New York City

The types of associations prevailing among Puerto Ricans and other Spanish-speaking ethnics are similar in structure and function to those of other immigrant groups in American society. Associations to promote education, mutual aid, orientation into the host society, and social amusement have been active among Puerto Ricans and other Spanish-speaking ethnics since the early twenties. Most organizations tend to strengthen the bonds with the home and at the same time help to integrate the group into the greater American social life.

Besides exclusive nationalistic associations of Puerto Ricans and of other Spanish-speaking ethnics, there are some associations formed by Spanish-speaking peoples crossing above national lines. The exclusive nationalistic associations of Puerto Ricans devote themselves to mutual aid, educational activities, social amusement, and political activities related to the city and homeland. Some of the political associations of Puerto Ricans in New York are branches of parent associations in the island. Among these, the *Congreso Pro Independencia,* the *Partido Liberal,* and the *Partido Nacionalista* are very active. Such institutions as the Puerto Rican United Front Party for the elections of Puerto Ricans to the Municipal Assembly of the city operate locally and without any connection to other organizations in the island. Associations composed by Puerto Ricans and affiliated with American organizations of the same type also exist. There was, in the thirties, a Porto Rican Democratic Club, Inc. with branches in the districts where Puerto Ricans were numerically important. A Liberty Republican Club backing Puerto Ricans for political positions in the State Legislature was operating during the thirties. In 1945, a native Puerto Rican was a member of the State Legislature representing a district of high concentration of Puerto Ricans and other Spanish-speaking American citizens. There are clubs named after Puerto Rican patriots, leaders, and poets, etc. Clubs to promote solidarity among those who came from the same hometown in the island like the *Club Caborrojeño* have been in existence. Labor groups have been organized into such associations like the *Alianza Obrera Puertorriqueña.*

Cooperation between exclusive nationalistic associations of Spanish-speaking ethnics is evident. The *Club Azteca,* a Mexican exclusive organization, for instance, sponsored a dance to raise funds for the victims of a hurricane in Puerto Rico. The mixed associations of Puerto Ricans and other Spanish-speaking ethnics operate also for mutual aid, social amusement, and the general welfare of all the Spanish-speaking ethnics. In these groupings, the nationalistic feelings are broken and language and the feeling of a common social heritage strengthen the bonds of solidarity among these ethnic groups.

The *Liga Puertorriqueña Inc.,* which later in its life changed its name to *Liga Puertorriqueña e Hispana,* was a parent association founded by Puerto Ricans and other Spanish-speaking peoples. In its beginning, in the early twenties, six hundred individuals applied for active membership in this organization. The association devoted itself to promoting social solidarity among all the Spanish-speaking peoples in New York City. This aim was pursued by offering a general and varied program of interest that would satisfy many of the social needs of the immigrants. Membership to the *Liga* was secured by payment of thirty-five cents weekly, and in exchange the *Liga* would provide economic aid in case of illness, would pay the expenses of burials, would grant legal aid, make loans at a reduced interest, sponsored dances, picnics, and other kinds of amusements, published a magazine, and sponsored English and Spanish classes as well as lectures on diverse educational topics and courses in vocational training for factory workers. The *Liga* also offered to back Congressional action to solve the social and economic problems of Puerto Rico and to protect publicly the Spanish-speaking ethnics from prejudice and unfairness. The *Liga* had planned to construct the House of Puerto Rico in America but did not succeed. The *Liga* had several branches in different sections of the city as well as specialized satellite-clubs where only certain aspects of its general program would be emphasized. Among these the *Club Jóvenes del Vals,* the Puerto Rican Social Club Inc., the *Hijos de Borinquen* Social Club, etc., had much popularity among the Spanish-speaking peoples during the thirties. At present, the *Liga* is a very weak organization with no more than fourteen members who meet irregularly.[12] The *Liga* decayed due to conflicts between the older and the younger generations.

> The older people wanted the *Liga* to be a nationalistic organization exclusively for Puerto Ricans. The younger people—the Puerto Rican–Americans—disagreed. They wanted the *Liga* to be internationalistic in its membership. The older people, besides, were dying very rapidly and most of the funds were used for burials, and so the younger people left the *Liga* and joined the IWO. Later the *Liga* tried to join the IWO but it was rejected.[13]

The story of the *Liga* is significant in relationship to the development of many associations of Spanish-speaking ethnics in New York City, and particularly of the Puerto Rican societies, clubs, lodges, brotherhoods, etc.

Other associations of Spanish-speaking people in New York in which Puerto Ricans were active were the *Ateneo Hispano Obrero de* New York, the *Unidad Fraternal Hispana,* the *Logia Amparo Latino,* the *Logia Voluntad y Unión,* etc., which operated for mutual aid, labor rights and claims, and social amusement. The *Frente Unido Contra la Discriminación a los Puertorriqueños y Latinoamericanos en General* operated as a block against discrimination and unfair treatment to the Spanish-speaking ethnics in New York City.

No exclusive Puerto Rican schools or churches exist in New York. The Puerto Ricans living in the colony usually go to the churches where other Spanish-speaking people go.

Puerto Rican Press

Newspapers and magazines in Spanish are owned and published by Puerto Ricans in New York. In the papers, information about the colony and the island are abundant. Among the newspapers, *El Antillano, El Universal, El Nuevo Mundo, Eco Antillano, El Curioso, El Pueblo, Alma Boricua, La Nación Puertorriqueña,* and *El Machete Criollo* were exclusively devoted to propaganda for the final solution of the status of the island and to political problems of the city of New York that would affect the colony. All of these papers defended strongly the unity of the Spanish-speaking peoples and claimed that the situation of the ethnics in the city required the full cooperation of all these groups. The fact must also be remarked that different organized groups would form a block in the critical moments. This is shown by some public manifestos signed together by different independent organizations. Manifestos addressed to the Puerto Ricans and other Spanish-speaking ethnics are frequently written and distributed without charge among the members of the colony. Manifestos deal chiefly with political issues, which call for immediate action, such as urging congressional solution to the political and economic problems of the island, backing individuals for political positions, thanking individuals for their contribution to the welfare of the colony or to Puerto Rico, etc. A manifesto signed by several organizations was published and distributed widely asking the members of the colony to help the police force in the capture and arrest of someone who had committed a sexual crime against a Puerto Rican girl. The act seemed to have been reproved with great strength as is indicated by the general emotional tone of the manifesto.

> We regret for many reasons, the horrible crime that has been committed on the person of the innocent girl M.R. (RIP) by the work of a human monster. Being this, the first crime of this nature ever committed, where the victim has been a member of our colony, we think it is our duty and the inescapable duty of every good citizen, and particularly of our countrymen, to cooperate with the authorities in an effective manner, so that the guilty parties [are] captured and treated as they deserve.[14]

Another manifesto was published asking the colony to cooperate economically in the legal defense of a Puerto Rican who had been accused of murder. The manifesto specified:

> We are not defending a murderer. We defend a Puerto Rican whose honor and dignity of Puerto Ricans were defamed and fate forced him to kill the man who tried to abuse of his condition as a foreigner, as a Latin, and as a Puerto Rican *jíbaro.*[15]

Associations, newspapers, and public manifestos indicate as well as the ecological distribution of the Puerto Ricans in New York that (1) there exists a strong sense of solidarity among the Puerto Ricans themselves, and (2) that this solidarity is extended to other Spanish-speaking neighboring groups in the city of New York.[16] The type of colony life and its sub-system of social control within the greater society operate in a twofold way: as agents of resistance to assimilation, and as agents to increase acculturation. Colony life gives an identity to the group, preventing thus its opportunity to merge with the larger society, and at the same time helps the individuals in organizing their relationships with the larger society as is demonstrated by those formal organizations that channelize participation in American politics, the learning of English, and in training factory workers.

Conflict between Puerto Ricans and Other Ethnics

It has been stressed by Chenault[17] that conflict between Puerto Ricans and neighboring American Negroes is frequent.

> The Puerto Rican worker who lives in Harlem and does unskilled work is bound to encounter group conflicts of one sort or another. The American Negro is inclined to resent all of the people from the West Indies because of their competition in the labor market. . . . the American Negro especially resents the worker from the British West Indies. His feeling may be shown by some of the terms he applies against him, such as "superior," "high hat," "a pessimist," and "stiff British attitude." Because the Puerto Rican speaks Spanish, he is apt to encounter some of the same resentment.[18]

Puerto Ricans, on the other hand, seem to resent American Negroes, and this attitude was found to exist even among colored Puerto Ricans.[19] There is the belief that Puerto Rican Negroes descend from "better" African lineages than the American Negroes, and together with this superstition, the adoption of the European aesthetic norms by the Puerto Rican Negroes and the fear of being identified with other colored people against whom racial discrimination is too strong explains in part this attitude of the Puerto Rican Negro toward the American Negro.[20]

Puerto Ricans are discriminated against by white Americans on the basis of color, and Puerto Ricans resent it. Color visibility, nevertheless, does not seem to be a barrier among the Puerto Ricans living in the colony, insofar as residence areas are concerned. No segregation pattern seems to operate in the selection of residence areas by Puerto Ricans in New York. It is said that among white assimilated Puerto Ricans in New York, an "American attitude" towards race exists. These individuals are supposed to have changed their social relationships with Spanish-speaking peoples who are noticeably colored.[21] This group of Puerto Ricans assimilated to the white structure of American society seems to form an upper-class group that operates discriminately against lower-class Puerto Ricans regardless of color. This pattern persists in Puerto Rico. The lower-class Puerto Ricans in New York settle social life around members of their class and are held down socially as long as their economic conditions remain low.

The general social situation of the lower-class Puerto Ricans in New York City was briefly summarized by Mrs. Baez to the Welfare Council of New York.[22]

> I have worked among the Porto Ricans for over 12 years. I feel I know them thoroughly without mentioning these needs which are not known to everyone. I will say, out of my experience, the following: (1) Porto Ricans do not go to the hospital for medical care, because not being able to understand the language, they resent the impatient mood of the nurses and hospital workers. (2) They will not go to homes or camps, to get a much needed rest and fresh air, for almost the same reason, with the condition that they do not like American food. The International Institute has opened a camp for Spanish speaking people during the month of July and we have been able to keep these Porto Rican women and children who would not stay for a day in another camp, just because they spoke Spanish and the food was cooked by a Porto Rican. (3) Working Porto Ricans will not go to public schools to learn English because in many cases they do not read and write Spanish and it takes a teacher with infinite patience willing to befriend them and talk to them in Spanish to make them understand things, and a teacher in public school could not give them that kind of attention. (4) Porto Ricans will not have any church connections here unless an understanding worker approaches them, one who they are able to understand, who would be willing to talk, and teach and persuade them to do the things that will solve their problems.

The above document reflects some of the basic problems faced by the mass of Puerto Ricans in New York that contribute to bar the acculturation and assimilation of the Puerto Ricans in that city. Acculturation of the lower-class Puerto Rican who is unable to speak English and whose income is very low takes place at a relatively lower rate if compared to that of the Puerto Rican who can speak English fluently, who is able to move away from the colony, and who enjoys a higher economic status. Due to the fact that the colony is continually receiving new influxes of peoples, the possibilities of increasing the rate of acculturation are still more limited. The Puerto Rican in New York who is able to speak English and who is engaged in business or in the professions and whose socio-economic status is at least higher than that of the average for the colony compares to the Puerto Rican in Chicago occupied in business or in the practice of a profession in respect to the fact that his conflicts with the host society are relatively low and his acceptance by the host society offers more possibilities in a lesser amount of time than that generally taken by the lower-class Puerto Ricans in New York.

NOTES

1. Lawrence R. Chenault, *The Puerto Rican Migrant in New York City* (New York: Columbia University Press, 1935), p. 156.

2. Florence G. Cassidy, *Second Generation Youth* (New York: The Woman's Press, 1930). Quoted by Alain Locke and Bernhard J. Stern in *When Peoples Meet* (New York: Committee on Workshops, Progressive Education Association, 1943).

3. Chenault, *op. cit.*, pp. 4 and 62.

4. Quoted in *ibid.*, p. 63, f. The figure calculated by Rice was corroborated by Chenault in unpublished data supplied to him by the Bureau of the Census.

5. Carey McWilliams says that in 1940 "census figures, while not clear, would seem to confirm the fact that the number in New York is between 125,000 and 150,000." See McWilliams, *op. cit.*, p. 214.

6. *Ibid.*

7. Baur, *op. cit.*, p. 1.

8. Chenault, *op. cit.*, pp. 74 ff.

9. *Ibid.*

10. *Ibid.*

11. Personal communication from Jesús Colón, President of the Spanish section of the International Workers Union, March, 1945.

12. *Ibid.*

13. *Ibid.*

14. Manifesto from the collection of Jesús Colón, translated from Spanish (no date).

15. Unsigned manifesto from the collection of Jesús Colón (no date).

16. Cf. Providencia Cintrón, "The National Status and the Social Traits of the Puerto Ricans" (Unpublished M.A. Essay, Department of Sociology, Columbia University, 1936), p. 22 f.

17. Chenault, *op. cit.*, p. 82.

18. *Ibid.*

19. Tomás Blanco, *op. cit.*, p. 3 f.

20. *Ibid.*

21. Chenault, *op. cit.*, p. 151.

22. Part of a report presented by Mrs. Thalia B. Baez, Spanish representative of the International Institute, Y.W.C.A., Brooklyn, to the Welfare Council of New York, April, 1930 (Unpublished document from the collection of Jesús Colón).

CHAPTER FIVE

The Puerto Rican Migrants in Chicago

This chapter summarizes data on the acculturation and assimilation of Puerto Rican migrants in Chicago. The story of the Puerto Ricans in this city is different from that presented by the Puerto Ricans in New York City in two ways: (1) the number of migrants, and (2) the trends in ecological distribution.

The migration of Puerto Ricans to Chicago has been of two types, namely that which may be termed "an old migration," and that which may be termed "a recent migration."

The "old migration" of Puerto Ricans to this city is composed of a scattered and reduced number of native Puerto Ricans, their non–Puerto Rican spouses, and their descendants who have established their residence in this city. The "recent" migration is composed of contract workers who were recruited in the island by a Chicago employment agency during 1946 with the official approval of the insular Department of Labor.

The exact number of Puerto Ricans in this city has not as yet been determined, a minimal population of eighty-six individuals being suggested for the members of the "old migration." The non–Puerto Rican spouses of married native Puerto Ricans and their descendants have been included in this figure insofar as the basic social relationships of native Puerto Ricans are structurally connected with them. Because Puerto Rican immigrants are American citizens, they do not appear either in the Federal or in the city censuses as a foreign group but are merged with the native American population.

The "recent migration" consisted of five hundred and ninety-four[1] white Puerto Ricans who started migrating in 1946 after they had signed contracts in the island to work in the Chicago area as general household workers and as laborers in a foundry. At present, at least half of them have abandoned

their contract jobs and have drifted by their own initiative into other types
of jobs. This condition has forced them to change their initial residential
distribution in the Chicago area. The prevailing tendency among them has
been to move into Mexican neighborhoods. The tendency to group themselves along their own nationality line does not seem to have been operating.
The ecological distribution of Puerto Ricans in Chicago, therefore, is to a
great extent amorphous. No area of major concentration of Puerto Ricans
as such is reckoned in the city. The general tendency operating among Puerto
Ricans with regard to ecological distribution has been to live scattered in the
community, with the exception of those who live in the Mexican neighborhoods who nevertheless are distributed in scattered forms within the said
neighborhoods. This condition has to a great extent been influenced by the
housing shortage prevailing in this city since the end of the war.

The Old Migration

From the point of view of time, the old migration of Puerto Ricans to this
city has covered a maximum period of no less than thirty years. Throughout
that period the number of Puerto Ricans was relatively stable, although part
of this population was replaced. For the purposes of this study, the Puerto
Ricans have been grouped into three categories based on a generational
axis. Native-born Puerto Ricans and their spouses have been grouped as
"parental," the first generation of Chicago-born Puerto Ricans and their
spouses as well as the native-born Puerto Ricans who migrated before their
adolescence have been grouped as "first filial," and their descendants as
"second filial."[2]

Reasons for Migration

The movement of these Puerto Ricans to Chicago was not a direct answer
to a surplus in the labor market. A partial explanation to this statement
is apparently found in the number of Puerto Ricans belonging to this old
migration and in the types of earning occupations they perform.[3] The migrations of these Puerto Ricans to Chicago have been intermittent and of
an individual character. They have occurred mostly as part of the general
interstate movements that are so characteristic of the United States. Most
of these Puerto Ricans came to this city after a period of residence in New
York or in Miami, two of the most accessible ports from Puerto Rico to
the United States. Some of the Puerto Ricans who reside in Chicago, and
who came directly from the island to this city or to any other city in the

Middle West, came with the purpose of continuing their studies, and in some particular point in their careers decided to establish their residence in Chicago. Some others have come to Chicago after having been asked to do so by other individuals, mostly by Puerto Rican friends and relatives already established in this city, and others came to work in Chicago on jobs offered to them while still in Puerto Rico.

Most of them came to the city as young unmarried adults. Among them, those who after having been established in this city decided to marry Puerto Rican woman residing in Puerto Rico, and either went back to the island, returning with their respective wives, or wrote their fiancées, asking them to come to Chicago, where the marriages were celebrated, no marriage by proxy having been celebrated between Puerto Rican women in Puerto Rico and Puerto Rican men in Chicago.

Ecological Distribution

Such a thing as a Puerto Rican colony, or community, or ethnic group does not exist in Chicago. The eighty-six Puerto Ricans of the old migration located for this study are not ecologically grouped with relationship to each other following any ecological patterns. Those who live in nearby areas are just obeying randomness or chance, but there is no tendency operating to condition their residential proximity. Only those Puerto Ricans who are members of primary family groups—parents and their children—live together in the same household.[4] Ten of the households occupied by Puerto Ricans are established in the suburb of Oaklawn and nearby areas in the western side of the city limits. These households are not grouped over specific blocks. No organized social relationships exist among these Puerto Ricans, to the point that some of them did not even know that there were any other Puerto Ricans living nearby. Those who knew or had heard that there were other Puerto Ricans in neighboring places did not seem interested in communicating with each other, and in some cases they showed an attitude of hostility towards their countrymen. Eleven households were occupied by thirty-four individuals in different sections of the North Side. Three households occupied by six Puerto Ricans were located within the limits of the Negro Belt. Three households occupied by five Puerto Ricans were located in the districts of greater concentration of Mexican immigrants in the South and West Sides of the city. Two households were occupied by four Puerto Ricans in the Hyde Park district of the South Side, and one Puerto Rican household occupied by one individual was located in the suburb of Evanston.

Numerical Distribution

The total number of Puerto Rican immigrants belonging to the old migration located in this study amounts to eighty-six individuals. In this figure are included native Puerto Ricans, their American or foreign spouses, and their American-born children. Only thirty-four of the individuals included in this study as Puerto Ricans were actually born in the island. Ten of the native-born Puerto Ricans of marriageable age are unmarried, divorced, or widowed. Only four married couples are native Puerto Ricans. Seven Puerto Ricans are married to white Americans, and ten are married to members of ethnic groups, not including American Negroes. In the first filial generation, eight members are the children of native Puerto Rican couples, ten members have one Puerto Rican parent and one American parent, and fourteen members have one Puerto Rican parent and another ethnic parent. In the first filial generation, the only married individuals are married to native Americans. In this generation, only two of the individuals of marriageable age are unmarried. The age of the remaining seventeen members of this generation range from childhood to early adolescence. The second filial generation is composed of three children under three years of age.

Education and Occupational Patterns

No unskilled laborers have been found among the Puerto Rican migrants in Chicago. Six Puerto Ricans came to Chicago with the aim of continuing study and returning to the homeland, after finishing their academic education. The other Puerto Ricans came in search of better opportunities than those available in the island. None of the Puerto Ricans planned beforehand to stay in Chicago the rest of their lives. Among those who have settled here and have decided to stay here forever, it is frequently heard that they would like to return to Puerto Rico to die, but not to continue living in the island.[5]

Formal education does not seem to have a determining factor in the acculturation and assimilation of Puerto Ricans in this city. A working knowledge of English has proven more advantageous for social and economic adjustment and acceptance by American society than any other single factor. A Puerto Rican lawyer, Tomás Sánchez S.,[6] who has lived in Chicago since 1919, reported that the liberal education he had acquired in Puerto Rican schools was of no use except for his knowledge of the English language.[7] Another Puerto Rican revealed that he had to do all sorts of menial jobs in New York City until he was able to speak English.[8]

Occupationally the Puerto Ricans tend to cluster in business of exportation, in the professions, in clerical work, and in factory work. Ten members of the first filial generation were in the military services during this study. Teaching Spanish and translation jobs are practiced by most of them either as a full-time or as a part-time job.

Social Relationships among the Puerto Ricans

Unlike most immigrants and ethnics in American society, these Puerto Ricans in Chicago have not tended to identify themselves as members of a distinct group. They live in relative isolation from each other, and they do not seem to show much interest in developing voluntary associations with each other either as individuals or as members of the Puerto Rican group.[9] There is not a single clique, and no formal associations composed exclusively of Puerto Ricans.

White native Puerto Ricans who know English relatively well and who enjoy a high socio-economic status have been accepted by native white Americans in their cliques and associations. The relationships of these Puerto Ricans are almost exclusively with other Latin Americans and North Americans engaged in professional and business occupational activities. These relationships have usually started as business relations and later on have been translated into friendship relations. Through these business and professional contacts, Puerto Ricans have been invited and accepted in clubs and societies whose registry is opened to Americans. Among this group of Puerto Ricans, the acquisition of the dominant American social values, attitudes, and moral standards of overt social behavior are noticeable after a short period of contact with them.[10] These individuals usually use English as a means of expression, and when using Spanish, they mix it with words and phrases in English. They participate in community activities. During the war, women belonging to this group had membership in different clubs for knitting, sewing, shipping materials to soldiers overseas, etc. Both men and women were interested in civilian defense programs and were active in this kind of work. Among these individuals the attitude towards Puerto Rico is almost invariably the same. They would like to visit the island, or go there to die, but don't want to live there permanently. They speak of Puerto Rico in an idealized sense, and when describing their relatives in the island, they usually claim relationship to old and wealthy Spanish families who because of some misfortune lost their wealth and prestige. This attitude does not prevail among some of the "self-made men" in this class.

It is within this group that the "American" attitude towards racial issues prevails. Dislike and contempt for American Negroes and Puerto Rican Negroes, and other ethnics, is frequently shown in their conversations. An informant said he chose Chicago as the place to establish his residence because he "knew that only selected people could come to Chicago, neither laborers nor Negroes from Puerto Rico could come."[11] Another member of this group reported in a conversation dealing with the racial situation in the United States that "Booker T. Washington was a conscientious Negro, when he was invited to lecture in a hotel in the loop he entered through the kitchen door, the doors Negroes use. . . . because such is the situation in this country."[12]

These professional and business men tend to live in different areas of the city although they tend to live in the North Side and in suburbs within a predominantly American neighborhood. They live in well-kept, medium-sized apartments, or in their own houses, in clean residential neighborhoods. They are not devout Catholics, although some of them claim to be Catholic. An individual in this group is a member of the Episcopalian church and goes to the services of this church regularly. Another individual goes to a Protestant church in the *Alliance Francaise* because she studies French and the services are conducted in this language. Marriages among these Puerto Ricans have been to white Puerto Ricans or to American whites, except for one case where a Puerto Rican lawyer married an Austrian woman. American wives married to these Puerto Ricans do not work outside their homes although some of them did during the Depression.

White Puerto Ricans who are able to speak in English but who occupationally are engaged in non-professional activities and admit coming from lower classes or from poor Puerto Rican families present a different picture from that of the Puerto Ricans in the professions and in business. Among the former, there is not a discriminatory attitude against members of other ethnic groups, or if this attitude exists it is in a less overt level than among the latter.

A member of this group in a conversation dealing with the patterns of segregation operating in many residential sections of this country stated that segregation areas "are crimes committed by most Americans. . . . I cannot understand why Americans can't see people, as if they were not human. . . . I particularly think about the Japanese-Americans and the Negroes. . . . Americans have said that we are not civilized, but we have proven we are beyond their understanding just because we have always felt the sense of true brotherhood."

The occupational statuses of this group range from skilled factory work to clerical, small trade, and shopkeeping. They live in apartments ranging from small to middle sized, and some of them own their own houses. These people tend to live in neighborhoods where other white ethnics and Americans live.

The neighborhoods are clean, and small unpretentious houses dominate in these areas. The contacts of these individuals with other Puerto Ricans in town are limited, and although they do not show hostility towards the members of their own occupational class, they do not seem to show interest in having contact or frequent relations with them. It is frequently heard from them, nevertheless, expressions of dislike in reference to the Puerto Ricans they think are much better off in the city.

White individuals, members of the lower classes in Puerto Rico and those who are unable to speak English, have found accommodation in the Mexican settlements in Chicago. Among these Puerto Ricans are found a seamstress, a small grocery co-owner, an employee in a radio shop, and a salesman in a retail store. These Puerto Ricans have developed loyalties towards Mexico and show interest in visiting both Mexico and Puerto Rico. Their relationships are mostly with the Mexican community. The Puerto Ricans in the Mexican colony did not know each other at the time this study was conducted but had heard about other Puerto Ricans in Chicago. They nevertheless had not had any contacts with Puerto Ricans in this city. Most of the lower-class Puerto Ricans who are able to speak English, and those who do not know this language, are Catholic and participate in activities sponsored by this church. Some of them are devout Adventist of the Seventh Day Church. The attitude of this group of Puerto Ricans toward other ethnic minorities in the United States, including the Puerto Ricans themselves, was sympathetic, except with reference to upper-class Puerto Ricans and American Negroes.

Very dark skinned Puerto Ricans who are able to speak English have found accommodations in different sections of the Negro Belt with the exception of a woman who lives in a white neighborhood where she works as a domestic.

The attitudes found in these Puerto Ricans on the racial issues of this country are much like those found among American Negroes in northern cities, namely, resentment and rebellion against the subordinated position imposed upon them by the superordinate white group on account of a peculiarity of the American social structure. This situation, nevertheless, is a new one for colored Puerto Ricans in whose home society "color visibility" was not rated in terms alike to those in American society.

There was not a single case of intermarriage between colored Puerto Ricans or between a colored Puerto Rican and colored American, at the time of this study. Marriages and tendencies to marriage among colored Puerto Ricans are towards members of other ethnic groups, namely, of a "Latin" background. A Puerto Rican school teacher is married to a Cuban mulatto who practices law; a Puerto Rican musician is married to a white Brazilian woman; and a bachelor was engaged to a white Italian girl at the time of this study.

The four colored Puerto Ricans in Chicago did not know each other, and had no contacts with other Puerto Ricans in the city. Their social relationships were netted mostly within the Negro substructure, their external contacts being mostly with other Latin ethnics and colored peoples from the West Indies. No Puerto Rican seemed to live around the districts pointed by the census reports as centers of residence of people from Cuba and other West Indies.

The attitude of these individuals towards the United States was one of combined hostility and submissiveness. They also resented the Puerto Ricans who had a discriminatory attitude towards people considered "colored" in this country. A colored Puerto Rican woman reported that she would not go to a certain Spanish Club that operates a restaurant in the city because she was too dark, and she had heard that dark people were not admitted in that club. What she objected to mainly was that this restaurant was operated by Latins who discriminated on the basis of color.

The attitude assumed by the colored Puerto Ricans towards their original society is an idealized one. They would like to go back to Puerto Rico where they feel they would not be discriminated against. They show antagonisms against other ethnics especially against the Mexicans living in this city. A colored Puerto Rican informed me that she did not like Mexicans because they speak like effeminates, and that she would love to go to Mexico if the people there were not Mexicans.

Second-Generation Puerto Ricans in Chicago

The data on the members of the filial generations of Puerto Ricans reveals that the family of procreation is the most important single factor conditioning the degree of assimilation, in a negative form. Children of both Puerto Rican parents are usually able to speak Spanish or at least have some knowledge of this language. In the families where both parents are Puerto Ricans and in the families where one of the parents is Puerto Rican and the other is another Spanish-speaking individual, the Spanish language is used in the family circle to some extent.

The children of one Puerto Rican parent and a non-Spanish-speaking parent tend to be more like the American children, insofar as English is the language of the home. This makes the contacts of these children with other English-speaking children much easier. These individuals are not able to speak or understand Spanish.

In the home where both parents are Puerto Rican the overt behavioral patterns dominant in Puerto Rican society are found to a higher degree than among those where only one of the parents is Puerto Rican. In the latter cases the dominant behavior of American society prevails.

Sentimental and idealized attitudes towards Puerto Rico are strongest in the homes where both parents are Puerto Ricans. In these homes the children are taught loyalties to both Puerto Rico and to the United States. Members of the second generation of Puerto Ricans with only one Puerto Rican parent do not develop sentimental attachments towards Puerto Rico, and their loyalties are mostly towards American society.

The second filial generation of Puerto Ricans is still a very young one—its three members are still in early childhood.

Case Histories

The following case histories are presented with the aim of illustrating the material presented on the old Puerto Rican migration to Chicago.

1. J. J. GROCCIO, A PUERTO RICAN EXPORTER WITH OFFICES IN THE LOOP   J.J. Groccio was born in Ponce, the second largest city in Puerto Rico, in 1882. He belongs to a Spanish family that distinguished itself in politics and journalism during the latter part of the last century. His family was respected and reckoned as a member of the upper class of insular society. They had some wealth but were never considered rich.

When J.J. was five, his mother died, and his elder sister brought him up. His first school experience was in a Catholic school for upper-class children in Ponce. His sister had great affection for her smaller brother, and because he looked unhealthy and he was an orphan and the youngest of the three children in the family, she petted him. When J.J. was thirteen, he fell in love with the daughter of the wealthiest man in his home town and proposed an elopement with her. While still a boy J.J. smoked and drank, two habits he hid from his family and their friends. At fifteen, his father sent him to Spain to start his law course, but J.J. stayed in Havana a couple of years before arriving in Spain.

In Havana, J.J. stayed for a short time with a friend of his father's, but soon moved away and was on his own. In Havana J.J. met young people who were interested in the political problems of Cuba and Puerto Rico, and in 1899, advised by a Cuban revolutionary youth, J.J. decided to go to Spain to study law. In Spain, J.J. lived among students, bullfighters, politicians, aristocrats, and artists and claimed that he could "learn from life" better than from the university. Six months after he registered, he quit it. He left Spain and traveled around France, Italy, and Switzerland for about thirteen years. In 1913 he came to the United States and decided to start earning a living. He remained in New York for six months, and after seeing a map of Chicago and assuming that neither colored Puerto Ricans nor laborers would come to this city, he decided to establish himself here. In Chicago he decided to teach Spanish privately. In 1914 he met three Puerto Ricans in Chicago with whom he has been friends, but with whom he has never wanted business relationships. In 1915 he met the daughter of one of his American students and three months later married her. From that marriage a son was born. A year after the marriage his wife divorced him, and J.J. married another American woman. This woman was ten years his elder. After this marriage he registered in the university and opened an office of foreign trade. After he finished his master's degree, he was appointed to teach in the same university where he studied. At that time he was also honorary vice-consul of a Central American Republic and started radio teaching of Spanish from the *Chicago Tribune* radio station. He was promoted to full consul of the Central American Republic. In 1928, he visited Puerto Rico, and after he returned he divorced his wife. The Depression forced him to reduce his office of foreign trade and he started teaching Spanish again. In 1934, he edited a book on foreign trade. In 1938, he married an American woman, and in 1939, he went to visit his relatives in Puerto Rico again. In 1944, he was separated from his wife and lived in a bachelor's apartment in one of the Chicago suburbs. By that time he kept an office of foreign trade and taught private lessons of Spanish.

The relationships of J.J. to other Puerto Ricans in Chicago are very limited. He knows most of the Puerto Ricans engaged in business, but he does not keep strong friendly relations with them. He says he does not trust Puerto Ricans because they are envious and gossip too much. He claims his friends are mostly Americans and South Americans. He dislikes Mexicans because "if you are frequently with them you get an accent in your speech habits," and claims he has no "racial prejudice," that it is necessary to realize that "the difference between a Chinese and a Negro to a white man is like that between heaven and earth." He says he would not like to return to live in Puerto Rico, but he likes to visit the island and would like to die there. The relationships J.J. has with Puerto Rico are very limited; he does not receive correspondence from anyone in the island. His contacts with his relatives are mostly with those who live in this country.

The Puerto Ricans who know Groccio say that this is a man who has "luck." He is criticized in many occasions by those who believe that "he does not like to work and [marries] women who would support him."

Today J.J. is an old man with gray hair, operating his office of foreign trade in the Loop and planning to write a book on exportation. His office is frequently visited by well-dressed, attractive women whose visits he explains with an evil smile.

2. A PUERTO RICAN WORKER IN CHICAGO WHO SPEAKS ENGLISH   Luis Hortas was born in a small community in the central mountainous slopes of the island. He belongs to a family that for generations has been tilling the soil for a living. The Hortas own a small farm devoted to raising minor crops, tobacco, and coffee. In his home town, Luis Hortas went to grade school and two years of high school. To find a better opportunity than that available in the fields, Luis came to New York with three other Puerto Rican youths. They worked as common laborers in factories, piers, and refineries. Because he did not know English, it was difficult for Luis to go beyond the tasks of common labor. He moved to New Jersey from where he decided to come to Chicago. It was in 1923 that he came to this city. By this time he was able to speak English, and he obtained a job in a factory devoted to processing and canning goods. At present, he is a foreman in one of the plants of this company. In 1926 he went to Puerto Rico for a visit. After he returned to Chicago he wrote to one of his first cousins asking her to marry him. She was then a student at the Normal School. She quit school and came to Chicago, where she and Luis were married in a Catholic ceremony. From this marriage two children have been born. Some years ago, Mrs. Hortas took her daughter to Puerto Rico where they stayed for three months. When they returned the girl was unable to speak English. At present, the Hortas live in their own two-storey house in a suburb of Chicago in a dominantly Irish-American neighborhood. Near their house is the Catholic Church with an adjacent school where both children of the Hortas study. The children are devout Catholics, and both of them and their mother go to church regularly. Luis never goes to church and is criticized by his neighbors. Mrs. Hortas, on the other hand, criticizes the policy of the church in its money collections as well as the men who get drunk during the week and go to church on Sunday. She likes her children to go to church because they are taught "punctuality." The Hortas know some of the Puerto Ricans in town but are aware of the fact that their Puerto Rican acquaintances do not like them insofar as they do not accept their invitations. Mr. Hortas criticizes those Puerto Ricans who have "racial prejudice" and criticizes the American system of segregation of other groups living in this country.

The social life of the Hortas centers mostly on the acquaintances they have made in the neighborhood through Mrs. Hortas and the children.

The Hortas like to eat Puerto Rican meals, and Mrs. Hortas prepares them on Sundays. The rest of the week the Hortas eat American food insofar as it takes less time to prepare it. Mr. Hortas does all the shopping for his wife, who stays at home as he thinks women should neither go out alone nor drive cars. The Hortas keep a henhouse in the basement of their home, and it is personally taken care of by Mr. Hortas. They also have a small vegetable garden in the backyard of the house.

The Hortas speak English to their children. Their older daughter is unable to speak Spanish but understands it. The Hortas think their children should learn Spanish, and plan to send them to Puerto Rico during vacations so that they can pick up the language. In their home they keep photographs, albums, and clippings about Puerto Rico. Mr. Hortas claims that he would like to visit Puerto Rico again but after having had established himself in this country he would prefer to continue living here permanently.

3. A COLORED PUERTO RICAN IN THE CHICAGO BELT   Laura Rondón is a colored Puerto Rican who has been in Chicago since 1935. She is a dark woman with predominantly Caucasian features. She was the third girl in a family of nine children. Her father was a schoolteacher who, after joining the local politics, became mayor of the town. Her mother was a very dark woman. The family was respected in the town, and although the father was a member of the local *casino,* neither his children nor his wife participated in the activities. Laura explains that "they were too dark" and were afraid of being criticized if they went to the *casino.* She says she did not have a feeling of being discriminated against in any other place in Puerto Rico. Laura studied at the University of Puerto Rico, from which she obtained her Normal School degree. She worked in Puerto Rico for a year as a school teacher. The following year she came to New York, where her elder sister lived. In New York she met Carlos Rondón, a Cuban mulatto whom she later married, and in the same year came to Chicago, where Carlos planned to open a law office with a friend of his. At present, Carlos and Laura live in a small apartment in a neat and well-cared-for neighborhood in the Belt. She teaches Spanish at night in a commercial school and keeps house during the day. Her husband practices law in Chicago and has his offices with two other Latin American lawyers. They have a son whom they teach to speak Spanish but who as yet is unable to speak it fluently. Laura is interested in the political problems of Puerto Rico and has a sympathy towards the independent movements of the island. She likes to see and talk to other Puerto Ricans and Latin Americans but feels they discriminate against her. She criticizes American women considering them "immoral." She thinks American influence on Puerto Ricans is "bad" because it gives them "all sort of corruptions." She has a great sympathy towards Cuba and plans to raise her child either in Cuba or in Puerto Rico. Most of the friends of the Rondóns are Cuban or from the other Caribbean islands. Laura dislikes Mexicans and American Negroes.

She keeps in touch with the events in Puerto Rico through a subscription to a Spanish weekly in New York that has a column on the island. She writes to her relatives in Puerto Rico once in a while, but she claims she does not miss them and is not interested in maintaining her relationships with them.

4. A PUERTO RICAN IN THE MEXICAN COLONY OF CHICAGO   Yolanda Torres lives around Ninth Street in a Mexican neighborhood. She is a dark, curly haired woman with round brown eyes and lacks a front tooth. She is the second of three girls born to a shoemaker and his wife in a Puerto Rican coastal city. Yolanda went to school in her home town. While in school, she learned to cook and take care of the home. In 1933 she went to New York with her aunt. She wanted to work and study. Her first job was as a seamstress in her own home. In the house where she lived she met a Mexican family who planned to move to Chicago and who asked her to come with them because in Chicago there were better jobs than in New York. Her aunt allowed her to come to Chicago. She lived with this Mexican family from the time of arrival to this city in 1934 until she married one of their relatives who worked in the steel mills. When Yolanda obtained a job she decided to go to night school, where she met the first and only Puerto Rican she thought lived in Chicago beside herself. This man was a student at Northwestern University who worked as a teacher in the night schools. In 1935 Yolanda married Pedro Velez. She quit school because her husband was jealous. She continued, however, at her job especially after her husband lost his job at the mills. Her marriage was not a successful one. Pedro complained because his wife was working and on many occasions reminded her that they were "living like Americans." He became a drunkard and had a mistress, and they divorced in 1938. Yolanda, who became a devout Catholic in Chicago, suffered much because of her divorce and lives rather isolated from people. She nevertheless is a member of a Mexican club for girls and visits some of her Mexican girl friends around the neighborhood. She has a sewing machine and makes dresses, which she sells from her home.

She loves Mexico and says she would like to go there some time. She has the same attitude towards Puerto Rico, which she says she would not like permanently. After being in Chicago since 1935, Yolanda is not able to speak English well, although she says she knows "enough to get along well."

Summary

The case histories presented here indicate some of the basic attitudes of four Puerto Ricans in Chicago towards both American society and their home society. They also show the basic forms of overt adjustment these individuals have developed to reduce their conflicts with their host society. The life history of J.J. Groccio shows the basic happenings in the life of this individual that prepared him to live in the United States and that conditioned his assimilation to American society. J.J. Groccio has adopted many characteristics that are more common to American society than to Puerto Rican society. His social world is American. He has lived in this country for over thirty years and regards it as the place to live in as compared to Puerto Rico, which is "the place where he would like to die."

The second case history is that of a lower-class peasant who came to this country to escape the rural setting of his homeland. He lacked a knowledge of English and was unequipped to adjust above the level of a laborer until he learned English. He is still attached to the land where he was born but realizes that he should stay in the country where his home is established. He married a Puerto Rican woman, and both of them want their children to learn Spanish and to know about Puerto Rico. They still preserve many aspects of Puerto Rican overt behavior: his wife has a place in the home, she does not like to go out alone, and she does not drive; he keeps the vegetable plot in the yard and the chicken house in their basement. They eat Puerto Rican food on Sunday. The wife and the children go to the Catholic church in the neighborhood, and the children receive their school education from the priests and nuns in the Catholic school. The Hortas realize that their upper-class countrymen do not care about maintaining friendly relationships with them, and they get along well with their Irish-American neighbors.

Laura Rondón has suffered the impact of "racial prejudice" in her home society insofar as she feels she was prevented from mixing with upper-class members of the *casino* in her home town. In the United States she has felt "racial prejudice" to the point of living in the Negro Belt. She resents color prejudice to a great extent and at the same time feels and expresses dislike for American Negroes and Mexicans. She has strong loyalties towards Puerto Rico and Cuba and shows a strong dislike for things American. She does not regard Chicago as the place where she is going to stay permanently, but says she wants to go to Cuba or back to Puerto Rico.

The case of Yolanda Torres is an example of acculturation and assimilation to a non-assimilated social sub-system within the American society. Yolanda does not speak English, and this condition limits her communications with the greater American society since her arrival to the United States. Her first contacts in Chicago were with the Mexican neighborhood, and having married into that group, she has been able to find accommodation in the larger American community through the channels it provides for Mexicans to become a part of it and to maintain their identity as an ethnic group.

The Recent Migration

By the middle of 1946, a private Chicago employment agency, Castle, Barton and Associates, in agreement with the Puerto Rican insular Department of Labor established an office in the island for the purpose of recruiting migrant workers to the Chicago area. Two types of work were offered: general household service, and foundry unskilled jobs. The employment agency offered contracts that guaranteed a full year of work for the migrants. The wages of sixty dollars a month for women engaged in household work and seventy dollars for men performing the same kind of work, plus room and board, sounded attractive to Puerto Ricans who were eager to leave the island because of the unemployment conditions prevailing there. Men were offered a minimum wage of thirty-five dollars a week to do unskilled foundry work. The employment agency would provide airplane transportation for the migrants, and the cost of transportation, as well as agency fees for the service, compulsory earnings, etc., would be discounted from their pay checks.

Castle and Barton contracted three hundred and ninety-six migrant household workers. The majority of them were women supposedly between eighteen and thirty-five years of age. Some married couples were also contracted.[13] A few of the migrants knew some English for communication purposes. About sixty-seven men were contracted to work in unskilled occupations in the Chicago Hardware Foundry Company in North Chicago. Most of these men were unable to speak or understand English.

The ecological distribution of the Puerto Rican workers in Chicago was originally determined by the ecological distribution of their employers who provided their housing accommodations. With the exception of about sixty-seven men assigned to work in the North Chicago foundry, and who were provided lodging in reconverted railroad cars on company property, the migrants were scattered in the Chicago homes where they were employed.

The branch of the Y.W.C.A. in Puerto Rico requested the Y.W.C.A. in Chicago to provide social activities for the Puerto Rican migrant workers. It was then agreed to offer tea for the workers on Thursday afternoons when they were supposed to have their day off. It was through the Y.W.C.A. that the Puerto Rican household workers could be contacted as a group. Early after their arrival the workers became discontented with their jobs. They learned that American household workers in Chicago were usually paid as much as twice the amount they had been offered in Puerto Rico, which theoretically was sixty dollars a month plus room and board. But the salaries actually amounted to forty-one a month after deductions for transportation and compulsory earnings.

The workers complained about the American families, food, the American food habits, the climate, the hours of work, wages, and their general status in the community. The Y.W.C.A. teas were not approved by them. They claimed they only drank tea when they were ill and never on their day off. Nevertheless, they went to the Y.W.C.A. on their day off and talked with each other about these problems.

After a short time in the city they learned there was a large Mexican neighborhood in Chicago. The *Rancho Grande,* a Mexican night club on the North Side, is located near a hotel where the Castle, Barton and Associates employment agency rented rooms to the migrants until they were placed on their jobs. The *Rancho Grande* became a center for the informal gatherings of the Puerto Rican household workers who, after the teas at the Y.W.C.A. were over, would meet there to chat, to eat Mexican food, and to dance to Latin American music. Through the *Rancho Grande* they started, to a large extent, their contacts with the Mexican community.

The Puerto Rican foundry workers in North Chicago, together with the household workers who lived in Chicago suburbs in the North Shore districts, used to meet in the reconverted railroad car that served as a dining room for the foundry workers. The Puerto Rican cooks would prepare special Puerto Rican dishes for the occasions, which were usually on Thursday and Sunday. After dinner, the workers would go to town to meet in the Happy Hour, an American night club frequented by other foundry workers. In the Happy Hour as well as in the foundry, the Puerto Ricans contacted many Mexican *braceros* with whom they developed certain kinds of social relationships that on some occasions manifest themselves as conflictual whereas on other occasions they were cliquish in nature. Some of the foundry workers established consensual relations of marriage with Puerto Rican household workers, moved out of the railroad cars, and rented rooms in Mexicans homes in town.

The Puerto Rican foundry workers started to become dissatisfied with their jobs largely because their cash pay checks after discount seldom were over one dollar for a normal day of work. They looked for other jobs in town, but apparently were rejected by employers or by the state employment agency.[14] About one-half of the workers have already abandoned their jobs and have come to the Loop or gone to New York City to stay with relatives or friends. Some of them were returned to Puerto Rico by the Chicago Hardware Foundry Company on the grounds that they were not physically fit to perform foundry work.

Those who remained in Chicago have tended to move into Mexican neighborhoods, and due to the housing difficulties many of them have had to live in transient hotels on South Clark and State Streets in the Loop, until they were able to find permanent places. The Mexican Civic Committee has been active in helping these Puerto Ricans to find accommodations in Mexican homes. Social service agencies have also referred these Puerto Ricans to Mexican neighborhoods insofar as they are Spanish-speaking peoples. Cliques of Puerto Rican men have tried to live in nearby places, but the general pattern of ecological distribution of Puerto Ricans seems to be amorphous. Puerto Ricans who have obtained permanent jobs have moved into Mexican neighborhoods as individuals and do not seem to concentrate in specific districts of the Mexican community.

The household workers who have discontinued working under contracts have tended to move into the Mexican community. Puerto Rican women in this group have shown the tendency to live consensually with Mexican men, while Puerto Rican men have shown the tendency to have marital relations with Puerto Rican women only.

Numerical Distribution

The figures on the recent migration of Puerto Ricans to Chicago are not very clear, especially in regard to those who have discontinued working under contracts. On January 16, 1947, Senator Géigel Polanco reported that of the 396 household workers who came to Chicago under contracts, 44 had returned to Puerto Rico and 65 had obtained other jobs or their location was unknown.[15] He also reported that only 36 men had remained working for the Chicago Hardware Foundry Company, 11 of whom lived in town. The situation is that since the government report of Senator Géigel Polanco, more and more workers have been abandoning their contract jobs. The exact figure of Puerto Rican migrants in Chicago at present cannot as yet be determined.

Educational and Occupational Patterns

It has already been stated that the recent migration of Puerto Ricans to Chicago was sponsored by a contract between the migrants and a Chicago employment agency.[16] The contracts were for two kinds of employment: (1) domestic or general household service, and (2) unskilled foundry labor. The formal education of the workers ranged from not having ever been in school to individuals with some college education. Household workers interviewed claimed they had never before worked in that occupational activity. Among them there were clerks, typists, practical nurses, sales ladies, housewives, maids, and students who thought they could continue their training in Chicago while working. Among the foundry workers were found men who were occupied in skilled trades or in clerical positions in

Puerto Rico, but none had ever worked in a foundry. Three Puerto Rican cooks were contracted in the island to prepare the meals for these workers. In Chicago, the company asked these workers to choose a supervisor, and they selected a Puerto Rican worker who was able to speak English fluently. The problems between workers and management were to be submitted to the Puerto Rican supervisor, who would act as an interpreter and a middleman between workers and managerial structure.

Most of the foundry workers who had abandoned their contracts tried to obtain jobs in the Loop through the United States Employment Service or by applying directly for such jobs as press-boy, dishwasher, etc., in restaurants in the Loop. The household workers, on the other hand, tended to look for factory jobs, and at present, the greater number of Puerto Ricans in factories are unskilled workers in plants like the National Biscuit Company, the Florsheim Shoe factories, and the Abbot Laboratories in Waukegan.

Social Relations of the Recent Migrants

The first contacts among the Puerto Ricans as a group in Chicago were those they established through recreation provided for them by the Y.W.C.A. on their day off. In the Y.W.C.A., the workers met, talked, and danced. Social contacts between them during the rest of the week were almost non-existent, since they were so scattered through the city and limited in their time off. Informal gatherings in the Mexican night club, the *Rancho Grande,* also created and strengthened social bonds among the Puerto Ricans who worked near the Loop and the North Side. A recently opened night club, the *Copacabana,* has also become a meeting place for the Puerto Ricans. Contacts between the workers and some Puerto Rican students in the city were mainly established in the Y.W.C.A. recreational activities and in the lodging cars in North Chicago. The Puerto Ricans working in North Chicago and nearby districts met in the dining car of the foundry workers, and in an American night club in town. In North Chicago there is a Mexican neighborhood, and most of the Mexicans are engaged as employees of the Chicago Hardware Foundry Company. The relationships between this group of Puerto Ricans and Mexicans were mainly established through their jobs and the limited recreational facilities provided in the town. All the Puerto Rican migrants who have moved out to the town are living in Mexican homes or in transient hotels.

The Puerto Ricans, however, dislike being identified as Mexicans. No open group conflicts exist between them, but individual disputes along nationality lines are frequently observed. Sources of disputes are usually related to matters of value attached to their particular cultural and social life. Among the migrants whose contacts with Mexicans started through their informal gatherings in the *Rancho Grande* night club, an attitude of dislike towards Mexicans is usually found.

The most significant single reason for this attitude is probably shown by the disorganizing effect that contacts between Mexican men and Puerto Rican girls have had. The non-permanent and illegal marital relations that have followed these contacts have resulted in situations not approved by Puerto Rican standards of social behavior. Illegal marital relations between Puerto Ricans have tended to show a more permanent character and seem to be approved by the Puerto Rican group. The social status of a Puerto Rican woman in Chicago, however, seems to be attached to the concept of virginity. Even women who married through the Catholic church, which probably is the most acceptable marriage ceremonial, have shown shame in admitting that they are not virgins. In the meetings of the recently arrived Puerto Rican women, the conversations center around the subject of virginity and other morals attached to womanhood.

Direct contacts between the "recent" Puerto Rican migrants and the "old" Puerto Rican migrants have been practically non-existent, although one of the members of the "old" migration seemed to have been acquainted with the project of the "new" migration as indicated by the publication of his picture with the first group of contracted household workers who migrated to Chicago in October, 1946. Personal social contacts between Puerto Ricans of the recent migration and the larger American society have been limited to the employer-employee type of relationships, and to their contacts with American co-workers in the factory and foundry. An attitude of dislike is indicated by verbalizations against American Negroes. A member of the new migration said, "not even Negroes were getting as low wages as the Puerto Ricans in Chicago." Another migrant claimed that "American Negroes were not like Puerto Rican Negroes because in this country, Negroes just were not equal to white people," so she would not even think of speaking to an American Negro.

This attitude toward the American Negro probably stems largely from the fact that the recent migration of Puerto Ricans theoretically only included white workers. Among the workers who came, nevertheless, many of them would be considered Negroes in the United States but were considered as white by the Puerto Ricans. No attitude of racial discrimination is found to operate against them by the lighter-skinned Puerto Rican migrants.

Social Welfare

The social conditions prevailing among the Puerto Ricans in Chicago attracted the attention of a group of Puerto Rican and American students from the University of Chicago who drafted a report[17] in English and in Spanish for the purpose of informing both the insular and the Federal governments, and to inform other organizations and individuals interested in the United States and Puerto Rico on these conditions. The students' report received wide publicity in the island. Miss Carmen Isales, a Puerto Rican social worker who had come to Chicago on a vacation trip, checked the data obtained and reported by the students' preliminary report and wrote another report addressed to the Governor of Puerto Rico confirming the conditions exposed by the University of Chicago students.[18] The Senate of Puerto Rico ordered an official investigation of the conditions of the Puerto Rican contract workers in Chicago, and the migrations were stopped until a new policy regulating migrant contract labor could be adopted by the insular Legislature.

The Council of Social Agencies of Chicago had a special meeting early in January, 1947, with the purpose in mind of drafting a policy of social action with regard to the Puerto Rican contract workers in the city. The Y.W.C.A. acquired the professional services of Miss Carmen Isales, who since January, 1947, has been administering the policy of social service aids sponsored by the Y.W.C.A. for the Puerto Ricans in Chicago.

Summary

The recent migration of Puerto Ricans to Chicago consisted of five hundred and ninety-four individuals contracted in Puerto Rico for household service and foundry unskilled labor in the Chicago area. The contracted workers were supposed to be white. The majority of the workers were women, although some married couples, as well, were recruited for household work. Only men were contracted for foundry work. The original ecological distribution of these workers was determined by their employers, who provided them with housing accommodations. All of the Puerto Ricans, with the exception of the men who worked at the foundry, lived scattered in the community. After a short period in the city the workers started drifting apart from their original work due to what they considered inadequate living and working conditions. This implied an ecological redistribution. The Mexican neighborhoods were mainly chosen as their new residential areas. The fact that most of these Puerto Ricans do not speak English explains largely their moving into Mexican neighborhoods instead of moving into areas occupied predominantly by Americans. Also, the relatively reduced number of Puerto Ricans and the unbalanced sexual ratio of the group have contributed to this shift into Mexican neighborhoods. The interest of the Mexican Civic Committee in helping the Puerto Ricans to find housing accommodations in the Mexican community helped to increase the mobility of the recently arrived Puerto Ricans in Chicago.

NOTES

1. *El Imparcial* (San Juan, no date).

2. Cf. W. L. Warner and L. Srole, *op. cit.*, pp. 30 ff.

3. Infra.

4. Two cases fall out of this general tendency: a bachelor lives in the same apartment as his brother and wife, and two brothers married to two sisters live in the same house although in separate sections. For the purpose of this study a household is defined as the dwelling place of at least one Puerto Rican or a direct descendant of a Puerto Rican. Under this definition, a room occupied by a Puerto Rican or a direct descendant of a Puerto Rican is considered as a Puerto Rican household.

5. From interview material.

6. Names of informants are fictitious in order to protect their identities.

7. From interview with Mr. Tomás Sánchez S.

8. From interview with Mr. Luis Hortas.

9. Mr. Moisés Ledesma informed the writer that only nine Puerto Ricans came to the meeting for the organization of a Puerto Rican Club founded by him in the thirties. Mr. Luis Hortas, a Puerto Rican immigrant in Chicago, informed the writer "that about ten Puerto Ricans came to the meeting and about six of them were students" (From interview material).

10. Infra.

11. From interview with Mr. J. J. Groccio.

12. From interview with Mr. Natalio Pérez.

13. V. Géigel Polanco, "Informe Sobre Las Condiciones de Vida y Trabajo de Los Obreros Puertorriqueños Contratados Por Conducto de la Agencia Castle, Barton Associates de Chicago," Washington, January 16, 1947 (Typewritten).

14. Written statement by Joaquín López Elías and confirmed verbally by Mr. Horner, C.I.O. United Steel Workers of America regional director.

15. V. Géigel Polanco, *op. cit.*, p. 1.

16. Supra.

17. Héctor Alvarez Silva *et al.*, "Preliminary Report on the Puerto Rican Contract Workers in the Chicago Area," November 25, 1946 (Mimeographed).

18. C. Isales, "*Situación de los Obreros Puertorriqueños Contratados por la Agencia de Empleos* Castle, Barton and Associates," Chicago, December 23, 1946 (Typewritten).

CHAPTER SIX

Conclusions

The Comparative Acculturation and Assimilation of Puerto Ricans in the United States

The main problem of this study has been to analyze the processes of acculturation and assimilation with particular reference to the double factor of size of the immigrant group and its ecological distribution. The Puerto Rican immigrants in Chicago, who compose a scattered and reduced population, and the Puerto Rican immigrants in New York City, who compose a large population and are distributed in consolidated neighborhoods or a colony, were chosen for purposes of comparison.

Data on both groups show that there is a correlation between the relative size of the immigrant group and its ecological distribution.

Acculturation as a process occurs in any situation where two people come into continuous and direct contact with each other.[1] The trend of this contact situation is towards the reintegration of the cultural life of either or both people involved. The final process of acculturation is therefore dependent on certain specific factors that tend to modify and to determine both its direction and speed. The factors of size of an immigrant group, its ecological distribution, and the length of time in the host community are of utmost importance. Assimilation is a process interdependent of acculturation, but the latter is not necessarily inclusive of the former. The time when an immigrant or ethnic group has lost its own identity to the point that it is accepted by the dominant American social system as one of its component parts assumes the immigrant or ethnic group has achieved ultimate assimilation into the native American society and can be safely described also as an acculturated group. Assimilation in the social level cannot occur without acculturation, properly speaking, while acculturation can exist to a large extent by itself. Cases in point are those of the American Negro and other minorities that through certain unrewarding phenomena such as "color visibility" are prevented full participation in the American social life.[2]

The Process of Acculturation in a "Colony"

Warner and his associates have shown how the residential patterns of ethnics develop[3] in the American society. Relatively small groups of ethnics of a common national, social, and cultural background tend to live scattered in the community, or mixed in already established ethnic neighborhoods. The colony situation is associated with the existence of a large number of ethnics of a common background. The former condition is the case of the Puerto Ricans in Chicago, and the latter of the Puerto Ricans in New York City. The colony situation affects the speed of the processes of acculturation and assimilation. The colony has its own semi-autonomous social structure and organization with its own mores and standards of social behavior that are a reflection of those prevailing in the original society of the ethnics. The development of a "colony" implies the appearance of institutions and usages that give internal coherence to the social life of the in-group. The structural conformations of the immigrants' associations and usages are the channels by means of which the immigrants relate with each other and with the native American society. To some extent the colony is a reaction against acculturation, insofar as it tries to keep alive the usages and traditions of the original society. The colony, on the other hand, does exemplify acculturation insofar as it is the structural contact between the ethnic and the dominant American community. Acculturation and assimilation, nevertheless, operate very slowly in ethnic communities that resist the changes in order to maintain themselves.

Evidence points to the fact that the Puerto Rican community in New York City is a hindrance to the acculturation and assimilation of Puerto Ricans there. The group of Puerto Ricans in New York City is large enough to maintain an organized Puerto Rican community organization whose function is chiefly to maintain and foster social solidarity of the in-group and to relate the Puerto Rican immigrants as a block to the larger community. The lower social status of the Puerto Rican group in New York City limits the social relations between members of that community and native Americans. The fact that in New York City the Puerto Rican community organization operates to maintain a live and functioning pattern of behavior dominant in Puerto Rico makes it a strong condition for curbing acculturation and thus assimilation.

Scattered Immigrants

The condition of scattered families and individuals who establish themselves in American communities in relative ecological isolation from each other varies from that of relatively large numbers of immigrants of a common traditional and national background who concentrate ecologically in "colonies." The absence of a collective ethnic structure reduces the contacts among the members of the ethnic group, promoting in this way wider relations between the ethnics and the host community. The trend is therefore towards a more direct integration with the host community, while in the colony situation, the dominant trend is towards the integration of the in-group. The factor of relative isolation among ethnics of a common traditional and national background seems to be very significant, therefore, in increasing the rate of the processes of acculturation and assimilation. The case of the old migration of Puerto Ricans to Chicago illustrates how a first generation of migrants have adapted themselves to the host community to the point of having no social identity as members of the Puerto Rican society. The case of the recent migration of Puerto Ricans to Chicago, on the other hand, shows how the ethnics tend to mix in a community more similar to their own than is the host community as represented by their tendency to live in the Mexican neighborhoods.

Such conditions as the lower social status of the recent migrants, as shown by the fact that most of their direct contacts with the larger society are those of employer-employee relationships, have influenced these Puerto Ricans to develop an attitude of resistance to personal contacts with the host society. The lack of a working knowledge of English and of the prevailing modes of behavior of the American social system has contributed to hinder their participation in the American community as such and to increase their social participation within the Mexican community. The social conditions of the recent migrants from Puerto Rico, however, are at present those of disintegration, but through the guidance of social welfare organizations they will probably crystallize into the development of a more rapid knowledge of American society, which in turn will produce an equilibrium towards the integration of these recent migrants to American life. This, of course, is contingent on the fact that the number of Puerto Rican migrants does not increase considerably enough so as to shape itself into a Puerto Rican community in Chicago. The acculturation and assimilation of the recent migrants who expect to stay permanently in this city will probably follow trends similar to that of the old migrants insofar as their direct contacts with Puerto Rican society are reduced and the systems of social control of Puerto Rican society will become weaker.

The tendency found among the recent migrants to move into the Mexican neighborhoods may result in either of the following situations before the ultimate end of the processes of acculturation and assimilation is accomplished. First, Puerto Ricans will tend to become Mexicanized. This condition will probably operate mainly with women who will marry into the Mexican group. The contacts between Puerto Ricans and Mexicans are mainly in an age level that ranges from adolescence to early adulthood. This circumstance is operative in the sense that this age group of Mexicans is probably undergoing a rapid process of Americanization, which will be reflected in their social relationships with the Puerto Ricans. Secondly, the accomplishment of the processes of acculturation and assimilation of these Puerto Ricans, if the group is not considerably increased by new migrations from the island, will probably be a more rapid one than in the Puerto Rican neighborhoods in New York City.

Summary

Data on the Puerto Rican immigrants in a situation of contact-continuum in two different areas of the United States show how the processes of acculturation and assimilation may operate at different relative rates regarding peoples of a common social and traditional background who migrated to basically similar areas as represented by the cities of Chicago and New York. The process of acculturation is limited by a colony structure, as is thus assimilation. This has been the case of the Puerto Ricans in New York. Acculturation and assimilation, on the other hand, occur more rapidly among immigrants who become ecologically "lost" in the host community. This is the case of the "old migration" of Puerto Ricans to Chicago.

The Puerto Rican migration to New York shows similar aspects to European mass immigrations to American industrial cities. The formation of the Puerto Rican colony in New York has followed the principle that because New York was in a direct shipping route from Puerto Rico and was the best-known American community in the island, it has attracted the majority of Puerto Rican migrants.

There are many Puerto Ricans who think New York is the entire United States, or that they are equivalents. New York offered opportunities to the Puerto Ricans that the island denied them. Continuous influxes of Puerto Rican families and individuals to New York who established residence there have resulted in a Puerto Rican colony. In Chicago a Puerto Rican colony was not formed by the "old migrants" because the group was too small and because they migrated as individuals and became "lost" in the city. Their social contacts are mostly with non–Puerto Ricans, and an in-group solidarity never developed among them.

The case of the "recent migration" of Puerto Ricans to Chicago represents an undetermined condition as yet for which a prediction is offered: there will not be a Puerto Rican colony in Chicago unless the number of Puerto Rican immigrants to this city increases by a large group of Puerto Rican family units or by the migration of large groups of unmarried adolescents and adults selected on a proportionate sex ratio. If the above minimal conditions are not granted, it can be hypothecated that the present Puerto Rican population in Chicago will not concentrate in certain exclusive districts of the city. The reasons are as follows: (1) the present population of Puerto Ricans is too small; (2) the sex ratio consists of one woman to five men, and complete Puerto Rican family units are numerically insignificant; (3) "recent migrants" have been encouraged to live scattered in the city if they want to succeed economically and socially in the United States.

Thursday meetings of Puerto Rican migrants held at the Y.W.C.A. are transitional in placing the Puerto Rican women within the particular clubs and associations of the Y.W.C.A. with mixed membership.

The fact that the "recent migrants" came to perform low-status work under the prevailing standard rates for this city is an added condition for the Puerto Ricans to aim at the loss of their ethnic visibility in this community.

The formation of an immigrant colony requires certain minimal conditions for its growth: such factors as size and balanced social units as provided by families or by potential marriages within the in-group are needed. The colony is an integrated society and functions if such minimal conditions are provided in its structural make-up. It is a natural system integrated by its parts, that is, the institutions and usages of the people who live within its structural make-up. The same social mechanisms that operate to place large numbers of immigrants together within an ethnic community organization also place scattered immigrants in the structure of the large society. People continue to search for their integration within a group that provides social orientation for their behavior.

Notes

1. Redfield, Linton, and Herskovitz, *op. cit.,* pp. 149 ff.
2. L. Srole, *op. cit.,* p. 6.
3. Warner and Srole, *op. cit.*

BIBLIOGRAPHY

Theory

Gardiner, B. B. *Human Relations in Industry.* Chicago: R. D. Irwin, Inc., 1945.

Linton, R. (ed.). *Acculturation in Seven American Indian Tribes.* New York: D. Appleton-Century Co., 1940.

Locke, A., and Stern, B. J. (eds.). *When Peoples Meet.* New York: Committee on Workshops, Progressive Education Association, 1942.

Park, R. E., and Miller, H. A. *Old World Traits Transplanted.* New York: Harper and Brothers, 1921.

Redfield, R. "Cooperation and Conflict as Modes of Social Integration in Cultural Change." Lecture delivered at the Oriental Institute, University of Chicago, November 30, 1945 (Mimeographed).

———. *Tepoztlan.* Chicago: University of Chicago Press, 1931.

———. *The Folk Culture of Yucatan.* Chicago: University of Chicago Press, 1941.

Redfield, R., Linton, R., and Herskovitz, M. J. "Memorandum on the Study of Acculturation," *American Anthropologist* (January–March, 1936), pp. 149–215.

Srole, L. "Ethnic Groups and American Society." Unpublished Ph.D. dissertation, Department of Anthropology, University of Chicago, 1940.

Thomas, W. I., and Znaniecki, F. *The Polish Peasant in Europe and in America.* 2 Vols. New York: A. A. Knopf, 1927.

Warner, W. L., and Srole, L. *The Social Systems of American Ethnic Groups.* Yankee City Series, Vol. III. New Haven: Yale University Press, 1945.

Ethnic Backgrounds

Abbad y Lasierra, Fray I. *Historia Natural, Geografica y Civil de la Isla de San Juan Bautista de Puerto Rico.* Comentada y anotada por D. Jose Julian Acosta. Puerto Rico, 1865.

Alvarez, H., et al. "Preliminary Report on the Conditions of the Puerto Rican Contract Workers in the Chicago Area." Chicago, November 25, 1946 (Mimeographed).

Baur, E. J. "Delinquency among Mexican Boys in South Chicago." Unpublished master's thesis, Department of Sociology, University of Chicago, 1938.

Blanco, Tomás. *El Prejucio Racial en Puerto Rico*. San Juan: Bibioteca de Autores Puertorriquenos, 1942.

Calcott, W. H. *The Caribbean Policy of the United States, 1890–1920*. Baltimore: Johns Hopkins University Press, 1942.

Cebollero, P. A. *La Linguistica-Politica Escolar de Puerto Rico*. San Juan: Consejo Superior de Ensenanza, Publications Pedagogicas, Serie II, Numero 1, 1945.

Chenault, L. R. *The Puerto Rican Migrant in New York City*. New York: Columbia University Press, 1935.

Cintron, P. "The National Status and the Social Traits of the Puerto Ricans." Unpublished master's essay, Department of Sociology, Columbia University, 1936.

Coeje, C. H. "*Nouvelle Examen des Langues des Antilles.*" *Journal de la Société des Américanistes de Paris*, XXXI (1939), pp. 1–129.

Degolia, Darwin Jack. *Problemas Tarifarios de Puerto Rico*. Translated and commented on by A. J. Colorado, San Juan, 1936.

Diffie, B. W., and Diffie, J. W. *Porto Rico: A Broken Pledge*. New York: Viking Press, 1931.

Federal Writers' Project. *The Italians of New York*. New York: Random House, 1938.

Fernandez, Garcia R. *The Book of Porto Rico*. San Juan, 1923.

Fewkes, J. W. The Aborigines of Porto Rico and Neighboring Islands. *Bureau of American Ethnology Annual Report*. Washington: Government Printing Office, 1907.

Flinter, Colonel George. *An Account of the Present State of the Island of Puerto Rico*. London: Longman, Rees, Orme, Brown, Green, and Longman, 1834.

Gamio, M. *Mexican Immigration to the United States*. Chicago: University of Chicago Press, 1930.

Gandara, R. *Land and Liberty*. San Juan: Bureau of Supplies, Printing, and Transportation, 1943.

Géigel Polanco, V. *El Despertar de un Pueblo*. San Juan: Bibliteca de Autores Puertorriquenos, 1942.

———. "Informe Sobre Condiciones de Vida y Trabajo de los Obreros Puertorriquenos Contratados por Conducto de la Agencia de Empleos Castle, Barton, Associates *de* Chicago." Washington: January 16, 1947 (Typewritten).

———. *La Legislación Social de Puerto Rico*. San Juan, 1944.

Isales, C. "Situacion de los Obreros Puertorriqueños Contratados por la Agencia de Empleos Castle, Barton and Associates." Chicago, December 23, 1946 (Typewritten).

James, P. E. *Latin America*. New York: Lothrop, Lee, Shephard Co., 1942.

McWilliams, Carey. "Puerto Ricans and Other Islanders," *Brothers Under the Skin*. Boston: Little, Brown and Co., 1942.

Mejías, F. *Condiciones de Vida de las Clases Jornaleras de Puerto Rico.* Monografías de la Universidad de Puerto Rico. Ciencia Social Numo. 2, Serie C, Universidad de Puerto Rico, 1946.

Paniagua, A. "Ethnologic Social Sketch." *The Book of Puerto Rico,* ed. E. F. García. San Juan, 1923.

Pattee, R. "The Puerto Ricans." *The Annals: American Academy of Political and Social Science,* CCXXIII (1942).

Pedreira, A. S. *Insularismo.* San Juan: Biblioteca de Autores Puertorriquenos, 1942.

Picó, R., and Haas, W. H. "Puerto Rico." *The American Empire.* Edited by H. W. Haas. Chicago: University of Chicago Press, 1940.

Puerto Rico Planning, Urbanizing, and Zoning Board. *A Development Plan for Puerto Rico.* Technical Paper No. 1. Santurce: Office of Information, 1944.

Rogler, C. C. *Comerio.* Lawrence: University of Kansas Publications, 1940.

———. "The Role of Semantics in the Study of Racial Distance in Puerto Rico." *Journal of Social Forces.* May, 1944, pp. 448–453.

Santullano, L. de. *Mirada al Caribe, Fricción de Culturas en Puerto Rico.* "Jornadas" 54. Mexico: El Colegio de Mexico, Centro de Estudios Sociales, 1945.

Seabrook, W. *These Foreigners.* New York: Harcourt, Brace and Co., 1938.

Spinden, H. "The Population of Ancient America." *Annual Report of the Regents of the Smithsonian Institute for the Year Ended June 30, 1929.* Washington: Government Printing Press, 1929. pp. 451–471.

Tugwell, R. G. *Changing the Colonial Climate.* Edited by John Lear. San Juan: Bureau of Supplies, Printing and Transportation, 1942.

———. *The Stricken Land.* Garden City: Doubleday and Co., 1947.

United States Bureau of the Census. *Fifteenth Census of the United States: 1930. Population,* Vol. II. Washington: Government Printing Office, 1933.

———. *Statistical Abstract of the United States: 1944–1945.* Washington: Government Printing Office, 1945.

United States Congress. *Hearing before the Committee on Territories and Insular Affairs. Independence for Puerto Rico On Senate Bill 227,* 79th Congress, 1st Session. Washington: Government Printing Office, 1945.

———. House of Representatives. Hearings before the Subcommittee of the Committee on Territories and Insular Affairs, to accompany H.R. 159. *Investigation of the Political, Economic, and Social Conditions in Puerto Rico.* 78th Congress. Washington: Government Printing Office, 1944.

———. House of Representatives Investigation of the Political, Economic, and Social Conditions in Puerto Rico. *Appendix to Hearings before the Subcommittee of the Committee on Territories and Insular Affairs, to Accompany H.R. 159.* 78th Congress, 1st Session. Washington: Government Printing Office, 1943.

United States Congress, *Investigation of Political, Economic, and Social Conditions in Puerto Rico,* App. to Hearings before the subcommittee (Washington: Government Printing Office, 1944).

United States Congress. Senate, *Independence for Puerto Rico.* Hearing before the Committee on Territories and Insular Affairs, U.S. Senate, 79th Congress, 1st Session on S. bill 227, April 23, 24, 25, 26, 27, and May 1 and 8, 1945. (Washington: Government Printing Office, 1945).

Winter, M. O. *Mexico and Her People of Today.* (New revised edition) Boston: The Page Co., 1918.

PART TWO

Reflections on Puerto Rican Immigrants in New York and Chicago

Puerto Rican "Spatio-Temporal Rhythms" of Housing and Work

Zaire Zenit Dinzey-Flores

> The island of Puerto Rico is the smallest of the greater Antilles with an area of 3,435 square miles. It lies between the Atlantic Ocean and the Caribbean Sea at a distance of 950 miles from the coast of Florida and 500 miles from the coast of Venezuela. Seismically the island is in the earthquake and the hurricane belts. Climatically it is a tropical land. Its summer temperature averages eighty degrees Fahrenheit and its winter temperature averages seventy-six degrees Fahrenheit. Narrow alluvial plains skirt the island and a range of central mountains runs through it from east to west. The highest peak of the *cordillera* is 4,398 feet above sea level. Rainfall is varied and ranges from 26 to 145 inches in some areas: Showers generally last a few minutes and are followed by a bright, warm sunshine.
> —Elena Padilla, "Puerto Rican Immigrants
>   in New York and Chicago"

Because Puerto Rico is located in the tropics, Puerto Ricans are deemed to be tropical people. They come from a tropical island of sea, sand, cool breezes, and plentiful fruit and have used the island's fauna, topography, and geography to describe who they are and what they are like. It is no surprise, then, that in her 1947 master's thesis that Elena Padilla included a geographical description of the island of Puerto Rico and the cities where Puerto Ricans resided. She not only described a mass of land but also provided an image, a portrait of livelihood and culture between ocean and sea, in the plains and the mountains, across seasons of heat, more heat, and cyclical hurricanes.[1]

Beyond the natural environment, Padilla was concerned about the community and spatial built environment that shaped the lives of Puerto Ricans in Chicago, New York, and Puerto Rico. Her work represents one of the early writings documenting the ecological distribution of Puerto Ricans in New York and Chicago and reveals an explicit and implicit awareness that people's everyday lives are interconnected with their environment. Although Padilla's central interest is the assimilation and acculturation process of Puerto Ricans in the United States, she privileges space as an essential component for understanding the cultural, work, and home lives of ethnic and racial groups in the United States. Henri Lefebvre suggests that it is not sufficient to provide a description of space but is also necessary to elucidate the everyday social processes—the "natural rhythms"—and the interlocutors involved in the production of space.[2] Padilla's work, and her thesis in particular, provides rhythmic deconstructions of notes, keys, and tempo of everyday home and work life melodies etched on and produced by Puerto Rican residential settlements of mid-twentieth-century Chicago and New York.

Elena Padilla's Urban Latino Ecology

To understand Puerto Ricans' process of assimilation in Chicago and New York, Padilla uses the concept of "ecology"—the science that examines the relationships between organisms and their environments. Borrowed from the natural sciences, the best known early application of ecology to the social sciences was by the founders of the Chicago School of Sociology, Robert E. Park and Ernest W. Burgess, in the early 1920s.[3] Park, a student of Georg Simmel, was aware of the interaction of social action with the physical environment and used the concept of "human ecology" to explain urban populations in the United States. In their 1925 seminal work—*The City*—Robert E. Park et al. apply the fauna and flora definition of ecology to urban sociological processes. They define human ecology as

> a study of the spatial and temporal relations of human beings as affected by the selective, distributive, and accommodative forces of the environment. Human ecology is fundamentally interested in the effect of *position,* in both time and space, upon human institutions and human behavior. "Society is made up of individuals spatially separated, territorially distributed, and capable of independent locomotion." These spatial relationships of human beings are the products of competition and selection, and are continuously in process of change as new factors enter to disturb the competitive relations or to facilitate mobility.[4]

The ecological lens was transmitted to Elena Padilla through advisers at the University of Chicago. For her master's thesis in anthropology, Padilla's committee included thesis adviser Sol Tax and two thesis readers—Robert Redfield and Louis Wirth. These thesis readers were more directly responsible for her reach into the field of sociology for the concept of ecology.[5] Redfield, an anthropologist by training, was Robert E. Park's son-in-law and in his work paralleled the sociological methods and analysis modeled by his father-in-law, which he readily displayed in his study of Mexican immigrants in Chicago. On the other hand, Louis Wirth, a renowned urban sociologist who was integral in developing the concept of the "ghetto" in sociology, encouraged Padilla's analytical sensibilities for studying immigrant populations in an urban setting. Together, Redfield and Wirth paved a path for Padilla's ecological analysis of immigrant populations and her adoption of Parkian models in her study of Puerto Ricans in the United States.

Padilla strictly borrows from Park and Miller's *Old World Traits Transplanted* in exploring the relationship of ecology with acculturation. In what I call her view of "ecological assimilation," Padilla suggests that there are stages of ecological concentration that correlate with the degree of assimilation of ethnic immigrants. She lists three stages of immigrant "ecological assimilation." The first stage, "ecological concentration," is characterized by early migration. In this stage, migrants arrive, settle, and interact with an established ethnic neighborhood that is typically located close to work opportunities. According to Padilla, members of the same nationality or social group concentrate and become residential nuclei or colonies, as exemplified by communities like Little Italy, Little Warsaw, and Little Greece, among others.[6] In the second stage, Padilla argues that American society has a "disorganizing effect" on the social subsystem of an immigrant colony because the group relies on the larger American society for basic social and economic needs.[7] At this stage, the disorganizing effect paves the road for acculturation. In the third and final stage, "disintegration" of the consolidated residential area occurs, resulting in a "crystallization of a broader perspective" and "partial acceptance of the social orientation as provided by American life."[8] At this stage, assimilation has occurred.

The three stages of assimilation that Padilla proposes have a precise ecological and spatial component. In order to be assimilated, she contends, immigrants progressed through colonies toward being spatially integrated in American structure. She corroborates this perspective of Park and Miller in her extensive citation of B. B. Gardner.[9] Her comments display the ecological component of acculturation, which emphasizes the movement from the "poorest districts" to the "own neighborhood" or "islands" (which Padilla also referred to as "colonies") to a reduction of "separation and its barriers" to "new neighborhoods":

Each new group tended to move in at the bottom of the community structure. The latest comers always had the lowest status; they moved into the *poorest districts;* they were looked down upon by all the older groups and were considered the poorest, dirtiest, least intelligent and less desirable group in the community. Each new group formed its *own neighborhood,* speaking its own language, and living its own culture, and generally formed a *little island* generated from the groups around it. The passage of time, however, gradually *reduced this separation and its barriers.* The children learned new ways and *moved to new neighborhoods.*

Thus, Padilla's view of acculturation, like Park's, depended on ecological integration and an erosion of the ethnic community, colony, and enclaves. She clearly states this position: "Assimilation, then, does not occur in the organized immigrant colonies. . . . Assimilation occurs when the colony starts a process of breaking down, and social solidarity increases with the larger society, whereas it is diminishing within the colony. This usually happens to members of the second or third generation of immigrants in this country."[10]

Elena Padilla applies her concept of ecology by comparing two "test cases"—Puerto Rican immigrants in Chicago and Puerto Rican immigrants in New York City. She identifies the Puerto Rican immigrants in New York as being a colony, which she attributes to the larger size of the community: "a rather large population of Puerto Ricans who have established their residence in consolidated neighborhoods or a 'colony' with a community organization of its own where contacts between the individual ethnics and the host society are less than those among the members of the ethnic community itself."[11] The Puerto Rican immigrants in Chicago, in contrast, "consist of a group of scattered families and individuals established in the city in relative isolation from each other, and of recently arrived contract workers recruited in Puerto Rico by a Chicago employment agency, who have tended to move into the Mexican neighborhoods in Chicago."[12] In her most clear statement of her objective in the thesis and her commitment to ecological analysis, Padilla states that she analyzes the two test cases "with reference to the double factors of ecology versus relative size of the immigrant group, and its determinants on the processes of acculturation and assimilation."[13]

Elena Padilla's thesis is extensive in its implications for the research of Puerto Ricans, migrants, immigrants, urban issues, assimilation, segregation, and the role that ecological analyses should play in future research on Latinos in the city. While it is possible to trace Padilla's ecological line to her predecessors at the University of Chicago, her thesis is an overlooked example of rich ecological social scientific research among communities of color. By underscoring the "ecology" and "ecological distribution" of Puerto Ricans in the exercise of racial and ethnic everyday relationships, Padilla exposed the symbiotic relationship between everyday actions and the geographic organization and characteristics of the built environment among Puerto Ricans in mid-twentieth-century urban centers of the United States. But beyond privileging the often ignored role and history of Puerto Ricans in urban centers, Padilla also infuses her analysis with a unique empirical view of the micro-level ecological dynamics, particularly those pertaining to home and work that inform settlement patterns of early Puerto Rican U.S. migrants.

Thus, Elena Padilla's work is an example of what Thomas F. Gieryn has called doing sociology in a "visual key."[14] That is, her thesis plays the symphonic, and sometimes cacophonic, "spatio-temporal rhythms" of everyday home and work life that provided for the residential settlement patterns of Puerto Ricans in New York and Chicago. She exhibits exactly what happens, where it happens, and how people interrelate in ways that allow us to see, feel, taste, and live the city that these populations experienced in their struggles and aims to find a sense of "home" in their new cities. Thus, the thesis stands as a model of rich social research that is attentive to the human and social environment contained in ecological research sensibilities. To revisit Elena Padilla is to record and reinvent ecological analyses of urban Latino life. Her analysis not only recognizes that Latinos exist within the scope of a U.S. urban social science tradition, but she also examines the everyday and in doing so recalibrates the urban ecological frame.

Inspired by Padilla's detailed focus on how people experience their environments, in the following sections I extend the boundaries of the illustration of urban Latino life. I build on her concern with the everyday, local rhythms of ecological distribution by identifying less audible but prominent institutional, spatial rhythms that have historically produced segregated spaces for racial and ethnic minority populations, and particularly for Puerto Ricans in Chicago, New York, and Puerto Rico. My aim here is to supplement rather than replicate Padilla's model. That is, with this supplemental ecological analysis, I hope to fill in her depiction of Puerto Rican life in Chicago and New York with additional spatial phenomena that shaped the home and work lives of Latinos and other communities of color. With this intervention, I not only underscore the very utility of her ontological ecological tool but also make the tool pliable in order to discover the very scales and categories that it silences, which are important for representing the everyday. Thus, the extension here is done in two ways: 1) by examining mid-range structural and physical planning policies that build on her analysis of Chicago and New York; and 2) by enlisting urban Puerto Rico as a case study to be considered in comparison to the conditions that Puerto Ricans faced in New York and Chicago. With this exploration, I hope to ecologically colorize and contextualize Padilla's rendering of Puerto Rican urban life.

Herein, I become an interlocutor with Padilla's findings to focus on the institutional ecological planning processes that shaped the home and work life of Puerto Ricans in the mid-twentieth-century United States. The production of urban physical spaces in the United States and throughout the world has been fundamentally determined by ideals and ideologies concerning the relationship of home and work.[15] Many modern city master plans are direct consequences of a preoccupation with the urban conditions that resulted from rapid, uncontrolled industrialization at the beginning of the century and the migrations of southern (within and beyond the U.S. borders) racial and ethnic laborers to northern cities. Attempts to civilize and control swelling population densities and the concomitant emergence of slums prompted numerous urban master plans that determined new relationships between home and work. These plans, their architects, their dictating ideologies, and their resulting social impact are the "spatio-temporal rhythms" that I here conscript in order to further understand the experience of Puerto Ricans. The rhythmic overture takes place in Chicago in 1893 with an elated urban celebration of Columbus's arrival in the Americas; it is followed by a crescendo and a chorus of the massive imposition of institutional housing for the poor in New York City in the 1930s and concludes with a *soneo* (improvisation) of the forced class and racialized segregation of residential spaces brought about by the Puerto Rican *caseríos* (public housing) of the twentieth century. With this analysis, I hope to provide yet another ecological angle—an ecology that was not popular in the 1930s urban community studies and that has grown as a result of a consolidation of the urban planning enterprise. Thus, here I combine critical macro-analytical planning research such as that employed by Jane Jacobs with Elena Padilla's local ecological understandings in order to listen to the intricate home and work rhythms that characterized the lives of Puerto Ricans in Chicago and New York.

Home and Work and the Production of Latino Space

Chicago

Daniel Hudson Burnham, the main architect for the 1893 World's Columbian Exposition and the 1909 Master Plan for the City of Chicago, wrote:

Before us spreads a plantation of majestic trees, shadowing lawns and roadways, upon the margin of the Lake. In contrast with it, the shining Lagoon stretches away to the north. Behind this the soft banks of the shore, and trains glancing in and out through waving willows. Behind all, the wall of a stately terrace, covered with clinging vines and crowned with statues, and upholding quiet lawns, surrounding lovely homes.

The Lake has been singing to us many years, until we have become responsive. We see the broad water, ruffled by the gentle breeze; upon its breast the glint of oars, the gleam of rosy sails, the outlines of swift gliding launches. We see racing shells go by, urged onward by bronzed athletes. We hear the rippling of waves, commingled with youthful laughter, the music swelling over the Lagoon dies away under the low branches of the trees. A crescent moon swims in the western sky, shining faintly upon us in the deepening twilight.

We float by lawns, where villas, swan-like, rest upon their terraces, and where white balustrades and wood-nymphs are just visible in the gloaming. The evening comes, with myriad colored lights twinkling through air perfumed with water-lilies, and Nature enfolds us, like happy children.[16]

The 1893 World's Columbian Exposition of Chicago, held between May 1 and October 30 to celebrate the four hundredth anniversary of the arrival of Christopher Columbus in the Americas, marks a transcendental period in the history of U.S., American, and international city design. The fair, and the 1909 Master Plan for the City of Chicago, devised by its main architect, Daniel Hudson Burnham, came to dictate the desired ecological reality for the modern, civilized city of Chicago. The fair serves as the catalyst for the American City Beautiful Movement, a derivation of majestic European cities involving a desire to obliterate the critical urban consequences of massive racial and ethnic migrations toward U.S. urban centers. Burnham's designs, as represented in the 1893 Columbian Exposition of Chicago and its "White City" on the shores of Lake Michigan, sought to restore or build anew the grandeur of the city of Chicago through the construction of grand buildings and large boulevards in a radial and axial form, the modernization of the transportation system, and the creation of waterfront beaches. The movement invoked a scientific management attitude intending to inject civilization through "beauty."

The idiom the City Beautiful leaders used in their ideal civic centers was the Beaux-Arts style, named for the famous Ecole des Beaux-Arts in Paris, which instructed artists and architects in the necessity of order, dignity, and harmony in their work. The first expression of this monumental style in the United States was found at the World's Columbian Exposition of 1893. The shimmering "White City," as the fair came to be known during that summer in Chicago, was a tour de force of early city planning and architectural cohesion. In the grand Court of Honor, architects, brought in from the East by Director of Construction Daniel H. Burnham of Chicago, put their Beaux-Arts training to use in the monumental and vaguely classical buildings, all of uniform cornice height, all decorated roughly the same, and all painted bright white. The beauty of the main court, the well-planned balance of buildings, water, and open green spaces was a revelation for the 27 million visitors. Not only was the White City dignified and monumental, it was also well-run: there was no poverty and no crime (so the visitors were led to believe), there were state-of-the-art sanitation and transportation systems, and the Columbian Guard kept everyone happily in their place. In contrast to the grey urban sprawl and blight of Chicago and other American cities, this seemed a utopia.[17]

In its pose of grandeur, the City Beautiful plan for Chicago has been aggressively criticized for using a "trickle-down urban development" approach that relied on "municipal cosmetic[s]" and had "no concern for the neighborhood as an integral unit, no regard for family housing, no sufficient conception of the ordering of business and industry themselves as a necessary part of any larger achievement of urban order."[18] Hence, the housing and urban density problems that were occurring amidst rapid urban industrialization were not addressed in the plan directly.

The impact of overlooking housing in the Chicago city plan would not be negligible, especially for those populations who relied on public investment projects to address housing supply and unsuitability. It is in the failure to address housing that Burnham's plan for Chicago reveals who his intended public was. The temporary international city of plaster that the Columbian Exposition brought to life, appropriately named the "White City," exhibited the inclusive segregationist character that American cities would come to display. The Midway Plaisance section of the fair was reserved for entertainment and for "the rest of the world" to be consumed by mainstream America. Here were the exhibitions and performances by countries in Europe, Africa, the Caribbean (Cuba, Haiti, Dutch Curacao), South America (British Guiana, Brazil), and Asia, and by local U.S. foreigners (African Americans). Although the midway has not been portrayed in today's literature as being a "freak" show of ethnic and racial diversity,[19] the black and brown of the world were crowded together in this entertainment hall that was six hundred feet wide and nearly a mile long. The rest of the White City represented undiversified technocratic and industrialist America, with an Administration Building, a Horticultural Building, an Agricultural Building, a Transportation Building, a Machinery Building, an Electricity Building, a Music Hall, a Casino, and a Fine Arts Building, among others. Thus, the relegation of the midway exotics to a specified and restricted spatial area of the fair, taken as a model of modern urban construction, showed a failure to understand diversity occurring within, not at the margins, of U.S. urban city design.

The plan for the city of Chicago has been described as "an aristocratic city for merchant princes."[20] Indeed, Burnham himself stated: "What would be the effect upon our prosperity if the town were so delightful that most of the men who grow independent financially in the Mississippi Valley, or west of it, were to come to Chicago to live? Should we not without delay do something competent to beautify and make our city attractive for ourselves, and especially for these desirable visitors?"[21] It became clear that Burnham's plan was not intended for the poor migrants and immigrants of color from the South. Instead it targeted financially desirable migrants. This lack of attention to diversity and "the poor" in planning would continue to plague urban design, even when housing became a central concern in urban plans.

The result of the outright ignorance of housing for the poor in the city of Chicago marked the initiation of the increasingly permanent, long-lasting, and acute segregation of the poor, and consequently African American and Latino populations, in Chicago. Here Elena Padilla observed two types of residential settlement patterns among Puerto Ricans. The "old migration" Puerto Ricans, those who emigrated early in the twentieth century, tended to be scattered in what she observed to be a "random" or "chance" ecological distribution in the North Side, the Negro Belt, the South and West Sides, the Hyde Park side of the South Side, and Evanston (see table 1).

However, the residential settlement of these Puerto Ricans—some of whom Padilla observed to be white educated, white poor, and "very dark skinned Puerto Ricans"—were dictated by their relative educational attainment, socioeconomic class, employment location, and race. Padilla observed that the residential distribution of the Puerto Ricans who migrated through work contracts in the foundry or household service industry—the

Table 1. Distribution of Puerto Ricans in Chicago Neighborhoods, 1947

Chicago Community	Number of Puerto Rican Households	Number of Puerto Rican Individuals
North Side	11	34
Negro Belt	3	6
South Side/West Side (Mexican)	3	5
Hyde Park District of South Side	2	4
Evanston (suburb)	1	1

Data Source: Elena Padilla, "Puerto Rican Immigrants in New York and Chicago: A Study in Comparative Assimilation" (master's thesis, University of Chicago, 1947).

"new migration"—was determined by the "ecological distribution of [the] employers who provided their housing accommodations."[22] In the case histories of these workers, a recurring theme is the residential constraints on the worker. Many lived with other color communities, predominantly Mexican and African American communities.

Padilla was privy to the rhythmic patterns of employment, race, and class that produced the ecological distribution of Puerto Ricans in the city of Chicago. Burnham's plan and subsequent Chicago city master plans, in their oversight of the role that poor people would play in Chicago, relegated Puerto Ricans, Mexicans, African Americans, and poor communities of color to the fringes of the economic and social lives of the city. A concern for beauty, order, and civilization made old and new people of color invisible in the economic life of the city and forced them into pockets of restricted social mobility.

New York

In contrast to Burnham's lack of attention to housing, the French architect Le Corbusier focused intently on the home and its relationship to work and industry. Le Corbusier had a functional ideological vision of the city where all formal urban uses, of which the most central were housing and industry, had to be logically accommodated to exist in an amicable relationship. Most central to his plan was the institutionalization of the home's function so that it was in harmony with industry. As Le Corbusier saw it, the "house is a machine to live in."[23] Interestingly enough, his solution to overcrowding, slums, disease, and chaos brought about by urban migrations was to increase density through the construction of superblocks of geometrically arranged high-rise buildings: "we must decongest the centers of our cities by increasing their density."[24]

Le Corbusier's design explicitly used the relationship of home and work to spatially segregate the city. Where people lived was dictated by where they worked. At the center of the city were to be built the offices for the elite *cadres*: industrialists, scientists, and artists. Outside that zone would be residential areas for the same *cadres,* and the workers would live in more modest households just beyond the residential areas of the *cadres.* The household units would all be uniform and contain the same furniture—they would be stripped-down "cells" that fulfilled basic human sentimental and physiological needs. All functions of the buildings would be institutionalized to fit the work day and the industrial interests.

Le Corbusier's vision of institutional housing would become the prime design pattern of housing for the poor in the United States. The onset of mass housing programs in the United States was driven by an attempt to do away with rapidly growing slums in the cities. The conditions of poverty and blight in the slums were thought, by this era, to produce socially deviant behavior among its inhabitants. Frederick Law Olmsted, the landscape architect and design partner of Burnham in Chicago's Columbian Exposition, had designed New York's Central Park in hopes of educating the tenement dwellers of the turn of the century, and Le Corbusier's home design was intended to establish order.

Le Corbusier's high-rise superblock design was welcomed in the 1930s and 1940s with the New Deal programs for housing. The 1937 Wagner-Steagall Housing Act established the United States Housing Authority (USHA), the first federal agency to deal exclusively with low-income housing concerns. The Housing Act of 1947 revived the 1937 Act and defined urban redevelopment and urban renewal as the official goals for housing. Robert Moses, who became known as "America's greatest builder," was responsible for $267 million in urban renewal investments in New York between 1940 and 1957. Moses was responsible for many of the public works—highways, bridges, and other improvements—that exist today throughout New York City. His top-down approach to planning was consistent with Le Corbusier's approach—clearing existing housing slums and building new high-rise superblock parks containing institutionalized and sterilized housing units. Corbusian design was embraced for housing for the poor, and public housing communities emerged all over the United States—in such cities as St. Louis, Chicago, Newark, and New York.

The construction of Le Corbusier's design in public housing, however, proved to be fatal. Public housing parks became ridden with crime. Many were abandoned, and to this day many continue to be demolished. It has been argued that the Corbusian failure was due to the fact that the design itself was meant for the "middle-class inhabitants whom he had imagined living their gracious, elegant, cosmopolitan lives in *La Ville Contemporaine,* but not for a 'welfare family.'"[25] However, amid its architectural failure as homes for the poor, the Corbusian public housing development was successful in segregating the poor from the rich—the black and brown from the white, and the jobs from the cities. In Manhattan, for example, public housing sites are located on the periphery of the island, close to the Hudson River along the west and primarily along the East River. Ironically, as these areas become more economically desirable today, public housing developments remain as the bulwark to gentrifying populations seeking to expand the metropolitan residential land mass.

The impact that job displacement and segregation has had on African American communities is well documented in African American urban research. Similar to African Americans, Puerto Ricans in New York undoubtedly were alienated from the economic and social life of the city as they came to occupy many of these public housing sites. Padilla notes that the formation of the New York Puerto Rican "colony" (as she refers to it) was instigated by a "natural system" of "institutions and the usages of the people who live within its structural make-up."[26] The colony in 1947 consisted of 44,908 Puerto Ricans, grouped racially into 34,756 whites and 10,152 "colored and members of other races."[27] The colony was industrially oriented toward factory work and service providers and had a series of cultural and church organizations to strengthen the bonds. Padilla notes that color visibility has little impact on residential settlement and that "[n]o segregation pattern seems to operate in the selection of residence areas by Puerto Ricans in New York."[28] However, the formation of the colony indicates overarching rhythms of city planning and the ecology of home and work that leads to segregation patterns. The implementation of Le Corbusier designs for the poor translated into a segregationist home-to-work spatial relationship for unskilled laborers. Again, housing plans for the poor, following the rhythms of industrial concerns, pushed Puerto Ricans into communities that would become increasingly segregated.

Puerto Rico

In Puerto Rico, housing has also been dictated by work and large-scale planning designs. In the 1940s, increasing industrialization led Puerto Ricans away from agriculture and the rural life into industry and city life. Increased migration to the cities led to the creation and continued growth of slum communities. Public housing in Puerto Rico emerged as a means to relief for the increasing number of slums in Puerto Rico. The purpose of the Puerto Rico Housing Authority, created in 1938 as a consequence of the 1937 U.S. Federal Housing Act, was to create adequate housing for workers primarily located in the urban centers of Puerto Rico—Ponce, San Juan, Mayaguez, Arecibo, and Rio Piedras.[29]

The slums in Puerto Rico were an increasing preoccupation among locals and U.S. visitors, including Eleanor Roosevelt and Rexford Tugwell during their 1934 visit to the island. In 1948, the national chairman of the Communist Party, William Foster, visited Puerto Rico and published a letter to President Truman in which he highlighted what he thought to be the imperialist repercussions of the U.S. presence in Puerto Rico as evident in the terrible conditions of a slum community located in San Juan called El Fanguito (The Little Mud):

El Fanguito is sprawled out over mosquito-infested, marshtide flats. The squatters' houses are thrown together of any material that comes to hand, and the shacks are incredibly over-crowded. Most of the places are unfit for hogs, much less for human beings. The houses have no toilet facilities, and there is no garbage collection. The water supply is entirely inadequate, consisting only of occasional community faucets, contrived by the people themselves. Whole areas are completely dark at night, having no street lights, and many of the people are too poor even to buy kerosene lamps or candles. Most of the inhabitants' homes are also practically destitute of furniture. There are not even streets in the horrible slum, except where the people themselves have carted in soil and rubbish to build up roadways of a sort.[30]

The approach of the Puerto Rican Housing Authority, to do away with slums, was not dissimilar to the one that had been employed in New York and Chicago following the top-down approach of Le Corbusier. The process was to eliminate slums and to substitute public housing project developments for them. The alternatives were not well received by the slum dwellers—many pleaded not to be removed from their homes and communities, and still others saw the new housing developments as being targeted for middle-class tenants.[31] Still more challenging was convincing slum dwellers to move to the new sanitized and foreign versions of their slum communities. In this sense, Oscar Lewis's ethnographical study of migration patterns among Puerto Ricans provides us with a glimpse of the housing realities of Puerto Ricans in the middle of the twentieth century.[32] Forcefully critiqued by Padilla in a 1967 review, Lewis's work displays this transition from slum to public housing:

> The social worker told me it would be a good idea to get the children out of La Esmeralda because there's so much delinquency there. Moving here to the housing project was practically her idea; she insisted and insisted. Finally one day she came to me and said, "Tomorrow you have to move to the caserío in Villa Hermosa." . . . You should have seen this place when I moved in. It was spilling over with garbage and smelling of shit, pure shit. Imagine, when the social worker opened the door that first day, a breeze happened to blow her way. She stepped back and said, "Wait, I can't go in. This is barbarous." . . . And this place isn't like La Esmeralda, you know, where there's so much liveliness and noise and something is always going on. Here you never see any movement on the street, not one little domino or card game or anything. The place is dead. People act as if they're angry or in mourning. Either they don't know how to live or they're afraid to. And yet it's full of shameless good-for-nothings. It's true what the proverb says, "May God deliver me from quiet places; I can defend myself in the wild ones."[33]

At the initiation of the Puerto Rican public housing programs, reluctance by slum residents to move into public housing had forced the government to develop alternative programs to provide adequate housing. According to scholars, the Puerto Rican slum dweller was oriented toward home ownership even if it was in a slum, and not paying rental fees even if it was a new and sterile setting. As a result, multiple innovative and diverse approaches, instead of one-shot remedies, were created in Puerto Rico.[34]

In 1948, twenty-seven housing developments, accommodating 5,768 families, had been built or were under construction on the island. The design of public housing in Puerto Rico departed slightly from the developments being built in Chicago and New York. Nevertheless, the structural orientation of buildings in a superblock, with formally defined open spaces, was replicated, although the high-rise component was not. Hence, the Le Corbusian plan was altered for Puerto Rico. Medium high-rise buildings and low-rise buildings became the preferred architectural form of public housing in Puerto Rico. The modernist movement toward high-rise public housing design that took over the United States evaded the majority of Puerto Rican public housing projects. This tendency, along with the fact that public housing projects in Puerto Rico were usually smaller, averaging three hundred units (although some of the largest public housing projects were built in Puerto Rico), destined Puerto Rican housing projects to avoid the structural determinist negative outcomes that U.S. public housing project designs are thought to provoke.

Nevertheless, the institutionalized superblock design of the Puerto Rican public housing segregated the poor and typically Black Puerto Ricans from the rich and the white single-family dwellers. Through the 1990s, when Pedro Rossello's crime-fighting policy *"mano dura"* resulted in fenced-off public housing sites, the separation of public housing residents from the rest of society, via their renovated housing built environment—not necessarily their city plan design—became evident. This segregation is partly evident in the racial identification fault lines that emerge along neighborhood lines. Exploratory analysis reveals that the San Juan police sectors containing public housing sites that had been "rescued" by the *mano dura* policies showed a slightly higher percentage of people who had identified themselves as Black in the 2000 census when compared to sectors that had not experienced Rosello's *mano dura* intervention. Furthermore, geographic analysis of race identification at the neighborhood level displays how these public housing sites have contributed to disproportionate representation of poor and Black Puerto Rican communities in public housing. Class and race are additionally actualized in residential environments resulting in stark class and racial segregation patterns between Puerto Ricans living in public housing.[35] Therefore, the construction of public housing developments as consolidated and large housing parks contributes to the segregation of communities. Hence, policy interventions and planning designs have played a central role in constructing the racial, class, and segregationist character of space in Puerto Rico.

Conclusion

Elena Padilla serves as a historically distant, yet very modern, application of how we can come to understand how space becomes racialized and ethnicized. Lefebvre states: "The departure point for this history of space is not to be found in geographical descriptions of natural space, but rather in the study of natural rhythms, and of the modification of those rhythms and their inscription in space by means of human actions, especially work-related actions. It begins, then, with the spatio-temporal rhythms of nature as transformed by a social practice."[36] Padilla gives us the rhythms and the melodies involved in the production of the ecological distribution of Puerto Ricans in mid-twentieth-century Chicago. Beyond validating her contributions to a historical narrative of Puerto Rican migrants, her thesis presents methodological and epistemological variations to our conceptualization of segregation and what produces segregation. Padilla explicitly links space to social, economic, and intimate rhythms of everyday life. Through her thesis we become privy to the process whereby our built environment becomes embossed with the rhythms of ideology and of living. Her thesis also makes us aware of the often unnoticed centrality of housing and its ecological and spatial distribution for understanding disadvantaged urban communities of color. An examination of her thesis induces us to re-examine texts for what they tell us about the production of urban space and urban living.

In this essay I have examined how mainstream planning and architectural ideals influenced the spatial housing segregation for Puerto Ricans in New York and Chicago. Furthermore, I have attempted to shed light on the impact of design ideologies on Puerto Ricans in Puerto Rico and contemplated the racial impressions of those designs, even for a society that commonly overlooks the racial quality of daily life. Understanding the processes that inform space is essential today for affecting urban dynamics of gentrification, gated communities, new-urbanist developments, mixed-use structures, and cultural neighborhood tourism renewal efforts that have a direct impact on the social health of communities of color. The understanding of the distribution of space and the production of space through rhythms of city planning in conjunction with the micro-rhythms of city life can lead to new directions in social and political movements, as well as new policy interventions to address segregation and covert forms of institutional racism. The production of the built environment in Puerto Rico, as well as that for Puerto Ricans and other ethnic and racial groups in the United States, can be investigated in order to understand the urban policies, practices, and designs of home and work that create and perpetuate racial and ethnic spatial segregation. The creative extension of Padilla's urban ecological tool, thus, is fruitful for revising the conceptual reaches of tried and true concepts, as well as for rediscovering life as experienced by Puerto Ricans in New York, Chicago, and Puerto Rico.

NOTES

1. F. W. Knight and C. Palmer, eds., *The Modern Caribbean* (Chapel Hill: University of North Carolina Press, 1989).

2. H. Lefebvre, *The Production of Space* (Oxford: Blackwell, 1991).

3. Catton notes that earlier uses of the term and concept of "ecology" were made by Charles C. Adams in 1913 and in the 1914 Summer Meeting of the British Ecological Society. W. R. Catton Jr., "Foundations of Human Ecology," *Sociological Perspectives* 37, 1 (1994): 75–95.

4. R. E. Park, E. W. Burgess, R. D. McKenzie, and L. Wirth, *The City* (Chicago: University of Chicago Press, 1925), pp. 63–64. A briefer definition provided by W. R. Catton is "the study of ecosystems that involve humans." Catton, "Foundations of Human Ecology," p. 77.

5. In the field of anthropology, "ecology" also had begun to gain currency, as a result of Julian Steward in the late 1930s. "Cultural ecology," also known as "anthropological ecology," specifically focused on explaining how environmental qualities informed culture, and vice versa. However, it was not until the latter half of 1947 that Elena Padilla met Julian Steward and his view began to have an impact on her work. Thus, Padilla's ecological sensibility remained firmly grounded in the discipline of sociology.

6. E. Padilla, "Puerto Rican Immigrants in New York and Chicago: A Study in Comparative Assimilation" (master's thesis, University of Chicago, 1947), p. 35. The thesis is reprinted in part 1 of this volume; all citations are to the reprint.

7. Ibid., p. 36.

8. Ibid., p. 36.

9. Ibid., pp. 36–37.

10. Ibid., p. 36.

11. Ibid., p. 44.

12. Ibid., p. 44.

13. Ibid., p. 44.

14. T. F. Gieryn, "A Space for Place in Sociology," *Annual Review of Sociology* 26 (2000): 463–496.

15. Space theorists such as David Harvey are especially privy to the relationship of capital, economics, and labor to the production of space. D. Harvey, *Justice, Nature, and the Geography of Difference* (Cambridge, Mass.: Blackwell, 1996).

16. Burnham cited in P. G. Hall, *The Cities of Tomorrow: An Intellectual History of Urban Planning and Design in the Twentieth Century,* rev. ed. (London: Blackwell, 1988), p. 195.

17. J. K. Rose, "City Beautiful: The 1901 Plan for Washington, D.C., Spring 1996, http://xroads.virginia.edu/~CAP/CITYBEAUTIFUL/dchome.html (accessed April 24, 2010).

18. Hall, *Cities of Tomorrow,* p. 181; Lewis Mumford cited in ibid., p. 182; L. Mumford, *The City in History: Its Origins, Its Transformations, and Its Prospects* (London: Secker and Warburg, 1961), p. 401.

19. C. R. Reed, *All the World Is Here! The Black Presence at White City* (Bloomington: Indiana University Press, 2000), p. xxvii. I would argue that more work on the midway's racial significance should be done.

20. Hall, *Cities of Tomorrow,* p. 183.

21. Burnham cited in ibid., p. 180.

22. Padilla, "Puerto Rican Immigrants," pp. 82, 90.

23. Fishman cited in Hall, *Cities of Tomorrow,* p. 205.

24. Hall, *Cities of Tomorrow,* p. 207.

25. Ibid., p. 240.

26. Padilla, "Puerto Rican Immigrants," p. 101.

27. Ibid., p. 68.

28. Ibid., p. 73.

29. Puerto Rico Housing Authority, *Housing Progress in Puerto Rico, 1938–1948* (San Juan: Puerto Rico Housing Authority, 1948), p. 1.

30. W. Z. Foster, *The Crime of El Fanguito: An Open Letter to President Truman on Puerto Rico* (New York: New Century, 1948), pp. 5–6.

31. Ibid.; K. W. Back, *Slums, Projects and People: Social Psychological Problems of Relocation in Puerto Rico* (Durham, N.C.: Duke University Press, 1962); C. Alvarado, *Public Housing in Puerto Rico: Housing for a Lower Segment, a Special Case* (New York: Halsted Press, John Wiley & Sons, 1974); H. I. Safa, *The Urban Poor of Puerto Rico: A Study in Development and Inequality* (New York: Rinehart and Winston, 1974).

32. O. Lewis, *La Vida: A Puerto Rican Family in the Culture of Poverty—San Juan and New York* (New York: Random House, 1965).

33. Ibid., pp. 661–662.

34. Back, *Slums, Projects and People*; Safa, *Urban Poor of Puerto Rico*; Alvarado, *Public Housing in Puerto Rico,* p. 172.

35. Z. Dinzey-Flores, "Fighting Crime, Constructing Segregation: Housing Policy

and the Symbolic Badges of Puerto Rican Urban Neighborhoods" (Ph.D. diss., University of Michigan, 2005).

36. Lefebvre, *Production of Space*, p. 117.

WORKS CITED

Alvarado, C. *Public Housing in Puerto Rico: Housing for a Lower Segment, a Special Case.* New York: Halsted Press, John Wiley & Sons, 1974.

Back, K. W. *Slums, Projects, and People: Social Psychological Problems of Relocation in Puerto Rico.* Durham, N.C.: Duke University Press, 1962.

Catton, W. R., Jr. "Foundations of Human Ecology." *Sociological Perspectives* 37, 1 (1994): 75–95.

Dinzey-Flores, Z. "Fighting Crime, Constructing Segregation: Housing Policy and the Symbolic Badges of Puerto Rican Urban Neighborhoods." Ph.D. diss., Sociology and Public Policy, University of Michigan, 2005.

Foster, W. Z. *The Crime of El Fanguito: An Open Letter to President Truman on Puerto Rico.* New York: New Century, 1948.

Gieryn, T. F. "A Space for Place in Sociology." *Annual Review of Sociology* 26 (2000): 463–496.

Hall, P. G. *Cities of Tomorrow: An Intellectual History of Urban Planning and Design in the Twentieth Century.* Rev. ed. London: Blackwell, 1988.

Harvey, D. *Justice, Nature, and the Geography of Difference.* Cambridge, Mass.: Blackwell, 1996.

Knight, F. W., and C. Palmer, eds. *The Modern Caribbean.* Chapel Hill: University of North Carolina Press, 1989.

Lefebvre, H. *The Production of Space.* Oxford: Blackwell, 1991.

Lewis, O. *La Vida: A Puerto Rican Family in the Culture of Poverty—San Juan and New York.* New York: Random House, 1965.

Mumford, L. *The City in History: Its Origins, Its Transformations, and Its Prospects.* London: Secker and Warburg, 1961.

Padilla, E. "Puerto Rican Immigrants in New York and Chicago: A Study in Comparative Assimilation." Master's thesis, Anthropology, University of Chicago, 1947.

———. "Review of La Vida: *A Puerto Rican Family in the Culture of Poverty—San Juan and New York* by Oscar Lewis." *Political Science Quarterly* 82, 4 (1967): 651–652.

Park, R. E., E. W. Burgess, R. D. McKenzie, and L. Wirth. *The City.* Chicago: University of Chicago Press, 1925.

Park, R. E., and H. A. Miller. *Old World Traits Transplanted.* New York: Harper, 1921.

Puerto Rico Housing Authority. *Housing Progress in Puerto Rico, 1938–1948.* San Juan: Puerto Rico Housing Authority, 1948.

Reed, C. R. *All the World Is Here! The Black Presence at White City.* Bloomington: Indiana University Press, 2000.

Rose, J. K. "City Beautiful: The 1901 Plan for Washington, D.C." A project of American Studies, University of Virginia. Spring 1996. http://xroads.virginia.edu/~CAP/CITYBEAUTIFUL/dchome.html (accessed April 24, 2010).

Safa, H. I. *The Urban Poor of Puerto Rico: A Study in Development and Inequality.* New York: Rinehart and Winston, 1974.

Footnotes of Social Justice

Elena Padilla and Chicago
Puerto Rican Communities

Mérida M. Rúa

Trained by a historian, in an interdisciplinary doctoral program, I was accustomed to hearing "sometimes the story is in the footnotes." Although reading footnotes was nothing new, I had never been fascinated by footnotes until I read and reread Elena Padilla's 1947 University of Chicago master's thesis, "Puerto Rican Immigrants in New York and Chicago: A Study in Comparative Assimilation."[1] Scattered at the bottom of the pages in three separate chapters, these notes grabbed my attention:

> —The data collected among the recent Puerto Rican migrants in Chicago were obtained in collaboration with Miss Muna Muñoz-Lee.
> —Personal communication with Jesús Colón, President of the Spanish section of the International Workers Union, March 1945.
> —Héctor Alvarez Silva, *et al.,* "Preliminary Report on the Puerto Rican Contract Workers in the Chicago Area," November 25, 1946 (Mimeographed).[2]

I decided to look for the story in the footnotes.

It is likely most readers of the thesis would assume the names or works cited are footnoted because they hold some significance; they must mean something, or else why place them in the margins? In Padilla's thesis, indeed, her footnotes form a semi-public transcript, marginal notes worthy of consideration by all readers concerning academic literature, archival collections, or expanded thoughts on theoretical frameworks while also prompting other meanings and critical linkages for readers with degrees of proficiency in

Puerto Rican and Caribbean history and culture. Fine-tuning James Scott's formulation of the offstage articulations of public dissent, historian Earl Lewis suggests that between the offstage or hidden transcript and the public one, the semi-public transcript is potentially available, identified as the poem, song, or folktale, among other forms. He writes, "This coded message is audible but indecipherable to those outside the community of reference because most outsiders do not understand the importance of certain symbols, cues, and events." The ability to read and comprehend these cues, Lewis acknowledges, is acquired knowledge; one is socialized through cultural practices.[3]

It is in Padilla's marginal notes, that is, her semi-public transcript, where we can detect what anthropologist Virginia Dominguez calls a "politics of love and rescue," or the discrete ways in which researchers have shown that they truly care for and about the people they study. The partial descriptions of relationships and deeds found in the footnotes of Padilla's work serve to frame and politicize the stakes of the research and thus are a strategic location from which she makes her extra-anthropological interventions: the use of her academic skills and credentials combined with her political commitments to improve the daily lives and employment conditions of Puerto Rican contract workers in Chicago.[4]

Taken together these footnotes provide a unique window not only into some of Padilla's intellectual influences and interlocutors but also into her early scholarly and personal commitments to social justice. As the first footnote reveals, Padilla collaborated politically and intellectually with Muna Muñoz Lee, her classmate and roommate at the University of Chicago. Muñoz Lee was the daughter of the president of the Puerto Rican Senate, Luis Muñoz Marín, who in 1948 became Puerto Rico's first popularly elected governor. At the University of Chicago, Padilla and Muñoz Lee studied under anthropologists Sol Tax and Robert Redfield, while Padilla also worked with sociologist Louis Wirth. Along with the Chicago social science luminaries, Padilla consulted periodically with New York Puerto Rican labor activist Jesús Colón, as indicated in the second footnote. She made use of his extensive personal archive—which included community publications such as local newspapers, organization manifestos, and reports—as well as the political knowledge he gained in years of in grassroots organizing.[5] Padilla even called on Colón personally to assist dissatisfied Puerto Rican contract workers from Chicago who decided to leave for New York City. Clearly, Padilla relied on and highly respected Muñoz Lee's and Colón's perspectives in her deliberations of her scholarly activism. The third footnote suggests that the unjust treatment of workers kindled her interest in researching the

experiences of Puerto Rican migrants in Chicago; nevertheless, it was an issue in which she took more than academic interest. One of seven co-authors,
listed in alphabetical order, Padilla was a main contributor to a report on
the working conditions and unfair contract arrangements of Puerto Rican
workers recruited for general household work and foundry labor.[6] Attention
to Padilla's footnotes offers valuable insight into who she was as a young
graduate student in her early twenties studying in Hyde Park, as well as into
who she is as a semi-retired scholar and committed mentor to a younger
generation of scholars.

In many ways, my fascination with the subtle yet intricate relationship
between research and activism found throughout Padilla's work inspired
the goal of this volume: extracting Padilla from the footnotes of the discipline of anthropology. The contributions to comparativist research and
scholarly activism by Padilla, a woman, a Puerto Rican, and a "native investigator," as well as her contemplations of the role of the researcher in the
research process, have been unjustly neglected in a field almost exclusively
committed to positivism and claims of objectivity. Stated another way, the
kind of ethnographic and scientific authority endorsed by the discipline of
anthropology reinforces hierarchies of race, class, and gender. Likewise, in
the burgeoning field of Puerto Rican studies, the lack of critical dialogue
with Padilla's work as foundational to Puerto Rican studies verges on the
shocking, as the field emerged in the 1960s and 1970s from concerns that
closely paralleled Padilla's. In both cases, in addition to rigid identity politics, Padilla's marginalization can also be attributed to the fact that she
saw relevance in and was intellectually curious about topics often deemed
inconsequential and unworthy of scholarly or political attention, such as
the labor rights and political potential of female domestic workers.[7] A close
reading of Padilla's thesis offers scholars and activists important ways to
think critically, not only about the kinds of work we undertake but also
about the stakes involved in what we study.

The second part of this essay turns to my own ethnographic work and how
reading and researching Padilla's thesis have influenced my own thinking
on Puerto Ricans in Chicago. I extract what would normally be relegated as
footnotes in the daily lives of members of the pioneering generation of Puerto
Rican female migrants to provide a more fine-grained portrait of the ways
in which their interventions in community affairs, however small, illuminate
how these women conceive of social justice in an urban environment and
the relationship between these "footnotes" and academic endeavors. Read in
tandem, the interventions of Padilla and the Puerto Rican women I came to
know make evident, not only their refusal to accept the social abandonment

of their communities by the state, but also the ways in which they sought redress from the state in their attempts to attend to the conditions of and in their communities.

Elena Padilla's Extra-Anthropological Interventions

When Jaime Benítez, chancellor of University of Puerto Rico and alumnus of the University of Chicago, decided that he should sponsor some of his most promising students for graduate study at elite U.S. institutions, the largest number of migrant students became a cadre at his alma mater in Chicago. Among those students was Elena Padilla, the spirited fledgling of the 1944 group. She was nineteen at the time, too young to enter medical school at the University of Michigan at Ann Arbor. Padilla had won a fellowship from the University of Puerto Rico to study the "Great Books" through the famed Chicago Program in Social Thought, directed by the president of the University of Chicago, Robert Hutchins, and the philosopher Mortimer Adler. Through this program, Padilla was introduced to Sol Tax, a specialist of Native American cultures, and to Robert Redfield, an authority on folk culture. She told me that she "became captivated by anthropology," gave up her plan for medical school, and enrolled in the university's graduate program in anthropology. Her compatriots, Muna Muñoz Lee and Ricardo Alegría, a future founding member of the Institute of Puerto Rican Culture and the Center of Advance Study of Puerto Rico and the Caribbean, joined Padilla in the anthropology program.[8] As a graduate student in anthropology from 1944 to 1947, Padilla conducted fieldwork among the Winnebago in northern Wisconsin with Sol Tax and served as a research assistant for Louis Wirth on the Committee on Interracial Relations (1946–1947).[9] The youthful girl who arrived in Chicago to gain an appreciation of the "great books" before venturing into medical school was not only stretched intellectually and politically at the University of Chicago, but she also made her own interventions. Padilla connected her new analytic tools and access to prominent scholars and institutions to investigate a troubling matter: the importation of Puerto Rican contract workers to Chicago.

In September 1946 Padilla came across a "help available" posting in the employment section of the *Chicago Daily Tribune* placed by Castle, Barton and Associates advertising the services of "white" Puerto Rican contract workers for general household or service work. Unsettled by the ad, she and Muñoz Lee decided to investigate and rode from the University of Chicago campus in Hyde Park, on the South Side, to the North Side of the city, the location of the employment agency and the Lincoln Park Hotel, temporary residence for the Puerto Rican migrants, to look into the matter and to speak with recruited workers. They made their way, too, to the North Chicago foundry site to speak with men hired by the Chicago Foundry Company.

On October 3, Padilla sent an impassioned letter to Jesús Colón, a New York social and political activist, about the precarious situation of these Puerto Rican workers, who benefited neither from minimum wage legislation nor from union membership that could defend their rights as workers. Even more troubling, Padilla learned through Ricardo Alegría that the Department of Labor of Puerto Rico sanctioned this arrangement. She closed her letter to Colón promising a social visit but only after having "done something to abolish the importation of Puerto Ricans who head straight to their own demise as well as contribute to the poverty and hunger of other workers."[10]

Padilla's early collaboration with Muñoz Lee investigating the daily lives of Puerto Rican contract workers became the foundation for her master's thesis research. Using her credentials as a University of Chicago graduate student as an entry to question and gather information from representatives of the private employment agency, she likewise drew on her social position as a Puerto Rican student-migrant interested in her compatriots to gather information on their work and social life in the city. Her political sensibilities and resulting unease with the recruitment program prompted her thesis research interest in Puerto Ricans in Chicago, which she refined to an investigation of the character of Puerto Rican identity and community formation in the United States, comparing the settlement and integration of the New York and Chicago populations. In Padilla's words, the thesis was concerned with "processes of acculturation and assimilation with particular reference to the double factor of size of the immigrant group and its ecological distribution."[11] In light of how she came to this project, a formidable section of the thesis is dedicated to the Puerto Rican contract workers who arrived in Chicago during her tenure at the University of Chicago.

In what follows, I focus on Padilla's observations of and actions on behalf of members of the "recent migration," contract workers recruited by the private Chicago-based employment agency Castle, Barton and Associates in the fall of 1946. This group of laborers was hired to cheaply remedy the domestic worker shortage and the "manpower" shortage at a foundry plant in Chicago.[12] Padilla's thesis provides critical historical knowledge of these contract workers, while her extra-anthropological interventions—efforts to help individual workers, to illuminate their plight, and to produce immediate changes in policy concerning migrant workers—indicate her refusal to accept the social abandonment of destitute Puerto Rican migrants by the state, both the government of Puerto Rico and the federal government of the United States.

Padilla's study sheds light on, and left a historical record of, an assembly of recruited Puerto Rican workers who might otherwise have remained in the shadows.[13] Castle, Barton and Associates, with the support of Puerto Rico's insular Department of Labor, contracted approximately four hundred domestic workers; the majority were single women. Also recruited were some seventy men to work for the Chicago Hardware Foundry Company in North Chicago, while Inland Steel Company in East Chicago employed another eighty male workers. The men remained fairly concentrated, housed either in reconverted boxcars on the grounds of the foundry or in a hotel near the steel mill. The female household workers, in contrast, were randomly scattered in the city and nearby suburbs determined by the residential distribution of their employers.

Given the considerable number of young female migrants and the fears of them becoming "lost" in the city, the Young Women's Christian Association (YWCA) in Puerto Rico promptly called on the Chicago branch to "look out for the girls."[14] For Puerto Rican household workers near the Loop—Chicago's downtown commercial district—the YWCA decided to host Thursday afternoon teas. Because of their scattered work and living arrangements, the recreational activity implemented at the YWCA was how Puerto Ricans first came together as a group in the midwestern city.[15] During the rest of the week, social relations among migrants were almost nonexistent. Although the women objected to the concept of "tea time"— they drank tea only when sick—they still used the space at the YWCA and the occasion of their day off to engage in ordinary conversation, to foster friendships, and to evaluate their unfavorable work conditions: unconscionably long workdays for little pay with hardly any time off.[16] The domestic workers became acquainted with a few of the Puerto Rican students at the University of Chicago, namely Elena Padilla and Muna Muñoz Lee, at the Thursday social gatherings. Padilla tells us that soon after the arrival of the recruited laborers, the women (and men) in households and the men in the foundry became increasingly dissatisfied with their work conditions and low wages.[17] Some breached their labor contracts and searched for factory or service work in the city; others decided to try their fortunes elsewhere. Those who abandoned their employment but who resolved to stay on in Chicago found interim living quarters in transient hotels in the Loop or in the homes of Mexican friends.[18]

As graduate students in their early twenties, Padilla and Muñoz Lee found themselves limited in the kind of assistance they could offer aggrieved work-

Reminds me of Dorothy Day

ers, but nonetheless they did not let their own circumstances prevent them from looking for viable work and living options for their compatriots in grave need. In letters to Jesús Colón, Padilla made evident her active role in assisting workers to abandon their contracts, especially the women. "Munita and I are operating a non-profit employment agency to find them factory jobs and rooms to live," she wrote. "Many want to leave for N.Y and we plan to do what is possible so that the women can achieve their objective. Our poverty prevents us from doing something [more], but that is no reason to be discouraged."[19] She humbly asked Colón to help migrants who wanted to move to New York find sponsors and also asked him to send applications for the Merchant Marine. Colón took their efforts seriously, opening his home in Brooklyn to Evangelina Serrano, a young domestic worker to whom Padilla and Muñoz Lee had lent a helping hand, and even invited her to address a radio public about the situation of domestic workers in the industrial heartland. Serrano wrote to Muñoz Lee: "Don Jesús wants me to talk on the radio on the Puerto Ricans in Chicago and I'm writing to see if you can send me some details about how they are being treated so that I can complete what I'm going to say."[20]

To help aggrieved and stranded migrant workers, the roommates engaged in a series of conspicuous and inconspicuous activities. In a later (authorized) biography, *Ricardo Alegría: Una Vida,* Alegría, a housemate of theirs in the International House at the University of Chicago, recalled, "Both [Padilla and Muñoz Lee] were conscious of the increasing influence of Puerto Rican migrants to the city," especially the young women recruited as maids, who had problems with their employers and were either thrown out or ran away. Muñoz Lee, so he said, "picked them up and would take them to her room in the International House without permission to do so." They "had created a commune with those girls." Five or six girls were sleeping on the floor in the room Muñoz Lee shared with Padilla, resulting in "problems with the administration."[21] Padilla admitted that she and Muñoz Lee brought girls to the International House when they had nowhere else to go, indicating this was less frequently and more spontaneously than Algeria's recollection suggests. "We were not going to leave anyone out in the cold. It was more accidental than routine," she told me in 2005.[22]

They also served as the primary interpreters for individuals willing to offer testimony of work-related abuses for the November 25, 1946, report, "Preliminary Report on the Puerto Rican Contract Workers in the Chicago Area," drafted with the intention of circulating it among those with influence.[23] Foundry workers, such as Leonides Algarín and Miguel Rivera, provided handwritten testimony of "being forced to work Saturdays to pay my debt during the time I was ill."[24] Written in both English and Spanish, the report was sent to both insular and federal government officials, such as Manuel A. Pérez, the commissioner of labor in Puerto Rico, to organizations, such as the Welfare Council of Metropolitan Chicago and the Immigrants' Protective League, and to the local press.[25] Prominent individuals within and beyond Chicago concerned with these matters, such as Padilla's adviser Sol Tax, Jesús Colón in New York, and Luis Muñoz Marín in San Juan, also received copies of the report.[26]

In coordinated letters written on December 9, 1946, to Jesús Colón and Muñoz Marín, introducing the report, Padilla and Muñoz Lee also included word of a domestic worker strike. On the last Thursday in November of 1946, more than fifty domestic workers with support from Puerto Rican graduate students at the University of Chicago and representatives of other student and labor organizations picketed the offices of Castle, Barton and Associates demanding "a day off, a raise, less work hours."[27] "The demonstration was impressive: it looked like a CIO line with how well it was organized.... On Thanksgiving Day the maids refused to work or to speak English," Padilla wrote to Colón.[28] Muñoz Lee, in her letter to her father, noted, "People with vast experience in workers organizations assured us that even in veteran workers struggles they had not observed more order, or more enthusiasm in a picket line."[29]

Letters to Luis Muñoz Marín from Muñoz Lee served as updates about the educational, social, and political activities of his daughter, but they had a larger purpose.[30] Surely the president of the Puerto Rican Senate would want to weigh in on the situation of contract workers, considering his own political aspirations for higher office, and in light of the pending U.S. congressional approval of legislation to allow the first popular election of the island's governor. In view of her father's political influence and ambitions, Muñoz Lee assured her father that she had made no promises in his name to the contract workers, but she *had* committed herself to relay word of their circumstances to him. In addition, she urged him as president of the Senate to take immediate measures to improve the conditions of labor migrants in Chicago.[31] Puerto Rican workers had already aroused resentment among their North American counterparts, as domestic workers had been accused of being "strike-breakers." Explaining the stance of the students who signed the report, Muñoz Lee insisted that, in principle, the group was not against migration as a strategy to alleviate Puerto Rico's problems. Nevertheless, a migration such as the one underway in Chicago, where workers least protected by law (as the case of domestics) were sent out under contracts that did not protect their rights and that made it impossible to earn a living wage, was no help in resolving the island's problems and in fact created new ones.

Muñoz Lee reminded her father that, in their advertisements, Castle, Barton and Associates "specified that they only wanted white workers for the area of Chicago," and told him that she and Padilla consulted Chicago sociologist C. Everett Hughes, president of the Commission on Race Relations and Industry, on the racial implications of recruited Puerto Rican labor migration. Hughes had speculated, "The poison of racial prejudice, injected by means of this kind of advertisement can be tremendously dangerous for the solution of the economic problems of Puerto Rico."[32] Hughes's warning suggested that U.S. notions of racial inferiority could hamper the viability of migration as an instrument for the economic development of the island. The case of Black Puerto Ricans shipped to the South was identified by Padilla and Muñoz Lee as especially remarkable; but they chose not to discuss it in their public report for fear that "the reactionary press would use it to create more diversions" to "stimulate racial divisions among Puerto Ricans."[33] Their omission points to the ways in which the subject of race in Puerto Rico has been glossed over with the pretext of not transporting and confounding U.S. racial ideologies to the island.[34]

More telling were the ways in which U.S. racial ideologies hampered the potential of political affiliations among workers of color at the local level. As Padilla noted in her thesis:

> An attitude of dislike is indicated by verbalizations against American Negroes. A member of the new migration said, "not even Negroes were getting as low wages as the Puerto Ricans in Chicago." Another migrant claimed that "American Negroes were not like Puerto Rican Negroes because in this country, Negroes just were not equal to white people," so she would not even think of speaking to an American Negro.
>
> This attitude toward the American Negro probably stems largely from the fact that the recent migration of Puerto Ricans theoretically only included white workers. Among the workers who came, nevertheless, many of them would be considered Negroes in the United States but were considered as white by the Puerto Ricans.[35]

In her December 9, 1946, letter to Colón, dispatching the report and expressing concern over the racial issues that had emerged, Padilla wrote, "I am prepared to write however many articles you like, in English or Spanish—let me know how you want them," reiterating a proposal she had made in an earlier letter in which she had referred to the recruitment of Puerto Rican workers to Chicago as a "scandalous act," "one of the greatest betrayals" of the Puerto Rican people by their government.[36] Scholars since have claimed that Puerto Rican migrants did not represent an economic threat to black and white workers in Chicago because of their small numbers, but the targeted labor recruitment of Puerto Rican women tells a different story.[37] It was a recruitment that attempted to undermine workers' rights, as well as labor organizing, and it was a significant event in Puerto Rican labor migration history.

In Puerto Rico, government officials responded defensively to the University of Chicago students' report. Manuel A. Pérez, commissioner of labor, warned Muñoz Marín, "I am afraid that the activities of these kids, as well intentioned as they may be, can be obstructive to these projects of migration that began to develop rather satisfactorily."[38] In a letter to Muñoz Lee, carbon-copied to Muñoz Marín, he requested that the students send "all of the evidence you have concerning contract violations, signed by the workers, and the mistreatment that, allegedly, they are receiving from their employers and from the employment agency." Further, he wanted the names of the workers, their employers or ex-employers, and postal addresses for all, along with information on the average salary and work hours for maids in Chicago, and a copy of a document or law regulating household labor or that established some kind of standard to substantiate the complaints of workers recorded by students. He asked for some proposed alternatives for migrant workers from the student committee, reminding them, all the while, of the poverty and unemployment in Puerto Rico. Perez questioned why not a single one of the female picketers spoke with a representative from the Illinois Department of Labor who was in a position to assess and likely ameliorate work standards; he also found the reticence inexplicable given the denunciations made by the domestic workers concerning their circumstances. Other investigations received by his office, Pérez noted, had also not included interviews with foundry administrators, representatives from the private employment agency, and the employers of the household workers. "It would have been useful and fair to hear from all parties before formulating the complaint," he suggested. "Nonetheless," he concluded, "I hope you continue studying the situation, bringing to light all the factors and circumstances, keeping in mind the unemployment rate level in the island and with an eye to the best labor opportunities you can suggest for our compatriots over there."[39] In his reply to Muna Muñoz Lee, Pérez enclosed a copy of an editorial from the island newspaper *El Imparcial,* perhaps as a lesson in "bringing to light all the factors and circumstances" in a debate and perhaps also to show the political uproar the student report had generated on the island.

The editorial in *El Imparcial* forcefully criticized Pérez for his apparent alignment with Illinois government and business interests rather than supporting the protest of "our migrant workers." Pérez, so the paper said, accepted the posture of an Illinois official and a representative of Castle, Barton and Associates, both of whom dismissed the allegations made in the report. Frank Graves, the Illinois official, had claimed that "there were few female workers" on the picket line in the protest, comprised mainly of "sympathizers recruited from other places," describing "the group of Puerto Ricans who channeled the protest . . . as 'small and petty.'" The representative from the employment agency was accusing the students of "falsifying the facts" and of "trying to organize all the girls we have brought from Puerto Rico." *El Imparcial* said Pérez had attempted to undermine the students' organizing efforts, treating the report as "sloppy and unfounded" and painting the students as "trying to create difficulties for the Insular Government." The editorial maintained: "It is not about minor differences between employers and workers that can be easily resolved. It is about fundamental violations of the rights of our migrant workers, violations that have all the marks of outrage and abuse." In contrast to Pérez's characterization, *El Imparcial* presented the students as "patriotically assum[ing] the task of organizing and defending . . . their humble migrant compatriots." The editorial called on the Department of Labor to enact protections for migrant contract labor instead of trying to justify their position in the press.[40]

Less than two weeks after receiving Commissioner Pérez's letter, Padilla and Muñoz Lee responded to his charges and questions, sending their rejoinder to the editor of *El Imparcial* for publication as well. The letter opened with the two students describing Pérez and Frank Graves as "very naïve" if they "sincerely believed" that two Puerto Rican maids, interviewed by Graves, would "confess to questions that they were being mistreated" in their employers' homes. To the characterization of the maids and their allies who participated in the picket as "small" and "petty," Padilla and Muñoz Lee countered that the majority of the maids who picketed the agency did so "fully recognizing that their protest was because of the contract's conditions, and that other Puerto Rican maids, satisfied with their situation, joined the protest in solidarity with their compatriots, along with a group of Puerto Rican students, and an even larger group of American students and representatives of the 'Workers' Defense League.'" They challenged Graves's claim that the maids had refused to be interviewed by him at the picket line. Muñoz Lee had, in fact, called his office to request a meeting in which students and workers could participate. When Muñoz Lee identified herself as Puerto Rican to one of Graves's staff members, he, "assuming that he was speaking with one of the protesting maids," reprimanded her: "If you did not like the contract, why did you sign it?" The students' noted, "Commissioner Pérez knows well that no such law exists in the State of Illinois for the protection of domestic service. And so, what legal guarantee could the Department of the Labor of Illinois offer them?"[41] The controversy over the conditions of contract workers and the report of the University of Chicago graduate students suggests that despite receiving financial sponsorship from the Puerto Rican government to study abroad, Elena Padilla and her comrades did not defer to or accept government policy that was inherently unjust in terms of the poorest of their fellow citizens.

The publicity garnered by the workers' protest and the report and letters authored by Elena Padilla and Muna Muñoz Lee (among others) prevailed upon the Puerto Rican Senate to order an official investigation into the matter. Labor migration from the island was suspended until the insular legislature adopted a new policy regulating migrant contract labor.[42] Government and business bureaucrats could not have imagined that isolated migrants would have any allies. Padilla and Muñoz Lee's collaboration with female workers, as well as the strategic use of their academic credentials and personal access to public officials, academics, and activists, to make the contract labor experiment an issue worthy of scrutiny and revision speaks to the ways in which women used the limited resources they had available to them to "direct the men in their communities and the affairs of those communities," as historian Earl Lewis has noted in another context.[43] The footnotes in "Puerto Rican Immigrants in Chicago and New York," I believe, point to the fact that Padilla's scholarship was very much driven by "a politics of love and rescue." In other words, Padilla's scholarship was also a powerful motion on behalf of the people in her study, her people, to be treated justly.

Foregrounding the Deeds of Puerto Rican Women

My own work continues, in some ways, where Padilla's left off.[44] I, too, crossed paths with Puerto Ricans who arrived or had family members who arrived in Chicago as part of the contract labor experiment while I was a graduate student at the University of Michigan (where Padilla was to have enrolled in medical school). By foregrounding the deeds of Puerto Rican women, this section continues the complex story of the diverse and at times antagonistic struggles of ordinary folks to find a way to live decent lives, struggling with forces far beyond their control even as they collectively work to shape their local context. Much like Padilla and her collaborators, who sought redress from the state and policymakers to defend the rights of the least protected community members, Puerto Rican women from Chicago's Near Northwest Side also refused to give up the right to a decent and just community or to absolve the state from assisting their efforts to do so. Specifically, this section focuses on a repertoire of what might be considered small-scale actions by Puerto Rican women who took an active interest in the betterment of daily life in their communities.

My landlady, Gina Bishop, owner of Caribe Funeral Home, the first Puerto Rican funeral home in Chicago, came to the city in the latter half of 1950 from Humacao, Puerto Rico. When asked why she migrated, Gina responded simply, "a buscar arroz y habichuela" (to look for rice and beans). Her sister, Medelicia, made arrangements for her to work for a year as a *niñera* (nanny) for a Jewish family. Medelicia Rios had worked for this family as part of the contract labor experiment. In the fall of 1946 Medelicia boarded a cargo plane in San Juan bound for Chicago's Midway Airport. "Yo era de la' primera'" (I was one of the first ones), she proudly claimed, perhaps even of the "recent migration" of domestic workers Elena Padilla observed in her 1947 master's thesis. When many of the recruited laborers abandoned their contracts, they looked for work and residence in the area near the YWCA. Eventually, a distinctly Puerto Rican social and geographic community emerged in the proximity of the Loop, which became a core community of Chicago Puerto Rican activism—the famed Lincoln Park/Old Town neighborhood of the Young Lords.[45]

On a variety of occasions in the front office of Caribe Funeral Home or at different social gatherings, Gina and her longtime friend Ana La Luz reminisced about their old neighborhoods, areas that are now considered the trendy and upscale areas of the city, areas where *los pobres* (the poor) are now policed. Ana spoke forcefully about her old neighborhoods, the Puerto Rican communities of the Near North Side, Lincoln Park, and Old Town: "It was poor peoples . . . during that time. But not now. Forget it, we Latinos can't go over there. Even here [Logan Square] we hardly can't." This coupling of Puerto Rican–ness, latinidad, and *los pobres* reveals a comprehension of Puerto Rican–ness and latinidad that is class based and shaped by discriminatory, racializing practices mapped onto space and affixed to people in that space.

The radical transformation of Old Town and Lincoln Park from "poor peoples" to some of the most elite neighborhoods in the city began in the 1960s when the city of Chicago put into action the renewal plan for the area. The populations most adversely affected by these changes were Puerto Ricans and African Americans, who were displaced by the loss of affordable rental units or were priced out of the housing market altogether.[46] For Ana La Luz and her family, the move from the Old Town neighborhood of the Lincoln Park community area in the late 1960s was a painful displacement. Unable to meet the high-end property demands or the changing racial aesthetic, the La Luz family sold their three-flat apartment building and bought a small single-family home in the Palmer Square section of Logan Square. The neighborhood was not an ideal choice, but it was what they could afford at the time. The house was in poor condition, in need of much repair, and "the neighborhood was very bad, full of gangs," Ana told me in 2002.[47] Although Ana spoke of how she and her family *sufrieron* (suffered) in Palmer Square, she did not paint a picture of a bleak or irredeemable community. Rather, she imparted a narrative of how "little by little—we worked hard to raise the neighborhood." Her understanding of community activism underscores the successive effects of small acts that set in motion the transformation of the neighborhood.

During the 1980s, the decade of intense gang violence, residents had to work two fronts in claiming their neighborhoods—one had to do with the intimidation tactics of gang members and the other with the response by law enforcement, which was either nonexistent or excessive. Ana recounted the almost daily gang harassment her youngest son, Santiago, faced in the early 1980s. Once Ana, widowed at the time, became aware of the situation, she kept a more watchful eye on him and sent him less frequently to run her errands. At first, avoidance was used as a strategy of protection from the gang. However, when Santiago witnessed a car accident involving one of the gang members and gave a statement to the police, avoidance was no longer possible. Aside from harassment as a recruitment tactic, the gang also deployed harassment as a means to protect their prized economic ventures— the distribution and sale of drugs in the area.[48] That night, someone called Ana's house to threaten Santiago. Panic-stricken, she packed her two youngest children's bags and sent them away for the summer the very next day. Early the following morning Santiago and Lucia, Ana's youngest daughter, were on a plane headed out of state to stay with one of their older sisters.

A deeply religious person, Ana did not resign herself to fate, "God's will." She went to her neighbor, a police officer, who told her "you alone can't do anything; me alone, even being a police officer can't do anything." The neighborhood needed to be organized. She vividly recalled, "The kids left Wednesday in the morning and Wednesday at 4:00, when I came home from work, I went door-to-door knocking on all the doors *in front* of those who were there. Therefore, I exposed myself to anything but . . . my kids came first . . . And I talked to the block." Plans were made for a community meeting at the police officer's house. Whereas previously avoidance was the tactic employed against gang harassment, Ana now used exposure to disrupt the gang dominance of the neighborhood. Coming to the realization that if she wanted to bring her children back home she could not do so alone, Ana operated from her intersecting commitments of labor, politics, and mothering, what sociologist Nancy Naples refers to as "activist mothering," to guide her understandings of her actions. This realization was a driving force in Ana's decision to go door-to-door telling her neighbors of her predicament and later calling on their involvement in neighborhood affairs. In effect, "cooperative self-help" blended with other strategies characterized the kind of community organizing in which Ana and her neighbors engaged to improve conditions in the neighborhood.[49]

With some degree of satisfaction, Ana recalled how residents responded to the beating of a neighbor by gang members because he told a group of young men congregated in the street to quiet down early one morning:

> In pajamas, in house dresses, or whatever . . . we came out and the police real-ized that we were united. When we went to the court date, a good group of us went . . . And the judge told the young man who hit the neighbor, the young man was one of *my son's* friends, well, he told him, "you see all these people here are united so do me a favor and leave these people alone." Therefore, the neighbors with this helped a lot. It didn't change it totally, but it did change a lot . . . And little by little the block was picking up and cleaning up . . . And so, I think that . . . we've improved a lot. I know that I exposed myself two times—but . . . the man next door also did.

Her account of community activism revealed a constellation of actions—from neighbors confronting gang members to residents coming out of homes to bear witness to altercations and law enforcement's response, to attending the court date as a community—that set in motion the transformation of the community. At the same time, attention was drawn to how law enforcement and the legal system took note of residents' conceptualization of themselves as a valued, viable community—a space worthy of defense. More broadly, it is also a defensive stance against the criminalized "culture of poverty" outlook held of Puerto Ricans that continually brings into question their respectability and national belonging, what Ramos-Zayas has described as a "politics of worthiness."[50] Celebrating small victories, Ana did not lose sight of the incredibly vulnerable position in which she and her accomplices placed themselves, using strategies of exposure to make the neighborhood a more decent place to live.

As residents contended with gang activity, there were individuals who believed the path to a better neighborhood was via the punitive expulsion of gang members. While Ana has supported the use of law enforcement in community affairs and while her statement that the neighborhood "was cleaning up" can be interpreted as an endorsement of the wholesale removal of gang members, it is important to note that she did not alienate wayward youth in her neighborhood by labeling them as "inherently bad" or "worthless." Instead, she recognized some of the young men as friends of her son, "good kids" heading down a wrong path, community members in need of guidance, especially given the failure of the school system and criminal justice system to serve their needs. Puerto Rican sociologist Marixsa Alicea, drawing on her family's intracity migration patterns to tell a story of racial domination and exclusion, argues that with such a grounding, "we had a quiet, tacit understanding and knowledge of the larger processes at work that led our youth to join gangs, and we also knew that not all young people in our community were in gangs."[51] An understanding of the larger process at work was visible in 1984 when Latina/o parents demonstrated against the unconscionable dropout rate of Latina/o students and gang violence in the schools and in communities.[52]

The state's blatant disregard for Latina/o youths' future presented a gruesome challenge for Otilia Irizarry, another longstanding community member. Otilia often found herself in the difficult position of having to deal with gang activity while also trying to protect the rights of youth in the neighborhood. Since the 1980s, Chicago, like other parts of the country, saw a marked shift in government policy from public services with the purpose of reintegrating youth into labor markets and educational programs to widely approved punitive strategies. The mass arrest of youth for petty crimes (like loitering and graffiti), harsher penalties for certain types of drug trafficking (disproportionately involving youth from low-income urban neighborhoods), along with the promotion of juvenile offenders to adult sentencing became the modus operandi of the new carceral state.[53]

Deeply involved in community affairs, especially issues with law enforcement, Otilia gave an account of the difficulties of not only building decent neighborhoods, but also equitable communities:

> So it's been very difficult because you have a meeting and the police come . . . and you invite a person to attend the meeting, but within that . . . the mother that goes there, the mother of the very kid that's in the gang. So how do you talk, how are you going to tell the police that look the gang is eating us up . . . Look at how difficult. If . . . there is a kid that has problems with the police, and then you speak out, you call the police with that problem and then what happens is that the police when they come they take that one and all that are with him even though they are not at fault. Or else . . . the police take him and

they drop him off in rival gang territory. They are going to give him a beating
. . . So then it is very conflictive for a person with a heart. Because if you don't
have a heart, if you don't care you say, "look put them in jail, all of them." But I
am a mother and I have nephews and furthermore . . . I love the people, I don't
want for anyone to have something bad happen that they didn't deserve . . . For
that reason, sometimes . . . if I can't give complete information . . . I've opted
to shut my mouth . . . And it's not that I say, "oh well, since they don't bother
me," because, yes, it does bother me that the other kids are losing themselves
to the drugs that they sell.

Compassion for youth is not for purely altruistic reasons. Women like Otilia
and Ana imagine an alternative way of life for themselves, their families,
and their community, and so to realize such a vision they necessarily involve
themselves in community affairs. Because they want to feel safe where they
live, they in turn seek to help others to feel safe in the process. The question
then becomes, how do we create safe spaces, and much more difficult, how
do we do so inclusively? Otilia pondered this dilemma when she considered
the position of a gang member's mother, as well as actual gang members,
when addressing issues of police involvement in neighborhood affairs. Sensitive to her listeners, Otilia assessed the repercussions of her comments
before expressing her apprehensions in a public forum. She prudently took
into account the role her public statements play in outside judgments of
her community, the geographic area and the people. Concomitantly, Otilia
tried to set up the possibility of a sympathetic space where even the most
unconceivable participants, from within, feel they can contribute in some
fashion. Rattled by the picture of "lost" youth, Otilia desperately searches for
ways to improve the quality of life in the community, in the hopes of assisting youth, without exiling them, locking them up, or, worse yet, sentencing
them to death.[54] She speaks out against mass incarceration as the remedy
for safe neighborhoods, precisely because of the suspension of justice for
underserved and systematically targeted youth, where the implementation
of heartless measures in the name of the public good only further exacer-
bates economic, social, racial, and educational disparities. Otilia's broader
sense of fairness stems from her ability to theorize from the personal, and,
I would argue, it is also based on a politics of love and rescue.[55] However,
the daunting realities faced in these communities can provoke, even in the
most dedicated, a degree of indifference.

Mayor Richard M. Daley once accused Puerto Rican parents of protecting
the criminal actions of Puerto Rican gangs. What some interpret as indifference or aiding in criminal activity, others interpret as a means to maintain
some sense of fairness for a population perceived as criminal. In Chicago,

regrettably, "being Puerto Rican and young has been made synonymous with being criminal."[56] Well aware of this, Otilia refuses to take part in an injustice in the name of justice and, therefore, sometimes has opted for silence in matters where she feels that cooperating with police will not produce beneficial outcomes for the community, in particular its systematically targeted members. By standing outside as police came to investigate the beating of Ana's neighbor, residents also witnessed the treatment of their youth by law enforcement. Thus, a further result, intentional for some and maybe not for others, of bearing witness to the arrest and attending the court date was the protection of neighborhood youth from excessive force.[57] As with Padilla many years earlier, residents like Ana were not just calling the police; they were calling on the state to act in a responsible and just manner. Ana's struggle was and is not to rid the neighborhood of unruly youth, but rather, to manage an environment where safety and communality (defined in certain and surely problematic terms) exist without the punitive expulsion of youth from the neighborhood.

Ana's goal

Otilia and Ana remind us that there is a responsibility in calling and involving the police in community affairs. This stance illustrates a very different understanding of the "we call police" flyers situated on the windows of homes in the area.[58] Policing for these women, in this context, requires much thought, tact, and negotiation; for Otilia, it is almost as a last resort to call police. Akin to Black feminist thought, their grounded Latina standpoint visualizes the world in which they live not as a place in which they manage to survive but as a place of which they feel possession and accountability.[59] Therefore, as community members, they underscore the urgency in acting responsibly to gain and to create a sense of social justice.

Journalist Ray Suarez, a celebrated former resident of Logan Square, wrote about how Latina/o residents worked toward stabilizing the community with homegrown revitalization. He paid critical attention to the real risks residents faced in efforts to create a safe, attractive neighborhood. Participation was a particularly dangerous matter in these cases where people exposed themselves to the potential of fatal retaliation, like Ana, whose home was targeted for arson. For Suarez, an indication of their accomplishment was the presence of "young white buyers, who wouldn't even have driven down this street a few years before." The residents with whom I spoke, however, were more critical of the movement of "young white buyers" into the neighborhood as a gauge of success. "I think that we've done a grand 'improvement' as white people say," Ana boasted cautiously. "Even though we are much happier in one sense," she continued, "but in another we're not . . . They are pushing us once again west." A feature article on Logan

Square in the "Apartment and Homes" section of a local paper serves as a reminder. The article indicates that some brokers believe that "prices will continue to appreciate rapidly in Logan Square, and that it will eventually look more like Lincoln Park than Humboldt Park."[60] Ana's brooding at the outset of this section concerning the diminishing prospect of Latinos to live or even walk around in Logan Square is quite legitimate indeed.

Today, balanced development and affordable housing have become urgent community concerns. Whereas previously community members questioned if these were viable areas to raise children due to issues of safety, now they question if these are areas average families can afford. In effect, they toiled tirelessly only to become strangers in their own communities. Women like Ana, Otilia, and Gina counter by charging affordable rent as a means to stabilize the area in their own way. I was able to conduct field research in the rapidly gentrifying neighborhood of my youth because Gina holds such beliefs. This new appeal makes evident a community's restorative ability as well as the new challenges that past achievements (large and small) generate. In short, the community about which these women spoke, critiqued with love, and fought so hard to transform epitomizes the kind of politics Dominguez calls for; it is the kind of politics Elena Padilla signaled in her footnotes.

Conclusion

While Dominguez argues for a politics of love and rescue from the perspective of scholars writing in the scholarly defense of the people they love, such a politics can also be extended to intellectuals outside of the academy, like the neighborhood intellectuals I came to know and respect in the city I call home.[61] Ana La Luz, Otilia Irizarry, and Gina Bishop, along with many other women and men, expressed their desire to help me, as they could, with my "school project" but nonetheless reminded me to be mindful of personal and communal discretion in the process.[62] Because of their willingness to engage the complexities of everyday life in the neighborhood, their caution should not be taken as an attempt to have me focus on the "positive" aspects of community. Rather, it points to the relationship these women have to the state, academic scholarship, and popular depictions of who they supposedly are and the places from which they come. They know what has been said and written about Puerto Rican communities, by "outsiders" and "insiders," and they know what is wrong with it. Their politics of love and rescue included an equally strong critique of our community as well as what I needed to pay attention to as a scholar. Perhaps Elena Padilla learned a similar lesson from her relationships with Muna Muñoz Lee, Jesús Colón, and the contract workers who shared their lives and perspectives with her.

Due to the prevailing inability of the social sciences to vulnerably engage and depict the subjects of their research or the complex relationship between the academy and communities of study, we lose an ability to make sense of the footnotes. Nonetheless, as the narratives in this essay indicate, the margins are an important place where people can express these alliances. Padilla's extra-anthropological activities highlight how the footnotes in scholarship need to be recuperated and examined for what they can reveal about the daily lives and struggles of individuals and collectives in an urban environment. Like the Puerto Rican women of Chicago's Near Northwest Side, who serve and protect their neighborhoods (beyond simply calling the police), Padilla had scholarly commitments that extended further than merely writing about the plight of Puerto Rican migrant workers; she incorporated her activism into her work and still lives the politics of her scholarship. This is evident in her follow-up study on Puerto Ricans in "Eastville," *Up from Puerto Rico,* and in her continued scholarship and activism concerning Puerto Ricans and public health.[63] More recently, one could spot Dr. Padilla on the streets of New York City protesting for health-care reform. It is also evident in her commitment to me as a young scholar and a Puerto Rican from Chicago, the place where she began her profession as an anthropologist and an activist scholar. She graciously accepted my phone calls and indulged my queries about her thesis and other aspects of her life, sometimes calling into question my ideas and interpretations. It is not likely she ever thought something she wrote in her early twenties would follow her into her eighties. Paying critical attention to the footnotes in scholarship and daily life, I argue, reveals how intellectual, political, and personal commitments powerfully refine our understanding of everyday activism in Latino urban communities and, more specifically, women's significant interventions in creating and promoting a fair and just sense of community.

NOTES

1. Elena Padilla, "Puerto Rican Immigrants in New York and Chicago: A Study in Comparative Assimilation" (master's thesis, University of Chicago, 1947). The thesis is reprinted in part 1 of this volume; all citations are to the reprint.

2. The first note appears in Padilla's method chapter (p. 49); the second in her chapter on Puerto Ricans in New York (p. 75, n. 22); and the final one in the chapter on Puerto Ricans in Chicago (p. 96, n. 17). Jesús Colón is cited at various times in the New York chapter. Before I came across Padilla's thesis I had seen a copy of the

preliminary report in a privately published book on Puerto Ricans in Chicago. See Manuel Martinez, *Chicago: Historia de Nuestra Communidad Puertorriqueña— Photographic Documentary* (Chicago: privately printed, 1989).

3. Earl Lewis, "Connecting Memory, Self, and the Power of Place in African American Urban History," *Journal of Urban History* 21, 3 (1995): 347–371.

4. Virginia R. Dominguez, "For a Politics of Love and Rescue," *Cultural Anthropology* 15, 3 (2000): 361–393.

5. Colón was also a member of the International Workers of the World and the Communist Party.

6. The list of those who signed the report consists of Héctor Alvarez Silva, Anne Duvendeek, Henry Goodman, Muna Muñoz, Milton Pabón, Elena Padilla, Albert Rees, and Manuel Zambrana.

7. Ana Y. Ramos-Zayas's chapter in this volume addresses this point in depth. Also see Judith Freidenberg, ed., *The Anthropology of Lower Income Urban Enclaves: The Case of East Harlem* (New York: New York Academy of Sciences, 1995); Gina M. Pérez, *Centro: Journal of the Center for Puerto Rican Studies* 13, 2 (2001), Special Issue on Puerto Rican Community in Chicago.

8. Jaime Benitez, chancellor of the University of Puerto Rico (UPR), sponsored cohorts of UPR graduates to attend elite U.S. institutions to groom the future faculty of the UPR system. Other groups of students were sent to the University of Michigan and Harvard University; however, the cadre of students at the University of Chicago was the largest group. Personal communication with Elena Padilla, October 20, 2005; see the introduction to this volume.

9. Louis Wirth, Sol Tax, and Everett. C. Hughes supervised the Committee on Interracial Relations, Division of Social Sciences at the University of Chicago.

10. Letter from Elena Padilla to Jesús Colón, October 3, 1946, Box 3, Folder 5, the Jesús Colón Papers, 1901–1974, Archives of the Puerto Rican Diaspora, Centro de estudios puertorriqueños, Hunter College, CUNY.

11. Padilla, "Puerto Rican Immigrants," p. 97.

12. "Fly Puerto Ricans to Chicago to Fill Jobs as Domestics," *Chicago Daily Tribune,* September 17, 1946, p. 24; "Foundry Solves Problem: Hires Puerto Ricans!" *Chicago Daily News,* September 28, 1946, p. 3; Lois Thrasher, "52 Pct. Success Marks Experiment of Imported Maid," *Chicago Daily News,* March 7, 1947, n.d. (circa March 1947), Section IV, Series 2, Sub-series 9B, Folder 277, Fundación Luis Muñoz Marín.

13. The letters of Muñoz-Lee and the letters and reports of Carmen Isales, a Puerto Rican social worker hired to work with the migrants (below), are also noteworthy. The contributions of these women as chroniclers of Puerto Rican community life are treated at length in my book-length project "A Grounded Identidad: Places of Memory and Personhood in Chicago's Puerto Rican Neighborhoods."

14. Thrasher, "52 Pct. Success Marks Experiment."

15. Tea times became a common social activity provided by the YWCA for Puerto Rican domestic workers in U.S. urban centers. Historian Carmen Whalen also docu-

ments the tea times among Puerto Rican domestic workers in Philadelphia as a time where women exchanged information and formed relationships. See Carmen Teresa Whalen, *From Puerto Rico to Philadelphia: Puerto Rican Workers and Postwar Economies* (Philadelphia: Temple University Press, 2001).

16. Presumably, the women recruited as domestics were between the ages of eighteen and thirty-five. However, since the Department of Labor did not require proof of age, some young women faked their ages to secure employment in the continental United States. Accusations of labor exploitation and other abuses included fifteen-hour workdays, lower wages than those received by other workers performing the same tasks, and impromptu transfers of domestic workers' employment locations. Padilla, "Puerto Rican Immigrants," pp. 84–86; also see Edwin Maldonado, "Contract Labor and the Origins of Puerto Rican Communities in the United States," *International Migration Review* 13, 1 (1979): 103–121; Maura Toro-Morn, "Género, trabajo y migración: Las empleadas domésticas puertorriqueñas en Chicago," *Revista de Ciencias Sociales* 7 (1999): 102–125.

17. The foundry workers were contracted to earn 88.5 cents an hour, with time and a half for overtime after forty hours a week. However, after various deductions, many Puerto Rican foundry workers received less a dollar in cash for a week's worth of work. Men who fell ill were nonetheless charged the full amount for their living expenses. Héctor Alvarez, Anne Duvendeek, Henry Goodman, Muna Muñoz, Milton Pabón, Elena Padilla, Albert Rees, and Manuel Zambrana, "Preliminary Report on the Puerto Rican Contract Workers in the Chicago Area," Welfare Council of Metropolitan Chicago Papers, Chicago Historical Society (now Chicago History Museum) Archives, November 25, 1946.

18. Padilla, "Puerto Rican Immigrants," pp. 90–93.

19. Letter from Elena Padilla to Jesús Colón, December 9, 1946, Folder 5, Jesús Colón Papers, 1901–1974, Archives of the Puerto Rican Diaspora, Centro de estudios puertorriqueños, Hunter College, CUNY.

20. Letter from Evangelina Serrano to Muna Muñoz Lee, May 19, 1947, private collection of Dr. Gloria Arjona, Puerto Rico.

21. Hernández, *Ricardo Alegría: Una Vida,* 96–97. Also see Reina Pérez, *La Semilla Que Sembramos: Autobiografía Del Proyecto Nacional.* At the Puerto Rican Studies International Congress held in San Juan in October 2008, Alegría referred to the near expulsion of his classmates Padilla and Muñoz Lee.

22. Personal communication with Elena Padilla, November 2, 2005.

23. Letter from Muna Muñoz Lee to Luis Muñoz Marín, n.d. (circa January–February 1947), Section IV, Series 3, Folder 397a, Fundación Luis Muñoz Marín.

24. Handwritten statement by Leonides Algarín and Miguel Rivera, personal collection of Gloria Arjona, Caguas, Puerto Rico.

25. "Puerto Ricans Charge Exploitation in U.S." *Chicago Defender,* November 30, 1946, p. 7; "Plight of Puerto Ricans Starts Dispute, Deplorable Conditions Denied by Employers," *Chicago Daily Tribune,* December 11, 1946, p. 30.

26. In my archival research in Chicago, New York, and Puerto Rico, Padilla and,

to a lesser extent, Muñoz Lee are the only individuals identified in relation to the report and its distribution. Padilla's co-authorship and other deeds were not hidden from her thesis committee. In fact, documents in Sol Tax's papers at the University of Chicago mention the report and the role of Puerto Rican students in publicizing the plight of the workers. Tax also wrote a proposal to continue a longitudinal study of Puerto Rican acculturation and assimilation based on Padilla's thesis. It appears this project was stalled due to plans for a Columbia University study on Puerto Ricans in New York headed by C. Wright Mills and Clarence Senior, which resulted in the book *The Puerto Rican Journey: New York's Newest Migrants* (New York: Harper and Row, 1950). See memo from Sol Tax and Everett Hughes to Social Science Research Committee regarding proposal for Puerto Rican Immigrants to Chicago Project, n.d., Sol Tax papers, Box 256, Folder 4, Special Collections Research Center, University of Chicago Library. While her advisers at the University of Chicago appeared supportive of Padilla's extra-anthropological activities, they seemed less encouraging when it came to the inclusion of such data and its implications in her thesis.

27. "Puerto Ricans Charge Exploitation in U.S." *Chicago Defender,* November 30, 1946, p. 7; letter from Muna Muñoz Lee to Luis Muñoz Marín, n.d. (circa January–February 1947); letter from Elena Padilla to Jesús Colón. December 9, 1946.

28. Letter, Elena Padilla to Jesús Colón, December 9, 1946.

29. Letter, Muna Muñoz Lee to Luis Muñoz Marín, December 9, 1947.

30. Ibid.; letter, Muna Muñoz Lee to Luis Muñoz Marín, n.d. (circa January–February 1947).

31. According to Padilla, Muñoz Marín used the pretext of a visit with his daughter to look privately into the condition of migrant workers in Chicago (personal communication).

32. Letter from Muna Muñoz Lee to Luis Muñoz Marín, n.d. (circa January–February 1947).

33. Ibid.

34. See Carlos Alamo Pastrana, "Racializing the Research Laboratory: Puerto Rico and the African American Intellectual Imaginary, 1940–1950," paper presented at 8th International Congress of the Puerto Rican Studies Association, San Juan, P.R., October 3, 2008.

35. Padilla, "Puerto Rican Immigrants," p. 94.

36. Letters, Elena Padilla to Jesús Colón, December 9, 1946, and October 3, 1946.

37. See Felix M. Padilla, *Latino Ethnic Consciousness: The Case of Mexican Americans and Puerto Ricans in Chicago* (Notre Dame, Ind.: University of Notre Dame Press, 1985), pp. 43–44.

38. Letter from Manuel A. Pérez to Luis Muñoz Marín, December 18, 1946, Section IV, Series 2, Subseries 9, Folder 251, Fundación Luis Muñoz Marín.

39. Letter from Manuel A. Pérez to Muna Muñoz Lee, December 17, 1946, Series 2, Subseries 9, Folder 251, Fundación Luis Muñoz Marín.

40. Notas Editoriales, "Nuestros Emigrantes Desamparados," *El Imparcial,* December 16, 1946, p. 16.

41. Jose Armindo Cadilla, "Estudiantes Chicago Contestan a Comisionado Pérez Señalando Caso De Violación De Contrato," *El Imparcial,* December 28, 1946, pp. 6–7.

42. Padilla, "Puerto Rican Immigrants," p. 95.

43. Lewis draws on the work of Elsa Barkley Brown to make this point. Lewis, "Connecting Memory," p. 363. See Elsa Barkley Brown, "Negotiating and Transforming the Public Sphere: African American Political Life in the Transition from Slavery to Freedom," *Public Culture* 7 (1994): 107–146.

44. This section is based on research from my larger project conducted from September 2000 through March 2003 and based on a combination of interviews, ethnographic observation, and archival investigation. I conducted formal and semi-formal interviews with one-time and present-day residents of Chicago's Near West Side, Logan Square, and Humboldt Park communities. Initially participants were selected based on my familiarity with families from these three communities. I asked individuals who shared their personal accounts with me to recommend other potential participants, applying what we in the social sciences term a "snowball approach" to "data collection." Individuals answered open-ended questions about family histories, neighborhood portraits and daily life in those vicinities, past and present community debates, and other institutional and social experiences that informed their life histories. Members of the pioneering generation of Puerto Rican migrants to Chicago, those who came in the 1940s and 1950s (about a third of the forty-four interviews conducted), were asked to describe life in Puerto Rico, explain why they migrated, and convey memories of early Puerto Rican life in the city. Casual interviews initiated during social and political activities were followed up with semi-structured interviews related to the individual's involvement in a particular event or in various events. In addition, I scribbled extensive notes and talked to folks in a variety of social settings (birthday parties, baby showers, and memorial services) and different events around the city (political protests and rallies, community meetings, and neighborhood festivals). I complemented my ethnographic investigation with archival research in Chicago, New York, and Puerto Rico. Almost all of the people who comprise the subjects of this project were given or selected a pseudonym. However, there are cases, such as local public figures, where real names are used.

45. The Young Lords, comprised mainly of second-generation Puerto Rican youth, were a former street gang transformed into a politicized youth organization in the late 1960s. The Young Lords led efforts against the displacement of Puerto Ricans from the Lincoln Park area (see Felix M. Padilla, *Puerto Rican Chicago* (Notre Dame, Ind.: University of Notre Dame Press, 1987; and Andrew Diamond, *Mean Streets: Chicago Youths and the Everyday Struggle for Empowerment in the Multiracial City, 1908–1969* (Berkeley: University of California Press, 2009).

Although today there are scant remnants of a Puerto Rican presence in Lincoln Park, stories abound of the once Puerto Rican neighborhood and the activities of the Young Lords on behalf of the community. My own father, a former resident of Lincoln Park, had commented about feeling disorientation with the transformation of Armitage Avenue, the main corridor of the area, when we drove in to pick up sushi for dinner one evening in November 2003. Carlos Flores, one of the Lincoln Park Young Lords, has an impressive photo collection documenting Puerto Rican life in Lincoln Park during the 1970s. See Carlos Flores, "Shades of Lincoln Park: Armitage Avenue in the 1970s," *Diálogo* 1, 1 (1996): 17–21; and Flores, "Photo Essay of Puerto Rican Chicago," *Centro: Journal of the Center for Puerto Rican Studies* 13, 2 (2001): 134–165.

46. Larry Bennett, *Fragments of Cities: The New American Downtowns and Neighborhoods* (Columbus: Ohio State University Press, 1990).

47. It was during the time of escalating gang violence (between 1980 and 1987) that Logan Square experienced significant racial changeover. Disinvestment and white flight gradually made available the least desirable sections of Logan Square and other neighborhoods on the Near Northwest side to Latinos and Blacks. See Janet L. Abu-Lughod, *New York, Chicago, Los Angeles: America's Global Cities* (Minneapolis: University of Minnesota Press, 1999); John J. Betancur, "The Settlement Experience of Latinos in Chicago: Segregation, Speculation, and the Ecology Model," *Social Forces* 74, 4 (1996): 1299–1324.

48. Ray Suarez, *The Old Neighborhood: What We Lost in the Great Suburban Migration, 1966–1999* (New York: Free Press, 1999).

49. For Naples, an examination of activist mothering enables a fresh understanding of the intertwined roles of labor, politics, and mothering. These are components of women's social lives traditionally investigated as separate spheres. Nancy Naples, "Activist Mothering: Cross-Generational Continuity in the Community Work of Women from Low-Income Urban Neighborhoods," *Gender and Society* 6, 3 (1992): 441–463. Also see Ruth Wilson Gilmore, "Mother Reclaiming Our Children," *Golden Gulag: Prisons, Surplus, Crisis, and Opposition in Globalizing California* (Berkeley: University of California Press, 2007).

50. Ana Yolanda Ramos Zayas, "Delinquent Citizenship, National Performances: Racialization, Surveillance, and the Politics of 'Worthiness' in Puerto Rican Chicago," *Latino Studies* 2, 1 (2004): 26–44.

51. Marixsa Alicea, "Cuando nosotros vivíamos . . . : Stories of Displacement and Settlement in Puerto Rican Chicago," *Centro: Journal of the Center for Puerto Rican Studies* 13, 2 (2001), p. 188.

52. E. R. Shipp, "Chicago's Hispanic Parents Protest 70% Dropout Rate," *New York Times,* March 28, 1984, A16; Pauline Lipman, "Chicago School Reform: Advancing the Global City Agenda," in *The New Chicago: A Social and Cultural Analysis,* edited by John P. Koval, Larry Bennett, Michael I. J. Bennett, Fassil Demissie, Roberta Garner, and Kiljoong Kim (Philadelphia: Temple University Press, 2006), pp. 248–258.

53. See, for example, Gilmore, *Golden Gulag*; Sudhir Alladi Venkatesh and Alexandra K. Murphy, "Policing Ourselves: Law and Order in the American Ghetto," in *Youth, Globalization, and the Law*, edited by Sudhir Alladi Venkatesh and Ronald Kassimir (Stanford, Calif.: Stanford University Press, 2007), pp. 124–157; Christian Parenti, *Lockdown America: Police and Prisons in the Age of Crisis* (New York: Verso, 1999). I thank Carlos Alamo Pastrana for introducing me to this literature.

54. Anthropologist Gina Pérez explores the adoption of exile as a means to rid communities of "problem" youth in her work on Puerto Ricans in Chicago. Gina M. Pérez, "The Other 'Real World': Gentrification and the Social Construction of Place in Chicago," *Urban Anthropology* 31, 1 (2002): 37–68.

55. Cherri Moraga and Gloria Anzaldúa, eds., *This Bridge Called My Back: Writings by Radical Women of Color* (Watertown, Mass.: Persephone Press, 1981).

56. John J. Betancur, "The Politics of Gentrification: The Case of West Town in Chicago," *Urban Affairs Review* 37, 6 (2002), pp. 811, fn33.

57. Venkatesh argues that this punitive approach was "facilitated by increasing levels of residential segregation that allowed law enforcement to target such harsh policing practices to specific communities." Venkatesh and Murphy, "Policing Ourselves," p. 136.

58. I thank Lorena Garcia for this observation.

59. Patricia Hill Collins, *Black Feminist Thought: Knowledge, Consciousness, and the Politics of Empowerment*, rev. 10th anniversary ed. (New York: Routledge, 2000).

60. Barry Pearce, "Logan Square," Apartment and Homes section, July 23, 1993.

61. See Ruth Behar, "Panel Comments: Challenging Disciplinary Acts through and within a Politics of Love and Rescue," comments presented at American Anthropological Association 100th Annual Meeting, Washington D.C., 2001.

62. At moments, however, they chose to expose themselves, as was the case with "Otilia," who at more than one of my public presentations in Chicago claimed her pseudonym and explained she selected the name in honor of her favorite aunt.

63. Elena Padilla, *Up from Puerto Rico* (New York: Columbia University Press, 1958; Padilla, "Retrospect of Ethnomedical Research among Puerto Ricans: Living at the Margin of East Harlem," in *The Anthropology of Lower Income Urban Enclaves: The Case of East Harlem*, edited by Judith Friedenberg (New York: New York Academy of Sciences, 1995).

Works Cited

Abu-Lughod, Janet L. *New York, Chicago, Los Angeles: America's Global Cities.* Minneapolis: University of Minnesota Press, 1999.

Alamo Pastrana, Carlos. "Racializing the Research Laboratory: Puerto Rico and the African American Intellectual Imaginary 1940–1950." Paper presented at 8th International Congress of the Puerto Rican Studies Association, San Juan, October 3, 2008.

Alicea, Marixsa. "*Cuando nosotros vivíamos* . . . : Stories of Displacement and Settlement in Puerto Rican Chicago." *Centro: Journal of the Center for Puerto Rican Studies* 13, 2 (2001): 166–195.

Alvarez, Héctor, Anne Duvendeek, Henry Goodman, Muna Muñoz, Milton Pabón, Elena Padilla, Albert Rees, and Manuel Zambrana. "Preliminary Report on Puerto Rican Workers in Chicago." Welfare Council of Metropolitan Chicago Papers, Chicago Historical Society (now Chicago History Museum) Archives, November 25, 1946.

Barkley Brown, Elsa. "Negotiating and Transforming the Public Sphere: African American Political Life in the Transition from Slavery to Freedom." *Public Culture* 7 (1994): 107–146.

Behar, Ruth. "Panel Comments: Challenging Disciplinary Acts through and within a Politics of Love and Rescue." Comments presented at American Anthropological Association 100th Annual Meeting, Washington D.C., 2001.

Bennett, Larry. *Fragments of Cities: The New American Downtowns and Neighborhoods.* Columbus: Ohio State University Press, 1990.

Betancur, John J. "The Politics of Gentrification: The Case of West Town in Chicago." *Urban Affairs Review* 37, 6 (2002): 780–814.

———. "The Settlement Experience of Latinos in Chicago: Segregation, Speculation, and the Ecology Model." *Social Forces* 74, 4 (1996): 1299–1324.

Collins, Patricia Hill. *Black Feminist Thought: Knowledge, Consciousness, and the Politics of Empowerment.* Rev. 10th anniversary ed. New York: Routledge, 2000.

Diamond, Andrew. *Mean Streets: Chicago Youths and the Everyday Struggle for Empowerment in the Multiracial City, 1908–1969.* Berkeley: University of California Press, 2009.

Dominguez, Virginia R. "For a Politics of Love and Rescue." *Cultural Anthropology* 15, 3 (2000): 361–393.

Flores, Carlos. "Photo Essay of Puerto Rican Chicago." *Centro: Journal of the Center for Puerto Rican Studies* 13, 2 (2001): 134–165.

———. "Shades of Lincoln Park: Armitage Avenue in the 1970s," *Diálogo* 1, 1 (1996): 17–21.

Friedenberg, Judith, ed. *The Anthropology of Lower Income Urban Enclaves: The Case of East Harlem.* New York: New York Academy of Sciences, 1995.

Gilmore, Ruth W. Wilson. *Golden Gulag: Prisons, Surplus, Crisis, and Opposition in Globalizing California.* Berkeley: University of California Press, 2007.

Hernández, Carmen Dolores. *Ricardo Alegría: Una Vida.* San Juan: Centro de Estudios Avanzados de Puerto Rico y el Caribe, Fundación Puertorriqueña de las Humanidades, Instituto de Cultura Puertorriqueña, Academia Puertorriqueña de Historia, 2002.

Lewis, Earl. "Connecting Memory, Self, and the Power of Place in African American Urban History." *Journal of Urban History* 21, 3 (1995): 347–371.

Lipman, Pauline. "Chicago School Reform: Advancing the Global City Agenda." In *The New Chicago: A Social and Cultural Analysis,* edited by John P. Koval, Larry Bennett, Michael I. J. Bennett, Fassil Demissie, Roberta Garner, and Kiljoong Kim. Philadelphia: Temple University Press, 2006, pp. 248–258.

Maldonado, Edwin. "Contract Labor and the Origins of Puerto Rican Communities in the United States." *International Migration Review* 13, 1 (1979): 103–121.

Martinez, Manuel. *Chicago: Historia de Nuestra Communidad Puertorriqueña— Photographic Documentary.* Chicago: privately printed, 1989.

Mills, C. Wright, Clarence Senior, and Rose Kohn Goldsen. *The Puerto Rican Journey: New York's Newest Migrants.* New York: Harper and Row, 1950.

Moraga, Cherri, and Gloria Anzaldúa, eds. 1981. *This Bridge Called My Back: Writings by Radical Women of Color.* Watertown, Mass.: Persephone Press, 1981.

Naples, Nancy. "Activist Mothering: Cross-Generational Continuity in the Community Work of Women from Low-Income Urban Neighborhoods." *Gender and Society* 6, 3 (1992): 441–463.

Padilla, Elena. "Puerto Rican Immigrants in New York and Chicago: A Study in Comparative Assimilation." Master's thesis, Anthropology, University of Chicago, 1947.

———. "Retrospect of Ethnomedical Research among Puerto Ricans: Living at the Margin of East Harlem." In *The Anthropology of Lower Income Urban Enclaves: The Case of East Harlem,* edited by Judith Friedenberg. New York: New York Academy of Sciences, 1995.

———. *Up from Puerto Rico.* New York: Columbia University Press, 1958.

Padilla, Felix M. *Latino Ethnic Consciousness: The Case of Mexican Americans and Puerto Ricans in Chicago.* Notre Dame, Ind.: University of Notre Dame Press, 1985.

———. *Puerto Rican Chicago.* Notre Dame, Ind.: University of Notre Dame Press, 1987.

Parenti, Christian. *Lockdown America: Police and Prisons in the Age of Crisis.* New York: Verso, 1999.

Pérez, Gina M., ed. *Centro: Journal of the Center for Puerto Rican Studies* 13, 2 (2001), Special Issue on Puerto Rican Community in Chicago.

———. "The Other 'Real World': Gentrification and the Social Construction of Place in Chicago." *Urban Anthropology* 31, 1 (2002): 37–68.

Ramos Zayas, Ana Yolanda. "Delinquent Citizenship, National Performances: Racialization, Surveillance, and the Politics of 'Worthiness' in Puerto Rican Chicago." *Latino Studies* 2, 1 (2004): 26–44.

Reina Pérez, Pedro A. *La Semilla Que Sembramos: Autobiografía Del Proyecto Nacional.* San Juan: Centro de Estudios Avanzados de Puerto Rico y El Caribe, 2003.

Suarez, Ray. *The Old Neighborhood: What We Lost in the Great Suburban Migration, 1966–1999.* New York: Free Press, 1999.

Toro-Morn, Maura. "Género, trabajo y migración: Las empleadas domésticas puertorriqueñas en Chicago." *Revista de Ciencias Sociales* 7 (1999): 102–125.

Torres, Arlene. "From Jibara to Anthropologist: Puerto Rican Ethnography and the Politics of Representation." *Identities* 1, 3 (1998): 107–122.

Venkatesh, Sudhir Alladi, and Alexandra K. Murphy. "Policing Ourselves: Law and Order in the American Ghetto." In *Youth, Globalization, and the Law,* edited by Sudhir Alladi Venkatesh and Ronald Kassimir. Stanford, Calif.: Stanford University Press, 2007, pp. 124–157.

Whalen, Carmen Teresa. 2001. *From Puerto Rico to Philadelphia: Puerto Rican Workers and Postwar Economies.* Philadelphia: Temple University Press, 2001.

"White" Puerto Rican Migrants, the Mexican Colony, "Americanization," and Latino History

Nicholas De Genova

> To articulate the past historically does not mean to recognize it
> "the way it really was". . . . It means to seize hold of a memory
> as it flashes up at a moment of danger.
> —Walter Benjamin, "Theses on the Philosophy of History" (1940)

It is one of the presumed functions of ethnography that it should produce a documentation of the present, so vividly descriptive that it can serve as an archive for a history of the present, as that present slips away and is inexorably consigned to the past. In the spirit of Walter Benjamin's Sixth Thesis on the philosophy of history, this essay considers the historical moment depicted in Elena Padilla's 1947 ethnographic thesis concerning the beginnings of Puerto Rican migration to Chicago.[1] In other words, this essay revisits Padilla's discussion of Puerto Ricans in Chicago, not to recapture the past "the way it really was," but rather to reanimate a moment of possibility suggested by her speculative analysis concerning the prospects for what she depicted as Puerto Rican "acculturation," "assimilation," and "Americanization." That moment of possibility concerns Padilla's description of Puerto Rican migrants' rejection of the social fragmentation that accompanied their initial spatial dispersion as contract laborers throughout the urban area, in favor of already established Mexican neighborhoods. Rejecting a condition that Padilla variously characterizes as being "scattered" or "'lost' in the city," Puerto Rican migrants, upon abandoning their labor contracts, initially sought the refuge of residence in the extant Spanish-speaking communities of Mexicans. And it is precisely the seeming elusiveness of such a prospect of communion and community between Puerto Ricans and Mexicans in the United States that continues to pose truly vexing questions and remains with us as an urgent present-day concern.[2]

Moments of Danger: (Our) History

There is an urgency in Walter Benjamin's "Theses on the Philosophy of History" that is inseparable from the particularity of Benjamin's circumstances and his historical moment, and that urgency informs his critical sensibility about what is at stake when we aspire to comprehend history. Benjamin completed the "Theses" in 1940, very shortly before he fled for his life from Paris as Nazi Germany subjugated France. Shortly thereafter, in a desperate attempt to escape the country, with a visa to the United States in hand, upon receiving the grim news that Spain had closed the border, he killed himself. Benjamin declares ominously: "The tradition of the oppressed teaches us that the 'state of emergency' in which we live is not the exception but the rule" (Thesis VIII; p. 257). Not only as a political sensibility about his own immediate sociohistorical political condition, Benjamin posits this insight as an enduring guide for our attempts to understand history. "Nothing that has ever happened," he contends, "should be regarded as lost for history" (Thesis III; p. 254). With far from an attitude of superstitious reverence about history with a capital "H"—indeed, precisely the opposite—he cautions us: "Every image of the past that is not recognized by the present as one of its own concerns threatens to disappear irretrievably" (Thesis V; p. 255). Indeed, Benjamin repudiates all presumptions of "progress" that would allow us to slip into a complacent and complicit treatment of the past as if all of history's disasters and defeats were simply necessary transitional steps in a forward march that delivered our own present as a kind of inevitable culmination of all that came before it.

Benjamin speaks simultaneously of the present and the past when he declares: "A historical materialist cannot do without the notion of a present which is not a transition, but in which time stands still and has come to a stop. For this notion defines the present in which he himself is writing history" (Thesis XVI; p. 262). One cannot inhabit the historical past as if it were merely a transition to what we already know ultimately followed; one can only truly comprehend the past by re-inhabiting the immediacy and irresolution of it as it truly was historically, as its own *present*, and as if its future were entirely up for grabs, much as we must inhabit our own present.

At this point, it seems necessary, or may in any case be appropriate, to examine more directly and explicitly the analogous but perhaps elusive ways in which Benjamin's text and my own, respectively, invoke a "we" that insinuates a certain identity, or at least a definite commonality of purpose, with its presumptive readers. In this sense, in addressing himself to the imagined audience of his text, Benjamin deliberately invokes a "we" that is situated in his own immediate "moment of danger," but also simultaneously prefigures a future in which *we,* as his ultimate inheritors, are beckoned into an intellectual dialogue that presupposes a political camaraderie with his own sense of purpose. Benjamin's "we," in other words, does not presume a fatuous universality in which all are invited and equally welcomed to muse upon grand abstract questions of historiography "in general," but rather presumptively treats us, his readers, as always-already on his side, and thus performatively (and emphatically) enlists *us* into his struggle—against fascism and, more generally, against all of the oppressions of capitalism. In this essay, I am in effect pursuing the same rhetorical strategy. In its most narrow sense, the "we" whom I invoke in addressing *you,* the reader, is the somewhat inadvertent "community" of scholars and students concerned with the interdisciplinary academic field of Latino studies. But inasmuch as one of the founding premises of all genuinely *critical* Latino studies and other so-called ethnic studies inquiries is precisely the enduring salience of specifically *racial* oppression for all people not racialized as "white" in the United States, what will serve for my purposes as a basic working definition of who may be validly considered to be the presumed "we" of Latino studies is precisely *not* those merely interested in research about Latinos, but rather those of us who self-consciously posit our intellectual enterprise as one that is politically committed to one or another project of radical social critique. Mine is therefore an expansive and inclusive understanding of the community of dialogue and debate that we share, but it does nonetheless require that we take a side, together. And the stakes for Benjamin, in his time—as for us, now—are indeed great.

The struggles of the oppressed in the past, Benjamin is arguing, must have an immediacy and presence in our own present and pressing concerns, and we must approach that past not as if it is already resolved once and for all, but rather as if the struggles of the past must be fought anew, so that our own history may not be relegated into the hands of the victors, and moreover, so that we ourselves may not be converted into simple mouthpieces for a view of history that culminates inevitably with our own oppression and misery in the present. Thus, he contends:

> To articulate the past historically does not mean to recognize it "the way it really was". . . . It means to seize hold of a memory as it flashes up at a moment of danger. . . . The danger affects both the content of the tradition and its receivers.

The same threat hangs over both: that of becoming a tool of the ruling classes. In every era the attempt must be made anew to wrest tradition away from a conformism that is about to overpower it. . . . Only that historian will have the gift of fanning the spark of hope in the past who is firmly convinced that *even the dead* will not be safe from the enemy if he wins. And this enemy has not ceased to be victorious. (Thesis VI; p. 255; emphasis in original)

Within every history, then, there are moments of danger that are simultaneously moments of possibility, and if we fail to fan the spark of hope contained there, even the dead will not be safe.

The manner in which we recognize the historical moment of danger is intimately and inextricably entangled with the immediacy and contingencies of our own. It is with just such an urgency that we ought to seek to appreciate precisely what is at stake in what by now has become a kind of historical archive, namely, Elena Padilla's study of the very beginnings of large-scale Puerto Rican migration to Chicago.

Re-Racialization: An Ethnographic Archive of Our Present

There is surely no point in rereading and evaluating Padilla's 1947 master's thesis merely to put it to the test of our retrospective judgments about "what really happened" and whether her speculations about conceivable Puerto Rican futures in Chicago turned out to be "right" or "wrong." Instead, what seems to me to be the crucial concern, following Benjamin's protocols, is rereading the images and impressions of the past with which Padilla supplies us, deliberately from within the urgency of our own moment of danger, from within a self-conscious and critical examination of the historical specificity of our own concerns in the present. This is why it matters less whether Padilla got it "right" or not, and more that her occasionally speculative posture invites us to confront a moment of possibility from which something else might have ensued. Rereading Padilla challenges us to see history not simply as a just-so story, in other words, but rather as its own moment of danger, which was radically open-ended and might have turned out differently.

When Padilla produced her thesis in 1947, Puerto Rican migration to Chicago, on any significant scale, was only beginning. The racialization of Puerto Ricans in the United States, notably, was for Padilla a defining feature of the specificity of their migrant experience. Predictably, Padilla was concerned with the (one might say, obligatory) theoretical problematic of "assimilation," which was a kind of ideological straightjacket indubitably imposed as an effect of her training under the direct supervision and also indirect influence of the famed Chicago School of Sociology.[3] Neverthe-less, Padilla explicitly distinguished and juxtaposed Puerto Rican migration from that of prior and contemporary European-origin migrations that had come to be racialized as white.[4] Invoking a theme sporadically formulated by Robert Park,[5] Padilla posited these questions of racialization in terms of a combined problem of "color" and "visibility": "There is . . . a stron-ger similarity between the Puerto Rican in New York and the Mexican in Chicago insofar as there is a great similarity in their background and both share to much extent 'color visibility,' which is a sociological phenomenon demanding a type of adjustment not required by American society for most European immigrants."[6]

By implication, Padilla seemed to posit the "assimilation" question in terms of a migrant group's prospects for vanishing, or "blending in," or in the idiom of the hegemonic ideology of "the melting pot," perhaps it seemed to her to be a matter of "melting away." In short, "assimilation" seemed to be obstructed by the awkward "visibility" of a migrant group's stubborn particularity, and probably no form of visibility was more obstreperous than the stigma of "color."

Notably, Padilla drew an analogy between this "color visibility" of Puerto Ricans with that of Mexicans. Furthermore, Padilla also called attention to the class-specificity of Puerto Rican labor migration as a concomitant type of visibility: "The fact that the 'recent migrants' came to perform low-status work under the prevailing standard rates for this city is an added condi-tion for the Puerto Ricans to aim at the loss of their ethnic visibility in this community."[7] That Puerto Rican migrants were stigmatized both as people of "color," so to speak, and also as "low-status" workers, then, contributed to a kind of high visibility that threatened to render them definitively and distinctly *"Puerto Rican"* outsiders in an "American society" where racial whiteness is normative.

Insofar as their racialization as something other-than-white required, in Padilla's account, a special "type of adjustment," it likewise becomes quite evident that these Puerto Rican migrants in the United States rather quickly apprehended those special demands in terms of an obligatory repudiation of African American Blackness. Citing Thomas Blanco's 1942 study, *El Prejuicio Racial en Puerto Rico*, Padilla noted:

> Puerto Ricans . . . seem to resent American Negroes, and this attitude was found to exist even among colored Puerto Ricans. There is the belief that Puerto Rican Negroes descend from "better" African lineages than the American Negroes, and together with this superstition, the adoption of European aesthetic norms by the Puerto Rican Negroes and the fear of being identified with other colored

people against whom racial discrimination is too strong explains in part this attitude of the Puerto Rican Negro toward the American Negro.[8]

Thus, even Puerto Ricans who did not disavow their own African ancestry were apparently insistent in upholding an effectively racialized distinction between themselves and U.S. Blacks. Elitist Afrocentrisms and colonized Eurocentrisms notwithstanding, what seems clearly to have been most salient was the palpable durability of racist hegemony in the United States that these "colored" Puerto Rican migrants encountered and the systemic discrimination that they sought to deflect from their own "visibility."

What was at stake, as Padilla was well aware, was precisely what I would characterize as a process of *re*-racialization. There was, after all, an important racialization that Puerto Ricans had universally undergone in Puerto Rico prior to migration, which was obviously grounded in the specificities of a distinct social history of Spanish colonialism as well as subsequent U.S. colonialism.[9] Indeed, in her own research on an earlier generation of Puerto Rican migrants in Chicago, whom she called "the old migration" and among whom, she maintained, "[s]uch a thing as a Puerto Rican colony, or community, or ethnic group [did] not exist," Padilla found some examples of "black" Puerto Ricans living with U.S. Blacks.[10] She offered the following depiction of these Puerto Ricans' responses to U.S. racism:

> Very dark skinned Puerto Ricans who are able to speak English have found accommodations in different sections of the Negro Belt. . . . The attitudes found among these Puerto Ricans on the racial issues of this country are very much like those found among American Negroes in northern cities, namely, resentment and rebellion against the subordinated position imposed upon them by the superordinate white group on account of a peculiarity of the American social structure. This situation, nevertheless, is a new one for colored Puerto Ricans in whose home society "color visibility" was not rated in terms alike to those in American society. . . .
>
> The attitude of these individuals towards the United States was one of combined hostility and submissiveness. [Colored Puerto Ricans] also resented the Puerto Ricans who had a discriminatory attitude toward people considered "colored" in this country. A colored Puerto Rican woman reported that she would not go to a certain Spanish Club that operates a restaurant in the city because she was too dark, and she had heard that dark people were not admitted in that club. What she objected to mainly was that this restaurant was operated by Latins who discriminated on the basis of color. . . . [Colored Puerto Ricans] show antagonisms against other ethnics especially against the Mexicans living in this city. A colored Puerto Rican informed me that she did not like Mexicans because they speak like effeminates, and that she would love to go to Mexico if the people there were not Mexicans.[11]

Thus, the re-racialization of "dark-skinned Puerto Ricans" in Chicago during the mid-1940s as people properly relegated to the denigrated and segregated social condition of African Americans ensured their estrangement not only from whites but also from lighter-skinned Puerto Ricans as well as other "Latins," especially Mexicans.

Finally, in Padilla's examination of various case histories of "the old migration," in her discussion of "a colored Puerto Rican in the Chicago [Negro] Belt," she notes that Laura Rondón, a Puerto Rican woman married to a "Cuban mulato" and very enthusiastic about Cuba, who was very sensitive to discrimination on the basis of her "color" by both Puerto Ricans and other Latin Americans, nonetheless established that she specifically disliked both "Mexicans and American Negroes."[12] One might infer that this particular "colored Puerto Rican" could neither evade nor tolerate the racializing disaffection of other Latinos, and yet she so repudiated the stigma of Blackness that she felt compelled to tenaciously sustain her own Latino difference from African Americans. It would seem that both Mexicans and Puerto Ricans had learned conclusively, despite the "color visibility" that they shared, that the worst thing to be in the United States was Black. Although this appears to have intensified the isolation and alienation of black Puerto Ricans from any viable identity or community they might have elaborated with other Puerto Ricans, and likewise from potential social formations of *latinidad* with Mexicans, these "dark-skinned" Puerto Ricans, in Padilla's account, also appear to have been decidedly averse to becoming Black. Predictably, among the great majority of the earlier generation of Puerto Rican migrants whom Padilla described as "white," those who came from more privileged class backgrounds seemed largely devoted to pursuing the prospects of their integration into racial whiteness in the United States by evading altogether any sustained contacts with other Puerto Ricans. For them, it seems, the putative "ethnic" option of a kind of "immigrant" would-be-whiteness, distinguished only by its Spanish accent, came with the compulsory requirement to effectively disavow any association with their actual "ethnic" community, whose racialization as not-white threatened to vanquish their tentative and tenuous claims to "American" whiteness.

"Colony"-zation

Working-class "white Puerto Ricans," however, had apparently begun to follow a rather more intriguing path. Padilla claimed:

> White individuals, members of the lower classes in Puerto Rico and those who are unable to speak English, have found accommodation in the Mexican settle-

ments in Chicago. . . . These Puerto Ricans have developed loyalties towards Mexico and show interest in visiting both Mexico and Puerto Rico. Their relationships are mostly with the Mexican community. The Puerto Ricans in the Mexican colony did not know each other at the time this study was conducted but had heard about other Puerto Ricans in Chicago. They nevertheless had not had any contact with Puerto Ricans in this city.[13]

In Padilla's examination of case histories of the old migration, in her discussion of "a Puerto Rican in the Mexican Colony of Chicago" (by which she referred to the Hull House barrio on the city's Near West Side), she relates the story of Yolanda Torres. Yolanda initially befriended a Mexican family who were her neighbors in New York in 1933, and they invited her the following year to join them in their plans to relocate to Chicago, where there were better jobs. In Chicago, she lived with the Mexican family for about a year until she married one of their relatives, with whom she remained only for three years. Yolanda's jealous Mexican husband had required her to quit night school. Although she had continued to work outside of the home out of economic necessity, he objected and complained that they were "living like Americans"; he ultimately became an alcoholic and became involved in an affair with another woman. Despite Yolanda's difficult marriage to this Mexican man, by the time of Padilla's study in 1946, Yolanda continued to "love Mexico" and dream of visiting the country, socialized primarily with Mexicans, and even participated in a Mexican women's club. Notably, Padilla's concluding remark in this section reveals that although Yolanda had been in the United States for over thirteen years, her long immersion as "a Puerto Rican in the Mexican Colony" had ensured that she was still not able to speak English well.

In her summary discussion, Padilla proceeds to characterize Yolanda Torres as "an example of acculturation and assimilation to a non-assimilated social sub-system within the American society," contending that Yolanda "has been able to find accommodation in the larger American community through the channels it provides for Mexicans to become a part of it and to maintain their identity as an ethnic group." This hypothesis of alternative and racially subordinate "assimilation" relied upon an analytic distinction that Padilla sustained between "assimilation," which, she contended, "cannot occur without acculturation," and "acculturation," which "can exist to a large extent by itself," for which the preeminent cases in point were African Americans and "other minorities that through certain unrewarding phenomena such as 'color visibility' are prevented from full participation in the American social life."[14] As we will see, in Padilla's discussion of what she called "the recent migration," this example and her analysis of it ultimately proved to be foundational for her speculations about the future of Puerto Ricans in Chicago.

To the extent that none of this earlier generation of Puerto Rican migrants in Chicago appeared to have any substantial links to other Puerto Ricans, which Padilla explained in terms of their miniscule numbers and their very individualized and "scattered" trajectories in Chicago, the predominant theme in her analysis, with respect to Puerto Rican identity, was fundamentally one of loss. These isolated Puerto Rican migrants of "the early migration" all appeared to be becoming, or seeking to become, something other than Puerto Rican.

What Padilla described as the "recent migration," which began in 1946, consisted of 594 contract laborers. Although there were some men contracted to work in a foundry in the far northern suburb of North Chicago, the great majority were young single women dispersed in private homes throughout the city where they were employed as domestic workers.[15] Moreover, Padilla affirmed, the new migration "consisted of . . . white Puerto Ricans." Of course, Padilla did indeed note that while "the recent migration of Puerto Ricans theoretically only included white workers" among the migrants, "nevertheless, many . . . would be considered Negroes in the United States but were considered as white by the Puerto Ricans."[16] These were working-class migrants, and while they may have been considered rather more "white" than not in Puerto Rico, they were often rather more "something else" in the U.S. context. Both the "color visibility" as well as the low-status class character that Padilla had already discerned among Mexicans in Chicago, in short, marked the Puerto Rican migration of the late 1940s. What exactly that nonwhite "something else" would eventually be counted as—Blackness or yet another racial category—was at the center of the unfolding Puerto Rican racial dilemma.

This newer Puerto Rican migration seemed to present a larger-scale manifestation of a trajectory that Padilla had already encountered. Due to what the migrants widely considered inadequate living and working conditions, significant numbers of them abandoned their contracts and sought jobs and housing elsewhere. "The prevailing tendency" among Puerto Ricans in Chicago, Padilla clarified, "has been to move into Mexican neighborhoods. The tendency to group themselves along their own nationality line does not seem to have been operating." Puerto Ricans quickly made their homes among Mexicans—above all, in Padilla's account, for reasons of language, but also for reasons of gender and (hetero)sexuality: "The fact that most of these Puerto Ricans do not speak English explains largely their moving into Mexican neighborhoods instead of moving into areas occupied predominantly by Americans. Also, the relatively reduced number of Puerto Ricans and the unbalanced sexual ratio of the group have contributed to this shift into Mexican neighborhoods."[17] Again, their relatively small numbers seemed to undermine the possibility of creating their own separate and distinct geographical community. Furthermore, the artificial selection of gendered contract labor migration had also ensured their disproportionately female sex ratio. Padilla identified a predominantly Mexican North Side nightclub, the Rancho Grande, as having provided a congenial space where Puerto Rican women, employed as domestic workers, would meet to socialize, eat Mexican food, and dance to Latin American music, and inevitably it served as a site where these Puerto Rican women made their first contacts with the Mexican community and sometimes became involved romantically with Mexican men. Notably, when Puerto Rican men and women socialized together in a north suburban nightclub called the Happy Hour, frequented mainly by white foundry workers but also by Mexican male migrants, the interrelations of Puerto Ricans and Mexicans tended to be more limited and sometimes conflict ridden.[18]

Nevertheless, as the Puerto Rican foundry workers moved out of the barrack-like accommodations provided for them in converted freight cars, most relocated to rent rooms, either as individuals or in married couples, in the homes of Mexicans in a small Mexican section of the suburban municipality of North Chicago. Likewise, whereas some of the Puerto Rican women eventually entered into "consensual unions" with Mexican men, many of the Puerto Ricans who first came into contact with Mexicans at the Rancho Grande "usually" developed "an attitude of dislike towards Mexicans":

> The Puerto Ricans . . . dislike being identified as Mexicans. No open group conflicts exist between them, but individual disputes along nationality lines are frequently observed. Sources of disputes are usually related to matters of value attached to their particular cultural and social life. . . . The most significant single reason for this attitude is probably shown by the disorganizing effect that contacts between Mexican men and Puerto Rican girls have had. The non-permanent and illegal marital relations that have followed these contacts have resulted in situations not approved by Puerto Rican standards of social behavior.[19]

Due specifically, then, to struggles over access to Puerto Rican women's bodies—or more precisely, their sexuality—Puerto Rican and Mexican men apparently encountered one another as rivals. Despite these palpable conflicts, however—and this is the truly remarkable and intriguing point—the vast majority of the new Puerto Rican migrants of the late 1940s sought residence, not only in Mexican communities, but within Mexican homes.

As Padilla saw it, "The tendency to group themselves along their own nationality line [did] not seem to have been operating."

The central theoretical problem of Padilla's study involved specifying what the case of Puerto Rican migration could illuminate about the larger conceptual framework devoted to rendering apprehensible social processes of "assimilation" and "acculturation." For Padilla, the steady movement of Puerto Ricans into Mexican neighborhoods demonstrated "how the ethnics tend to mix in a community more similar to their own than is the host community." She contended: "Acculturation and assimilation . . . occur more rapidly among immigrants who become ecologically 'lost' in the host community [than among those who live in a 'colony']. This is the case of the 'old migration' of Puerto Ricans to Chicago. . . . a Puerto Rican colony was not formed by the 'old migrants' because the group was too small and because they migrated as individuals and became 'lost' in the city." We will recall that the earlier migrants had been so completely scattered, or "lost" in the city, Padilla contends, that "such a thing as a Puerto Rican colony, or community, or ethnic group [did] not exist."[20] For these "individuals . . . 'lost' in the city," in Padilla's account, Puerto Rican identity was being inexorably vanquished, variously, by the competing enticements of racial whiteness, on the one hand, and the comforts of the kind of acculturation and assimilation to a non-assimilated "ethnic" social formation, principally exemplified by Mexicanization, on the other.[21]

This submersion into "the Mexican colony" involved a kind of partial "acculturation" without "assimilation." In her discussion of what she calls "the process of acculturation in a 'colony,'" Padilla explores further the implications of her proposition of "acculturation" without "assimilation":

> The colony has its own semi-autonomous social structure and organization with its own mores and standards of social behavior that are a reflection of those prevailing in the original society of the ethnics. The development of a "colony" implies the appearance of institutions and usages that give internal coherence to the social life of the in-group. . . . To some extent the colony is a reaction against acculturation, insofar as it tries to keep alive the usages and traditions of the original society. The colony, on the other hand, does exemplify acculturation insofar as it is the structural contact between the ethnic and the dominant American community. Assimilation and acculturation, nevertheless, operate very slowly in ethnic communities that resist the changes in order to maintain themselves.[22]

In her concluding remarks, furthermore, Padilla affirms the structural-functionalist commitments of her analysis of the migrant "colony" situation: "The colony is an integrated society. . . . It is a natural system integrated by its parts, that is, the institutions and usages of the people who live within its structural make-up. The same social mechanisms that operate to place large numbers of immigrants together within an ethnic community organization also place scattered immigrants in the structure of the large society. People continue to search for their integration within a group that provides social orientation for their behavior."[23] Thus, much as Puerto Rican migrants "lost in the city" may have sought their integration as "individuals" directly into the larger society, so also were Puerto Ricans—young single women, in particular—increasingly finding accommodation in the proxy society of "the Mexican colony."

All of this, Padilla was careful to emphasize, was contingent: "The social conditions of the recent migrants from Puerto Rico . . . are at present those of disintegration. . . . This, of course, is contingent on the fact that the number of Puerto Rican migrants does not increase considerably enough so as to shape itself into a Puerto Rican community in Chicago."[24] Insofar as Puerto Rican migration did not dramatically expand, however, those who had already migrated would, Padilla postulated, necessarily undergo a kind of "disintegration" of their Puerto Rican identity, as they sought integration into the unassimilated Mexican particularity of "the colony," which would mediate their further relations with the dominant society. If Puerto Rican migration did indeed accelerate, on the other hand, they might very well come to enjoy the holistic integration afforded by a "colony" of their own.

Here, however, one must consider whether the hypothetical increase of "Puerto Rican migration" was in fact presumed to signify an increased migration of Puerto Rican *men*, inasmuch as it was precisely their absence that seemed to truncate the prospects for young Puerto Rican women alone to constitute a veritable "community" of their own and doom their Puerto Rican–ness to disintegration. In this regard, the subordinate racial "colony" emerges not only as a structural effect of white supremacy but also as a sociospatial organization of patriarchal heterosexual reproduction, and the very notion of racialized "community" is revealed to be a thoroughly gendered site where the presumably stable production and reproduction of something like "Puerto Rican" identity may prove to be profoundly contingent upon the rigorous maintenance of a well-ordered (patriarchal, heteronormative) subordination of the sexuality and autonomy of women. But what if a continued migration from Puerto Rico had retained its disproportionately female composition, for instance, as the consequence of a colonial state-orchestrated wholesale export of Puerto Rico's "overpopulation problem"—in its most palpable form as the reproductive fertility of young women's migrant bodies?[25] Was it even plausible in Padilla's analysis that young women migrants could have created and sustained a Puerto Rican "community" of their own? In Padilla's more speculative moments, it would seem, the prospect of such gender disproportions in the migration process that she was studying could only ensure that Puerto Rican women would "disintegrate" into Mexican wives.

The Mexican community in Chicago was fairly well established and, despite forced repatriations during the prior decade, had already been reproducing itself in a "second generation." Thus, the relatively advanced condition of the Mexicans' "Americanization," in contradistinction to the comparatively delayed and prospectively more protracted process whereby Puerto Ricans might otherwise create a "colony" of their own, Padilla reasoned, would inadvertently accelerate the analogous process for the young Puerto Rican migrants who were seeking an orientation for their own behavior among their Mexican counterparts. First, however, and especially among the Puerto Rican women, they would tend to become Mexicanized. Padilla argued:

> The tendency found among the recent migrants to move into the Mexican neighborhoods may result in either of the following situations before the ultimate end of the processes of acculturation and assimilation is accomplished. First, Puerto Ricans will tend to become Mexicanized. This condition will tend to operate mainly with women who will marry into the Mexican group. The contacts between Puerto Ricans and Mexicans are mainly in an age level that ranges from adolescence to early adulthood. This circumstance is operative in the sense that this age group of Mexicans is probably undergoing a rapid process of Americanization, which will be reflected in their social relationships with the Puerto Ricans. Secondly, the accomplishment of the processes of acculturation and assimilation of these Puerto Ricans, if the group is not considerably increased by new migrations from the island, will probably be a more rapid one than in the Puerto Rican neighborhoods in New York City.[26]

Thus, the prospective Mexicanization of the Puerto Rican migrants that Padilla predicted was presumed ultimately, and inexorably, to resolve itself into a type of "Americanization," one specific to "minorities that through certain unrewarding phenomena such as 'color visibility' are prevented from full participation in the American social life."[27] The "colony" was merely the particular form of their racialized "Americanization."

And it is here that we must discern the moment of danger.

"American"-ization, or a Latino History?

One need not quarrel here with Padilla's theoretical commitments to the hegemonic "assimilation" problematic; one need only recognize that there was, and is, no way out of its teleology. One simply cannot set out to study "assimilation" without falling into the trap of its teleological presuppositions: by hook or by crook, *por las buenas o las malas,* the end of the process—however much delayed, detoured, or deferred—is inevitably "Americanization." And "Americanization" necessarily involves a negation of whatever it was that people started as—in this case, Puerto Ricans. Indeed, the U.S. nationalist logic of this "assimilation" schema is analogous to the segregationist metaphysics of the distinctly U.S. model of "miscegenation," historically—whereby "race mixing" was reduced to an oxymoron, producing not a new category of persons of "mixed race," but only more Blacks. Similarly, "assimilation" in its classic formulation was never conceived as a fusion of two "nationalities" or "cultures" that would generate something new, but rather only as the obliteration of one by the other—at least by implication, just more (white) "Americans." The racial logic was one of contamination, whereas the assimilationist rubric presumed an inexorable, irresistible subjugation and homogenization of difference, but neither could abide by any hybrids.[28]

What is intriguing about Padilla's assimilationist narrative of loss—namely, Puerto Rican migrants' loss of their Puerto Rican identities—is that it could only arrive at the obligatory "Americanization" by way of an alternate path that Padilla discerned in the Mexican "colony." In the absence of the material conditions of possibility for a Puerto Rican "colony" such as existed already in New York, the Chicago Puerto Ricans' incorporation into the Mexican "colony," Padilla hypothesized, might serve as an effective proxy for their ultimate structural "assimilation" as an "ethnic" group into "the dominant American society." Padilla seemed to reach the rather dismal but fairly accurate conclusion that Puerto Ricans (and by implication, all other migrants of color as well) would have no other alternative than to be located in one or another social and spatial ghetto from which to become "acculturated" in the face of a more basic impossibility of genuine "assimilation"; as racial "minorities," their "Americanization" would at best have to be a distinctly subordinate one.

From the vantage point of the present, it may seem rather implausible to many, if not frankly preposterous to some, to imagine Puerto Ricans becoming "Mexicanized" (whatever that might be taken to mean).[29] It is much too easy, however, to rush to reassuring historicist explanations that would simply take comfort in the retrospective certitude that, indeed, Puerto Ricans in Chicago did ultimately create their own little "colony," to use Padilla's terminology, and, by implication, that it could not have been otherwise. Indeed, one might even say that Puerto Ricans in Chicago not only came to create a distinctive and durable (pronouncedly racialized) neighborhood of their own in Chicago, but ultimately did so with a vengeance—complete with towering metal archways fashioned into Puerto Rican flags to mark the beginning and end of the officially "Puerto Rican" commercial district along Division Street. Of all the Puerto Rican migrations to the U.S. mainland, the Puerto Ricans in Chicago would end up with no sense of their Puerto Rican–ness!? Surely, we know that, more than in any other place, indeed more than in Puerto Rico itself, the Puerto Rican community in Chicago has been the epicenter of Puerto Rican nationalism.[30] Thus, in the aftermath of mass migration from Puerto Rico, a U.S. colony, the re-racialized production of a Puerto Rican racial "colony" in Chicago, a city on the U.S. Mainland, seems to have generated an at-best reluctant "Americanization" and arguably secured instead a quite robust "re–Puerto Rican–ization." But rereading Padilla reminds us that it might not have turned out this way—it could have been different.

Historicity: The Production of Difference

If indeed, in Padilla's estimation of that particular historical moment, Puerto Ricans could have conceivably been on their way to becoming (some kind of) Mexicans, then we must consider that moment not only as one of possibility, but also as one *where a certain possibility was defeated*. That is why it represents for us, in our own present, a moment of danger. Walter Benjamin offers us an image of history, personified as an angel: "This is how one pictures the angel of history. His face is turned toward the past. Where we perceive a chain of events, he sees one single catastrophe which keeps piling wreckage upon wreckage and hurls it in front of his feet."[31] The catastrophe that I am urging us to contemplate is not, of course, that Puerto Ricans did not become Mexicans. Nor is it necessarily a calamity that those Puerto Rican migrants ultimately "remained" Puerto Ricans—or in any case, merely became some *different* kind of Puerto Ricans. Rather, I want to consider that there was something at stake *prior to* Padilla's projected "Mexicanization" of Puerto Rican migrants in Chicago. That something, quite simply, was what we might retrospectively identify as an incipient sense of shared identity and commonality of interests between Mexicans and Puerto Ricans—as Latinos—which might therefore have confronted them with the prospect not merely of situationally adapting and aligning themselves with one another, while upholding their distinct and discrete respective identities, but even of going so far as actually *negating* their very identities as such, in the course of becoming something truly new.

There is nothing automatic, inevitable, or even necessary, after all, about the emergence of a shared sense of "Latino" identity among distinct groups of Latin American origin or ancestry, as indeed there are never any natural or self-evident positive grounds for *any* identity. Identities must be *produced* through social relations and struggle. In this way, they coalesce rather more negatively than positively, *relationally* instead of on the basis of essential a priori "truths," and always, therefore, emerge historically—both as the effects of prior histories and their accumulated consequences, but also as the contingent dispositions of people engaged in struggles over the their own indeterminate futures. As often as not—or perhaps more often than not—identities tend to become rigid and ossified and serve the ends of subverting the potential subversive force of people's struggles by inculcating in them morbid attachments to more or less fixed, thing-like, fetishistic notions of who and how they really "are" or are "supposed to be," privileging being over becoming, status and stasis over dynamic irresolution and sheer vitality. And it is really only the latter than can be genuinely subversive and emancipatory.

If we dispense with any and all culturalist essentialisms about the ostensible substance of Latino identity, then, we must examine what indeed could supply a material and practical basis for meaningful, historically specific commonalities between or among distinct Latino groups, such as the Puerto Ricans and Mexicans in Padilla's study. Moreover, we must consider whether or not such a sense of shared "Latino" identity would truly prove to be of some critical value for advancing the strategic position of those groups in the social struggles that they might conceivably seek to wage in coalition. Positing both the practical appeal of a shared community of Spanish language as well as analogous conditions of migrant labor subordination and racialized subjection on the basis of "color visibility," even while simultaneously affirming Puerto Ricans' disaffection for Mexicans' language and inclinations toward conflict with Mexicans, Padilla contended nonetheless that one paradoxical but plausible prospect for these Puerto Ricans was their imminent "Mexicanization."

We need not go that far, and yet we ought to go still further. What seems likely was that Padilla was discerning a kind of incipient *latinidad* between Puerto Ricans and Mexicans. Notably, it was a *latinidad* that was internally differentiated (perhaps irreducibly so), gendered, and constitutively conflicted. Furthermore, it was grounded in the substantive analogies that derived from the historical specificities of the two groups' respective experiences of labor subordination and racialized oppression. If Padilla initially sought to evaluate the prospects for those early not-quite-white Puerto Rican migrants' eventual "Americanization" and posited their imminent arrival at a crucial juncture where they seemed destined to have a decisive rendezvous of one sort or another with Mexicans, then it is precisely that crossroads, replete with ambiguities and uncertainties, that ought to be where we now retrospectively seek to dwell. After all, if we dispense with any and all culturalist essentialisms about the ostensible substance of "Latino" identity, then, we might also begin to be able to relinquish any such essentialisms about the presumed substance of "Puerto Rican" or "Mexican" identities as well.

Furthermore, if we may retrospectively identify an incipient sense of shared identity and commonality of interests between Mexicans and Puerto Ricans—as Latinos—then might we not begin to be able to fathom the historically counterfactual (and, regrettably, counterintuitive) possibility that those prospective "Latinos" (among the Puerto Ricans and Mexicans considered by Padilla) could have also exceeded and surpassed even the confines of their latinidad and embraced an incipient sense of shared identity and commonality of interests with African Americans, for instance? There was, therefore, a whole gamut of successive transformations that might have ensued. What was ultimately at stake, then as now, was nothing less than the prospect of becoming and incarnating that purely negative principal of world-making life, which would necessarily have been imbued simultaneously with a destructive and creative force—the creative capacity and productive power of humanity as such—of which every positive "identity" is but a pale, fragmentary, and inverted reflection.

The moment of danger, historically, never involved so much the accumulating wreckage and ruin of one or another identity project ("Puerto Rican" or otherwise), whereby each putative "group" could eventually be definitively identified and decisively located, but rather, precisely the contrary—that each group could indeed be thus encircled and partitioned, and thereby entrapped securely in its "proper" place. Against the sheer negativity and radically open-ended vitality of potentially becoming something so explosively transgressive and subversively expansive that it would have necessarily relinquished and repudiated morbid attachments to even its own prior ways of being ("identities," for example), the Puerto Rican historical movement (which Padilla's ethnography sought to comprehend) somehow got captured and channeled into the sociopolitical regime of "Americanization" that would finally spell nothing but re-racialized domestication and (re-)colonization. And that somehow is the ineffable stuff that constitutes our history. But the irresolution and incompletion that Padilla's study audaciously highlighted is the historicity—both theirs and also our own—which is finally the difference that history can, and should, make.

The historical moment depicted by Padilla represents a moment of possibility as intriguing and provocative as her somewhat tortured assimilationist hypothesis of Puerto Rican Mexicanization is arrestingly and unsettlingly counterintuitive. Insofar as the historical image of the past that it affords us should be recognized as one of our own concerns in the present, it must therefore be recuperated, following Benjamin, as a moment of danger, lest it be forfeited to an overpowering historicist conformism, and disappear irretrievably. Relinquishing the preemptive conceptual constraints of the "assimilation" teleology, it now may seem so much the more likely that the conceivable shared trajectory and eventual destination of those Puerto Ricans and Mexicans could have been altogether more fascinating and perhaps also more politically volatile than the already foreclosed dead-end of aspiring to become "Americans." Again, if we fail to fan the spark of hope contained in this history, even the dead will not be safe. Indeed, we will have become complicit in killing them, yet again.

If Benjamin posited his theses with regard to the study of history and how it gets written, however, Padilla's ethnography—and specifically, her more speculative reflections on her immediate historical moment—reveals to us some instructive ways in which we may go about writing histories of *the present*, and likewise confronts us with an enigmatic quandary that has not ceased to be our own immediate moment of danger. By unsettling in this manner our encrusted and brittle presumptions about *identity*, in general, and our own putative identities, in particular, Padilla's seemingly quaint or even antiquated ethnography challenges us to have the temerity not merely to fan the spark of hope that may be recovered from the past, but much more important, to recover the spark of hope that is nestled beneath the dry dead weight of History that smothers our present but that may yet be consumed by an unquenchable fire.

NOTES

1. Elena Padilla, "Puerto Rican Immigrants in New York and Chicago: A Study in Comparative Assimilation" (master's thesis, University of Chicago, 1947). The thesis is reprinted in part 1 of this volume; all citations are to the reprint.

2. For a consideration of the differences and divisions between the two groups, based on ethnographic research in Chicago during the 1990s, see Nicholas De Genova and Ana Y. Ramos-Zayas, *Latino Crossings: Mexicans, Puerto Ricans, and the Politics of Race and Citizenship* (New York: Routledge, 2003).

3. An elaborate critical comment and exegetical exposition on the Chicago School's sociology of "immigration" is beyond the interpretive scope and intellectual stakes of the present essay. For an extended critique of the conventions of the "assimilation"

problematic in the hegemonic sociology of "immigration" in the United States, as well as pertinent bibliographic references, see chapter 2 in Nicholas De Genova, *Working the Boundaries: Race, Space, and "Illegality" in Mexican Chicago* (Durham, N.C.: Duke University Press, 2005).

4. In this regard, Padilla's work was admirably engaged with theoretical questions that eluded the considerably more senior anthropologist W. Lloyd Warner and his research associates, whose expansive "Yankee City" research project on U.S. social inequalities was initiated during the same period. Whereas Warner was always care-ful to underscore the distinction between the social status of "ethnic groups" (which he associated principally with European migrant groups who came to be racialized as white) and the "racial caste" status of African Americans, he nonetheless readily subsumed Mexicans and Puerto Ricans into the "ethnic" category, attributing their low social status merely to the recentness of their migrations; see, e.g., W. Lloyd Warner, *American Life: Dream and Reality* (1953; rev. ed., Chicago: University of Chicago Press, 1962), p.183. Thus, the analytic category of "ethnicity" notably became an obstacle to identifying and critically examining the proliferation of ra-cialized distinctions and the extension of what Warner called "racial caste" status to migrant groups that did not come to be racialized as white.

5. For discussions of racial distinctions as dependent on "visibility," see, e.g., Robert E. Park, "Race Prejudice and Japanese-American Relations" (1917), "Behind Our Masks" (1926), and "The Race Relations Cycle in Hawaii" (1937), all reprinted in *Race and Culture: The Collected Papers of Robert Ezra Park,* vol. 1 (New York: Free Press, 1950).

6. Padilla, "Puerto Rican Immigrants," p. 68.

7. Ibid., p. 101.

8. Ibid., p. 73.

9. For an extended discussion of re-racialization in the experiences of Mexican migrants in Chicago during the 1990s and the reconfiguration of their conceptions of "Mexican"-ness, see De Genova, *Working the Boundaries.* More generally, also see Nicholas De Genova and Ana Y. Ramos-Zayas, "Latino Racial Formations in the United States: An Introduction," *Journal of Latin American Anthropology* 8, 2 (2003): 2–16.

10. Padilla, "Puerto Rican Immigrants," p. 78. For reasons of racial politics, I capitalize "Black" and "Blackness" as they refer to the social condition and histori-cal specificity of African Americans, but deliberately do not capitalize "white" or "whiteness." My usage takes a cue from Ralph Ellison, for instance, who referred to the capitalization of the term "Negro" as "one of the important early victories of my own people in their fight for self-definition"; see *Shadow and Act* (1953; re-print, New York: Signet, 1964), p. 253. In contrast, as David Roediger explains, "It is not merely that whiteness is oppressive and false, it is that whiteness is *nothing but* oppressive and false. . . . Whiteness describes not a culture but precisely . . . the empty and therefore terrifying attempt to build an identity based on what one isn't and on whom one can hold back"; see *Toward the Abolition of Whiteness: Essays*

on Race, Politics, and Working Class History (New York: Verso, 1994), p. 13. In contrast to African American Blackness, and due moreover to Puerto Rico's distinct social history and divergent economy of racial meanings, I do not capitalize references to the figurations of racial blackness for the Puerto Rican migrants depicted in Padilla's early study.

11. Padilla, "Puerto Rican Immigrants," pp. 82–83.

12. Ibid., pp. 87–88.

13. Ibid., p. 82.

14. Ibid., pp. 88–89, 98.

15. The large majority (329) of the 396 Puerto Ricans first contracted in 1946 by the Castle, Barton and Associates employment agency were young women who originally migrated as domestic workers and whose social activities were partly coordinated through the YWCA in Chicago; although there were some married couples contracted for domestic service, most of the Puerto Rican men were contracted for foundry work and were settled in North Chicago.

16. Padilla, "Puerto Rican Immigrants," pp. 76, 94.

17. Ibid., pp. 77, 95.

18. Ibid., pp. 90, 91–92, 93.

19. Ibid., pp. 93–94.

20. Ibid., pp. 77, 99, 100.

21. Although Padilla does not make the case as forcefully, inasmuch as the example is decidedly more idiosyncratic, there is nonetheless an implicit parallel to Mexicanization in the case of the "dark-skinned Puerto Rican" woman, married to a "Cuban mulato," who is analogously Cuban-identified—rejecting the "color" consciousness of other Puerto Ricans, but retaining a distinctly Latino identity in effectively racialized contradistinction to the stigma of African American Blackness.

22. Padilla, "Puerto Rican Immigrants," p. 98.

23. Ibid., p. 101.

24. Ibid., p. 99.

25. For a discussion of the "Chicago experiment" that sought to alleviate Puerto Rico's "population problem" by recruiting Puerto Rican women of child-bearing age for contract labor as domestics in Chicago during the 1950s, see Maura I. Toro-Morn, "Género, trabajo y migración: Las empleadas domésticas puertorriqueñas en Chicago"; see also Toro-Morn, "*Yo era muy arriesgada*: A Historical Overview of the Work Experiences of Puerto Rican Women in Chicago," *Centro: Journal of the Center for Puerto Rican Studies* 8, 2 (2001): 25–43.

26. Padilla, "Puerto Rican Immigrants," p. 100.

27. Ibid., p. 98.

28. This comparison is suggested by Walter Benn Michaels in *Our America: Nativism, Modernism, and Pluralism* (Durham, N.C.: Duke University Press, 1995), p. 61; for a more extended discussion of "race" and "miscegenation," see F. James Davis, *Who Is Black? One Nation's Definition* (University Park: Pennsylvania State University Press, 1991).

29. Again, for an examination of the differences and divisions sustained between the two groups in Chicago at the end of the twentieth century, see De Genova and Ramos-Zayas, *Latino Crossings*.

30. See Ana Y. Ramos-Zayas, *National Performances: The Politics of Class, Race and Space in Puerto Rican Chicago* (Chicago: University of Chicago Press, 2003).

31. Thesis IX, p. 257, in Walter Benjamin, "Theses on the Philosophy of History," *Illuminations: Essays and Reflections* (New York: Schocken Books, 1968).

Works Cited

Benjamin, Walter. "Theses on the Philosophy of History" (1940). *Illuminations: Essays and Reflections*. New York: Schocken Books, 1968.

Benn Michaels, Walter. *Our America: Nativism, Modernism, and Pluralism*. Durham, N.C.: Duke University Press, 1995.

Davis, F. James. *Who Is Black? One Nation's Definition*. University Park: Pennsylvania State University Press, 1991.

De Genova, Nicholas. *Working the Boundaries: Race, Space, and "Illegality" in Mexican Chicago*. Durham, N.C.: Duke University Press, 2005.

De Genova, Nicholas, and Ana Y. Ramos-Zayas. *Latino Crossings: Mexicans, Puerto Ricans, and the Politics of Race and Citizenship*. New York: Routledge, 2003.

———. "Latino Racial Formations in the United States: An Introduction." *Journal of Latin American Anthropology* 8, 2 (2003): 2–16.

Ellison, Ralph. *Shadow and Act*. 1953. Reprint, New York: Signet, 1964.

Padilla, Elena. "Puerto Rican Immigrants in New York and Chicago: A Study in Comparative Assimilation." Master's thesis, Anthropology, University of Chicago, 1947.

Park, Robert E. *Race and Culture: The Collected Papers of Robert Ezra Park*. Vol. 1. New York: Free Press, 1950.

Ramos-Zayas, Ana Y. *National Performances: The Politics of Class, Race and Space in Puerto Rican Chicago*. Chicago: University of Chicago Press, 2003.

Roediger, David. *Toward the Abolition of Whiteness: Essays on Race, Politics, and Working Class History*. New York: Verso, 1994.

Toro-Morn, Maura I. "Género, trabajo y migración: Las empleadas domésticas puertorriqueñas en Chicago." *Revista de Ciencias Sociales* 7 (1999): 102–125.

———. "*Yo era muy arriesgada*: A Historical Overview of the Work Experiences of Puerto Rican Women in Chicago." *Centro: Journal of the Center for Puerto Rican Studies* 8, 2 (2001): 25–43.

Warner, W. Lloyd. *American Life: Dream and Reality*. 1953. Rev. ed., Chicago: University of Chicago Press, 1962.

Gendering "Latino Public Intellectuals"

Personal Narratives in the Ethnography of Elena Padilla

Ana Y. Ramos-Zayas

Academic discussions concerning the role of "public intellectuals" have proliferated in the last decade or so, especially among scholars of color.[1] These discussions have particularly considered the "crisis of black public intellectuals" in the United States.[2] Some scholars have argued that intellectuals no longer exist and that the end of the Cold War, the opening up of the mainly U.S. university to legions of scholars, the age of specialization, and the commercialization and commodification of everything in the newly globalized economy have simply done away with the public intellectual.[3] Some scholars such as Russell Jacoby and Richard Posner, for instance, have insisted that the public intellectuals as a group are in decline or have altogether disappeared, or at least that the quality of their work is getting worse.[4] Such claims of decline rely on a particular understanding of who and what we mean by "intellectuals," in general, and "public intellectual," in particular.

The term "public intellectual" traces to Russell Jacoby's 1987 book, *The Last Intellectuals*, but it has outgrown its origins. The bare term "intellectual" is used to describe the sort of prominent individual engaged in social criticism. Some find the term "public intellectuals" tautological since all intellectuals are by definition public.[5] The public intellectual is generally some sort of specialist, most likely an academic, who finds a way of engaging in public, as opposed to exclusively academic, debates. It is the intellectuals' "publicness," their intervention into the public sphere, that defines the category.[6]

Tim Dunlop, for instance, argues that the traditional understanding of public intellectual needs to be challenged and replaced with "a more democratic, less elitist model, one that specifically ties the title to participation and citizenship."[7] Likewise, Edward Said stresses that "the absence of any master-plan or grand theory for what intellectuals can do" in fact "enables intellectual performances on many fronts, in many places." Hence, all the arts and all forms of writing can be considered intellectual endeavors and should be represented. The goal of the intellectual, then, is not only to define a situation but also to discuss the possibilities for active intervention and to sense that other people have a similar stake in a common project.

These conversations about the roles of "public intellectuals" have often-times excluded the role of women in general and women of color in particular in the production of knowledge and intervention in civic life. A Black-white racial binary prevails in these discussions, and when addressed, gender is subsumed under other social categorizations.[8] The role of Latino public intellectuals has been suspiciously absent from any discussions of intellectual production and community involvement in the United States, even when their Latin American and Caribbean counterparts have played active roles in their countries' politics and social life. An exception to this absence of Latinos in discussions of "public intellectuals" appeared in 2003 in the form of a theme issue in the journal *Napantla: Views from the South* (volume 4, issue 2). Published by Duke University Press, this theme issue consisted of a central article by Eduardo Mendieta titled "What Can Latinas/os Learn from Cornel West? The Latino Postcolonial Intellectual in the Age of the Exhaustion of Public Spheres," followed by a series of individual responses to the Mendieta article. It was particularly revealing that most of the response articles were celebratory of Mendieta's proposition that Latinos needed to follow Cornel West's model of intellectual practice, in particular West's appeal to religious faith, presence in multiple sites of intellectual production, and ability to synthesize the great intellectual traditions of all time (from "romantic Marxism" to literary criticism). Few respondents in fact question the very choice of Cornel West, a scholar who has been notorious for his general silence on issues of gender and patriarchy, as Mendieta's proposed "guide" for Latinos into the road toward public intellectualism.[9] Likewise, very few respondents challenged Mendieta's vague understanding of "public spheres" as spaces that needed to be generated by creating "a new transnational and hemispheric agenda able to include not just Mexican Americans, Puerto Ricans, Dominicans or Cubans, but also the broader group of Latinas/os that constitutes now over 12 percent of the U.S. population."[10] The unproblematic assumption of the existence (or desirability) of a "Latino" identity was only worsened by Mendieta's insinuation that we have already focused "too much" on some Latino populations and perhaps not on others. This aspect of Mendieta's work is critical to this essay, because Mendieta's perspective is illustrative of how the intellectual work of Puerto Rican women (and Latino women more generally) is actively and very concretely obliterated oftentimes by the very men who bemoan the "disappearance" of a public sphere and the invisibility of Latino public intellectuals.

This essay attempts to broaden the conception of the public intellectual to include not only the themes discussed by a legion of scholars engaged in social equality projects but also the spaces in which such discussions take place and from which such discussions emanate in the first place. Discussions of "public intellectuals" have historically tended to privilege the public sphere of organized political movements and nation-building projects, while often negating or undermining the projects that focus on the examination of beliefs systems, domestic life, or alternative spaces considered "private." These discussions have assumed that "real" politics are the realm of the public, while activities in the "private" realm are considered apolitical or not "political enough."

From the onset, it is important to note that this essay does not aim to reify an oftentimes ludicrous separation of "public" and "private," but precisely the opposite: by recognizing the problematic of determining and untangling these analytical categories and examining their sporadic salience, the essay hopes to shed light onto ways in which being a "public intellectual" is often, particularly in the case of subordinate groups, about reconfiguring conceptions of "academic work" and "real life" in more dynamic and fluid ways. A partial and decidedly incomplete examination of the scholarship and academic life of Elena Padilla, a Puerto Rican anthropologist conducting fieldwork in Chicago, New York, and Puerto Rico in the 1940s and 1950s, serves as a point of departure to generate and perhaps encourage further critical examinations of the ways in which private/public distinctions serve in fact to theorize racial and gender inequality in academia and public life.

Moreover, Padilla's work serves as a point of departure to documenting the roles that Puerto Rican, or even Latino and Latin American, women have performed in U.S. public intellectual life and academia more generally. Scholars such as Mendieta have denounced the lack of "Latino public intellectuals" (and have oftentimes proposed elitist criteria of admission into such a group), while in fact failing to recognize the ways in which their very conceptions of public intellectuals have historically truncated the contribution of Latina women in general and of women and men from specific Latino nationalities (in Mendieta's case, he lists "Mexican Americans, Puerto Ricans, Dominicans, or Cubans" in this group). By Mendieta's definitions, and by the definitions of the Puerto Rican and American male academics with whom Elena Padilla worked in the 1940s and 1950s, Padilla would not have been considered a "public intellectual." This is the case, even when Padilla spoke to a variety of audiences, indirectly challenged the Chicago School's views of urban neighborhoods as "natural areas," and, somewhat inadvertently, enhanced traditional methodologies in "fieldwork." Elena Padilla's very connections with the Puerto Ricans whom she interviewed also contributed to the creation of an alternative sphere—neither public nor private, yet both public *and* private—for discussions of citizenship, urbanism, and inequality.

The first section of this essay addresses the concept of "public intellectuals" as a U.S. construct that highlights the very rigidity of conceptions of intellectual life in the United States, in contradistinction to the way in which the term "public" is implied in Latin Americanist views of intellectual life. By focusing on Elena Padilla's connection to both Latin American and U.S. intellectual traditions, the goal of this section is to situate Padilla's involvement in civic life, her interest in fluid confluences of "private" and "public" in people's everyday lives, and her concern with her own professionalization.

The second section of this essay constitutes a closer textual examination of some of Padilla's earliest work, particularly focusing on her deployment of "personal narrative," the term I use to refer to the autobiographical interventions in her ethnographic text. This section discusses the methodological and epistemological elements of Elena Padilla's work, including her incorporation of the "backstage" aspects of fieldwork into the production of ethnography, the development of the role of the "native researcher," and her critical self-positioning as a middle-class, educated Puerto Rican woman affiliated with elite academic institutions.

Finally, the last section of the essay argues that the gender discrimination against Elena Padilla was not explained as such but was rather coded as "lack of political commitment" by her Puerto Rican male colleagues. These colleagues viewed her focus on the "private" realm as "apolitical" or as "not nationalist enough." Likewise, Padilla's academic and personal interests in the lives of "her own people" was viewed with professional suspicion by her American colleagues, who still measured a "true anthropologist" by the degree of distance between a researcher-self and an exotic-other. Consequently, this final section more broadly considers the very notions of "public" and "private" as categories used as proxy to sustaining the subordination of marginal groups in civic contexts and academic life.

Public Intellectuals in Latin America and the United States

Latino intellectuals belong at least as much to a Latin American public intellectual tradition, as they do to a professionalized U.S. academy, or perhaps even more so. A hemispheric approach to the conception of the "public intellectual" is particularly pertinent in the case of Latino and Latin American intellectuals who embody multiple scholarly and political traditions, given the common understanding that in Latin America and the Caribbean all intellectuals are and have always been "public."

Latin American and Caribbean intellectuals seem to have played a greater role in public discourse than their counterparts in the United States, regardless of their ideological position, and the operative definition of an intellectual in Latin America seems to be less restrictive than in the United States.[11] As Jorge Castaneda argues, in a region of the world where "societies are polarized, and knowledge and social recognition are rare, almost anyone who writes, paints, acts, teaches, and speaks out, or even sings, becomes 'an intellectual.' . . . The scope of the term is very broad, because the activities of those it is associated with are equally diverse."[12] The comparable conditions of marginality and social polarization seem pertinent also to U.S. Latino and African American communities, where public reflection, cultural production, and social activism have been often conflated and have contributed to multiple formulations of grassroots mobilization at least since the mid-twentieth century.

As is the case of Latin American intellectuals, what distinguishes Latino and African American intellectuals in the United States from their white counterparts is their intellectual and artistic efforts to decenter the racialized national subject, that is, to obliterate the correlations between whiteness, citizenship, and national subjectivity that have pervaded political discourse in Western Europe, Latin America, and the United States since the early twentieth century. In the process of national cultural development, Latin American and Caribbean intellectuals have long rendered the separation of "academia" from "real life" as preposterous. The University of Puerto Rico in the mid-twentieth century, for instance, was engaged in "nation-building" projects of various kinds and from an array of seemingly contradictory political angles. The tension between the identity of an "intellectual" expected of Padilla in her undergraduate training at the University of Puerto Rico was experienced in tension with the traditional academic personas Padilla was required to develop first in her master's program at the University of Chicago and then during her doctorate at Columbia University.

Around the time when Elena Padilla was completing her bachelor's degree, in the mid-twentieth century, the University of Puerto Rico (UPR) occupied an important place both in the strategy of the Partido Popular Democrático, the party under which the colonial relationship between Puerto Rico and the United States was consolidated in the form of a "free and associated state," and in the reformist project of the imperial state.[13] Since its founding as a teacher-training school in 1903, the public university in Río Piedras served as an instrument of the projects that were intended to modify Puerto Rican society and culture and orchestrate the shifts from agronomy to industry. The UPR served as training ground for teachers whose primary function was to "Americanize" the island and produce suitable Puerto Rican male and female workers that could, in turn, respond to the colonial aspiration of eventually launching the rapid industrialization project known as Operación Manos a la Obra (Operation Bootstrap). During the 1930s, the UPR had likewise been the site of attempts to pan-Americanize public higher education, using it as a bridge between the United States and Latin American countries. In the process, however, the UPR also became a center of Hispanic and literary studies, as well as a locus of anti-imperialist activity.

When a group of Columbia University researchers conducted the first area studies on the island in an effort to examine the impact of industrialization on agricultural communities in various towns in Puerto Rico, they promptly identified the peculiar position of the UPR in a pan-Americanist context. The leader of the Columbia research project, entitled *The People Of Puerto Rico,* of which Elena Padilla was a part, posited that "economic and political development under American [U.S.] rule" created a "cultural gap" between Puerto Ricans and other Latin American peoples, without "genuinely incorporating the island into American cultural life. Puerto Ricans are thus unable to identify fully either with North Americans or with fellow Latin Americans."[14]

In fact, at the time when Elena Padilla was pursuing her bachelor's degree, the UPR already had institutional links with various prestigious U.S. universities, including the University of Chicago, one of the centers of development of the emerging theory of modernization and of the tools of economic expansion and political manipulation.[15] Sponsored in part by the Centro de Investigaciones Sociales of the UPR, a team of young men and a woman, Elena Padilla, were placed in prestigious U.S. universities with the intention of training them to conduct research on the Puerto Rico later on. Consequently, Elena Padilla became a graduate student of anthropology at the University of Chicago, where she completed her master's degree in 1947, when she presented a thesis titled "Puerto Rican Immigrants in New York and Chicago: A Study of Comparative Assimilation." Moreover, Padilla would go on to pursue her Ph.D. at Columbia University, where she worked in Steward's *The People of Puerto Rico* project in the 1950s, on which she based her dissertation, "Nocorá: An Agrarian Reform Sugar Community."

By the 1950s the term "intellectual" carried a wider set of associations, many of them having to do with ideology, cultural production, and the capacity for organized thought and learning.[16] In the U.S. setting, intellectual work was characterized by a normative professionalism and emphasis on specialization to a much greater extent than it did in Puerto Rico and other parts of Latin America and the world. The cult of expertise ruled the world of discourse in a way unparalleled by the intellectuals in other countries.[17] For U.S. intellectuals the great separation of the political realm and the academic realm suggested that an academic involved in political life would have to be interested in running for office or achieving a government position.

Perhaps a caveat to this development of the "intellectual" in general and the "public intellectual" in particular in the United States was the struggles engaged by Black scholars in their efforts to invigorate a collective identity as descendants from "Africa." As Robin Kelley notes:

> For all their distrust of, or outright opposition to, United States nationalism, most of those early black historians were engaged in a different sort of nation-building project. Whether it was deliberate or not, they contributed to the formation of a collective identity, reconstructing a glorious African past for the purposes of overturning degrading representations of blackness and establishing a firm cultural basis for a kind of "peoplehood." They identified with a larger black world in which New World Negroes were inheritors of African as well as European civilizations. To varying degrees, they were products of the same political imperatives that led to the formation of Pan-African and other black international movements.[18]

The connection between Latin American intellectuals in the United States and academics in Latin American countries, however, appears less cohesive than what Kelley describes in reference to African Americans.

In the context of a growing interest in "nation-building" in 1950s Puerto Rico—a decidedly "public" sphere project—either by embracing the ELA (Estado Libre Asociado)[19] route of colonial cooperation or by rejecting it in favor of an anti-imperialist, nationalist stance, Elena Padilla's critical disengagement with both of these postures actually relegated her to a relatively marginal position among U.S. academics and (male) Puerto Rican colleagues alike. The racial and gendered dimensions of the relative marginality to which Elena Padilla was likely subjected were covertly presented through discourses that tacitly (or even explicitly) granted the "public" a privileged position as the only legitimate political site of struggle, while rendering any research that engaged the "private" sphere of people's lives irrelevant to the consolidation of either U.S. colonial control (under the commonwealth government) or complicit with the imperialist project (not "nationalist enough").

The academic discourse of the time viewed "nation building" either as something to be configured even under enduring colonial rule, as the commonwealth supporters (under Luis Muñoz Marín's leadership) did, or in the context of anticolonial struggle, as endorsed by nationalist figures of the time (most notably, Pedro Albizu Campos). Nevertheless, Elena Padilla's work suggests that she challenged the political party structure that was already gaining salience in Puerto Rican society, in favor of a more immediate focus on issues of poverty, inequality, discrimination, and subordination, which directly resulted from U.S. imperial domination over Puerto Ricans both on the island and in U.S. *colonias* alike. These issues continued to figure prominently in her scholarly interests in Puerto Rican migrants in the United States and displaced agricultural workers in Puerto Rico. Padilla began to uncover and elucidate the contest between a powerful system of interests and less powerful interests threatened by the system of the powerful, by focusing not on the development of electoral schemes or theories of industrial production. Rather, Padilla's scholarship and the policy reports she wrote (in collaboration with Muna Muñoz Lee) regarding the condition of the Puerto Rican contract laborer and domestic worker in Chicago aimed to challenge imposed silences and naturalized power inequalities regarding the condition of the migrants that the government of Puerto Rico, in its efforts to create a middle class by shipping out the poor, wanted to forget.[20]

The hemispheric perspective of Elena Padilla's intellectual engagement contributed to her success in incorporating or even privileging the domestic and spiritual lives of the "informants" with whom she worked in Chicago and later on in New York and Puerto Rico. A focus on the social interaction between Mexican and Puerto Ricans in Chicago and the role of witchcraft and *espiritismo* in rural Puerto Rico figured prominently in Padilla's understanding of anticolonial struggle and imperialism, even in an academic male–dominated climate that equated Puerto Rican–ness with "nation-building" and island nationalist or colonial politics. The tension between Elena Padilla's marginality from both the U.S. academics for whom scientism in the anthropological profession was pre-eminent, on the one hand, and the limiting views of nation-building politics among Puerto Rican male scholars, on the other, is evidenced by the methodological and epistemological uneasiness that tends to characterize Padilla's earlier work.

Personal Narratives as Intellectual Interventions in "Public" and "Private"

Contemporary anthropology has been concerned with the anguished and messy tangle of contradictions and uncertainties surrounding the interrelations of individual experience, personal narrative, scientism, and professionalism in ethnographic writing. Since the 1980s many anthropologists have argued that the messiness and the faux pas of fieldwork should not be limited to private conversations or edited out of ethnographies in the interest of creating an easily woven text, but rather this evidence of the researcher's involvement in the fieldwork process needed to be included in the text and subjected to scholarly scrutiny just like the rest of the ethnographic text.[21] Personal narratives would come to be considered "cutting edge" and an indispensable aspect of ethnographic texts in the mid-1980s, but as a "native researcher" Elena Padilla was exploring anthropological angst and the possibility of reflexivity from her first ethnographic endeavor in the late-1940s.

It is particularly critical to situate Elena Padilla's work in the sociohistorical context of the University of Chicago and, more importantly, of the so-called Chicago School, which has been reputed for laying the foundation for American sociology.[22] Using the city of Chicago as their laboratory, Robert Park, Ernest Burgess, Louis Wirth, and other members of the Chicago School defined local communities as "natural areas" that could presumably generate a comprehensive picture of contemporary urban life and that could produce understandings of "race" as thoroughly grounded in human ecology.[23] More significantly, as Mary Jo Deegan argues, early male Chicago School sociologists were frequently not interpreted as important figures in sociological thought because their more important ideas and contributions were evaluated as "nonprofessional" activities and interests.[24] In such a repressive context, early female sociologists fared even worse than their male counterparts. Although women flocked to the University of Chicago and to its Department of Sociology, they were unable to gain a foothold in academic sociology. Female sociologists were expected to be "practical" thinkers, capable of reaching out to strangers in a hostile world and in this way mimicking the female roles of wife, mother, and daughter in the home.[25] Padilla joined the Department of Anthropology of the University of Chicago in the decades immediately following the consolidation of the Chicago School as a precursor of "community studies."

In Padilla's study of Puerto Ricans in Chicago, the neighborhood was tangentially seen as fundamental to the broader system of stratification in the United States, although the connection between social relations as necessarily spatial relations did not figure prominently in Padilla's theorizing. Whether deliberately or inadvertently, Padilla's work in Chicago in fact problematized the facile and at times rigid associations between "race" and space that the Chicago School produced, without diminishing the role of spatiality in the production of "Puerto Rican"–ness. Padilla's ethnographic writing and methodology contributed to this expansion of conceptions of "the neighborhood."

Written over three decades prior to the "ethnography as text" school trends endorsed by James Clifford and others, the personal narrative in ethnographic text begins to surface, largely because of Padilla's own self-conceptualization as a "native investigator," even though she herself was not from Chicago. As she explains: "The material on the Puerto Rican immigrants in Chicago was obtained in the field through observation, participation, and the recording of verbalizations. Formal and informal interviews were an important aspect of this part of the research. In relation to the field work, a point to be discussed is that of the native investigator."[26] Even though Padilla viewed her personal narratives as authorial interruptions that were ambiguous, confusing, and lacking scientific rigor, she still drew on her own self-positioning as a Puerto Rican middle-class woman as an important condition that informed her interpretation of the lives of Puerto Rican migrants in Chicago. A University of Chicago graduate student in anthropology, Padilla certainly understood that the "formal" ethnography was the one that counted as professional capital and as an authoritative representation, and that personal narratives in ethnographic writing were often deemed self-indulgent, trivial, or heretical in other ways.

Nevertheless, while recognizing such disciplining of the personal narrative by the professional anthropological community, Padilla still insisted on drawing from her own background. As she explains in the introduction of her master's thesis, "Puerto Rican Immigrants in New York and Chicago: A Study in Comparative Assimilation": "The field material was collected by a native Puerto Rican who had lived in Chicago for about two years. This point seems important insofar as the field worker, since the beginning of the study, was aware of the fact that the rapport established with the informants would be very much influenced by this circumstance, as also would be the data obtained."[27] Fieldwork produces a kind of authority that is premised to a large extent in subjective, sensuous experience—the "being there" present in the everyday life of the subjects. One experiences the indigenous environment and lifeways for oneself, witnesses experiences firsthand, even plays some roles, albeit contrived ones, in the daily life of the community. Nevertheless, the professional text to result from such an encounter is supposed to conform to the norms of a scientific discourse whose authority has historically resided in the absolute effacement of the speaking and experiencing subject, as well as the sensuous memories produced from such encounters.[28] Padilla was aware of this backstage/public distinction.

Likewise, unlike male academics of her time, including Padilla's former husband, Eduardo Seda Bonilla, who virtually rejected the national belongingness of Puerto Rican migrants and subscribed to rigid notions of cultural authenticity,[29] Elena Padilla actually placed the plight of Puerto Rican migrants to Chicago squarely at the center of definitions of "the nation" and "Puerto Rican"–ness, thus challenging discourse that advertently or inadvertently aimed to erase Puerto Rican migration from the island's historical imaginary. Padilla did this not only by exploring the daily lives of the Puerto Ricans living in Chicago at the time of her fieldwork but also by introducing "personal narratives" into her ethnographic writing at a time when anthropologists still endorsed scientism and objectivity.

In Padilla's ethnography, the author's personal narratives are responsible for setting up the initial positionings of the subjects of the ethnographic text: the ethnographer, the native, and the reader.[30] In Padilla's case, the researcher's personal narrative was contained in a brief methodological chapter, in which she recognized the ways in which researcher subjectivities are inseparable from the fieldwork experience, even—or especially—in the case of so-called native anthropologists. Nevertheless, Padilla also reasserted the researcher/subject boundary by stating that native anthropologists are still anthropologists and thus challenged the exoticization of herself as a potential "other" in an overwhelmingly white professional academic setting of the University of Chicago in the 1940s and Columbia University in the 1950s. This, of course, indicated a greater conflict between her developing professional identity and her condition as a Puerto Rican woman inhabiting a powerfully gendered and racialized space.

Elena Padilla used "personal narratives" to anchor the problematic class, linguistic, and racial distinctions between herself and her audience and "informants." She also recognized the ways in which her "native" status made her connection to her informants profoundly complicated, particularly given Padilla's social class and institutional affiliation, and the privileged locations she occupied as an upwardly mobile young woman who arrived in the city of Chicago as a student in a prestigious and elitist university, rather than as an immigrant escaping poverty or subjected to the imperialist demand for cheap labor. Personal narratives, in this sense, represented a way of reflecting on the intense experience of fieldwork.

Although Padilla conferred various degrees of methodological significance to her middle-class "Puerto Rican"–ness to argue for the validity and unique insights produced by her research, she also appeared self-reflective about the ways in which her "Puerto Rican"–ness became simultaneously exoticized (in white academic settings) and naturalized (in her relationship with other Puerto Ricans). For instance, as Padilla explains in her Chicago study: "The field worker knew some of the informants quite intimately for a period of about a year before this research was planned. These individuals were visited and informed about the research, and nevertheless, they did not seem to accept the field worker in their role, but persisted in continuing their relationship with her on a friendly level."[31] A hybrid, a translator, an interpreter, and, in her own words, a "native researcher," Padilla created a space in academic life by recognizing and reflecting on her own racialization as "Puerto Rican."

What seems most ironic, however, is Padilla's insistence on being recognized as a "professional" by her fellow Puerto Rican interviewees, rather than demanding that recognition more forcefully from her academic colleagues. Not only does Padilla acknowledge the difficulty asserting herself as a professional researcher in relation to her informants because she knew them in friendly terms prior to the beginning of her research, but she also states that even those individuals whom she did not know refused to view her as a detached, objective researcher. Padilla remarks: "A different type of experience occurred with those informants the field worker did not know before the study was planned. These Puerto Rican informants, at the beginning of their relationship with the field worker, took her in this role, although they dropped it very soon, either in the first or second interview. . . . The data were checked and more information obtained from their Puerto Rican acquaintances in the city. Those Puerto Ricans who knew each other gossiped about their countrymen."[32] Hence, as she was undertaking her first fieldwork project, unquestionably a "rite of passage" for anthropology graduate students, Padilla realized that the relationships she had built and would continue to build "in the field" were conditioned by the researcher/ subject interaction oftentimes in implicitly racial and classed terms, while also expressing her social scientific understanding of triangulation (through a "gossip analysis" of sorts) as an important research strategy.

A particular passage in Padilla's master's thesis alludes to the social inequalities between researcher and "informants," and between Padilla's friends and the people whom she had met only as a consequence of her research. Padilla remarks: "This situation [of the individuals interviewed not accepting the field worker as a researcher, but continuing to see her as a friend] seems to have operated in two ways in relation to the data obtained from these individuals: 1) they tried to impress the field worker with their success and socio-economic status in Chicago and in Puerto Rico, and 2) they resisted giving information on subjects they would consider a negation of the above, i.e., actual incomes, unsuccessful relationships with Americans, etc."[33] Padilla shows how her informants are aware of the researcher's power to represent and interpret their lives as Puerto Rican migrants in Chicago—a largely unstudied population at the time. In particular, they exert certain claims to these representations by creating a portrait of themselves as "successful" and directing the researcher away from subjects who would challenge these images of social and economic prosperity. Nevertheless, Padilla never analyzes her position of class privilege as a critical stance for her evaluation of the informants' self-representations as prosperous. This seems to correspond to her training at the University of Chicago, where Robert Park and other members of the Chicago School drew connections between studying poverty and studying poor neighborhoods in such a fundamental way that it was rarely necessary to spell it out explicitly.

In this model, the assumption was that, given the high degree of segregation in U.S. cities, talking about the spatial context of poverty also meant talking about racial and ethnic segregation. Hence, while from the very beginning of her anthropological career Padilla viewed ethnography as indeed a collaborative project mutually (though never equally) undertaken by researcher and informants, the persistent power inequalities between herself and some of the Puerto Ricans whom she interviewed remains a problematic silence in Padilla's work. Although at some level Padilla interpreted her compatriots' responses as performances of variously classed identities, she did not examine how these responses could have been a reaction to the researcher's own middle-classness and affiliation to the elitist space of the University of Chicago.

In Padilla's study of Puerto Ricans in Chicago, the researcher's incorporation of personal narrative does not preclude the somewhat objectifying descriptions that characterized most ethnographic texts of the time and that reflected Padilla's insistence on mediating the contradiction within the discipline between personal and scientific authority, a contradiction that has become especially acute since the advent of fieldwork as a methodological norm in anthropology.[34] Nevertheless, the hue of her informants' skin and their English dominance become the significant, if somewhat limiting, rubrics that Padilla deploys to interpret the declarations of social success she noticed among some of her Puerto Rican interviewees, rather than presenting a view of a monolithic community of Puerto Ricans, as was the nationalist tendency. As Padilla writes: "It must be pointed out that the above observations [related to the ways in which the individuals interviewed tried to convey an overly successful and positive description of their condition as immigrants] are particularly noticeable in light-skinned Puerto Ricans who speak English relatively well and who are engaged either in business or in the professions."[35] Likewise, a recognition of a mythified ancestral homeland inflicted with recognition of the emotional role of language dominance and diversity contributes to Padilla's implicit understanding of problematic constructions of "cultural authenticity" among Puerto Ricans across generations. Padilla explains that being familiar with some of the interviewees' "relatives or friends or their home towns, or just [saying] something about Puerto Rico was very helpful in establishing rapport. The use of mixed Spanish and English in the conversations was also of much help insofar as it avoided embarrassments due to a certain inability of expression in using just one of the two languages throughout all of the conversations."[36] Padilla noticed the sophisticated ways in which language and linguistic creativity mediates the interaction and intimate identification between "native researchers" and informants in ways that are performed as strategically essentialist ways of being a "real Puerto Rican."

Although Padilla's personal narrative is circumscribed to the methodology chapter of her ethnography, it aims to mediate the contradiction between the intimate engagement called for in fieldwork and the self-effacement called for in formal ethnographic description. She not only inserts into the ethnographic text the authority of the personal experience out of which the ethnography was made, but more significantly, she draws consistent reference to the ways in which being a "quasi-native" or a "native researcher" produces unique contours in the production of knowledge.

Every discursive intervention, including ethnography, is specific to a particular occasion and assumes an existing consensus, paradigm, episteme, or praxis. The hallmark of the era in which Elena Padilla wrote her ethnographic works of Puerto Rican life in Chicago, New York, and the town of "Nicoro" (Barceloneta) in Puerto Rico was dominated by a mainstream-academic-government orthodoxy against which it was very difficult to go. In light of this context, an important aspect of Padilla's personal narrative is that it is not only circumscribed to a methodological commentary of the problems of being a "native investigator" but is actually in dialogue with her epistemology. She knows what she knows because she is Puerto Rican, but also because she has to examine her ethnographic materials in connection to her Puerto Ricanness and her professional identity. Padilla never seems to acknowledge that every situation she identifies in her descriptions of

Chicago (and later of New York and rural Puerto Rico) was embedded in a contest between a powerful system of interests and less powerful interests threatened with frustration, silences, incorporation, or extinction by the powerful. In this sense, perhaps Padilla was still never fully able to escape what Judith Brett explains as the nature of the structural divide between the intellectual (academic) and the citizen that arises as the result of the academic being forced to use a bureaucratized form of writing underpinned by the hegemony of empiricist and positivist models of truth as the goal of academic enquiry.[37] Nevertheless, Padilla was cognizant of this and was making decisions in the tense and at times crudely oppositional stance of a Puerto Rican woman in a male-dominated, white academy.

The issue of personal accounts and the exoticization of the native anthropologist as Other is a subtext to Padilla's remark. As Mary Louise Pratt argues, personal narratives, as a conventional component of ethnographies, appear almost invariably in introductions or first chapters, where opening narratives commonly recount the writer's arrival at the field site, for instance, the initial reception by the inhabitants, the slow agonizing process of learning the language and overcoming rejection, the anguish and loss at leaving.[38] However, in Padilla's case, the effort is not to create the image of her informants as exotic Others in the savage/civilized scheme of many anthropological accounts of the time, but rather to recognize that the distinctions between herself as a researcher and the informants were decidedly blurred and complicated and always retained messy configurations of power and subordination.

The opening narrative of Elena Padilla's Chicago study is given by way of explaining the limitations on the ethnographer's ability to carry out her scientific mission. Paradoxically, the conditions of fieldwork and the researcher's embeddedness in the private lives of other Puerto Ricans in Chicago are expressed as impediments to the task of doing fieldwork, rather than as part of what is to be accounted for in fieldwork and its "public" outcome, the ethnographic text. As Padilla concludes:

> To summarize: there are some advantages as well as disadvantages in being taken for a member of a group investigated. The main advantages lie in the fact that the investigator is in a better position than a stranger is to identify in a shorter period of time certain types of attitudes and overt behavior, namely, those that are individualities and those that are to a greater extent common to a larger number of members of the group. The main disadvantage of being a native investigator lies in the fact that biases are very difficult to check, and that the personal equation is probably greater than in the cases when the investigator is quite familiarized with the subject matter of his study but is not sentimentally or emotionally bound to it. . . . In regard to this particular research, an obstacle

was found in regard to the type and quality of the data obtained. It has been already stated that informants systematically tried to impress the investigator about their success in the United States. The investigator was always under the impression that they felt they had to act in that particular way because they thought it would not be pleasing to have a countrywoman and a friend have certain kinds of information about them. Of course, the possibility that the investigator was not sophisticated enough to handle the interview-situations in more suitable ways should not be forgotten."[39]

The scientific ideal seems to press on public intellectuals acutely, calling for codified field methodology, professional detachment, a systematic write-up. Nevertheless, Elena Padilla still alludes to the sentimentality and emotional boundedness of the native researcher in a way that transcends a public intellectual's knowledge of the subject matter. She in fact re-evaluates her own self-positioning in light of what she has already in the 1940s envisioned as the great reflective capacities of a research "self" that transcends a monolithic scientist-observer entity and becomes a multifaceted presence, participant, observer, and writer in an ever shifting academic production.

Puerto Rican Women as Public Intellectuals: Racial and Gendered Configurations of the "Public" and "Private"

Elena Padilla viewed her work in anthropology as an opportunity to examine and depict the reality of imperialism, not primarily in terms of dogmatic nationalist stances, but in the context of class formations and inequality in the everyday lives of Puerto Rican migrants to Chicago (and later to New York and peasants in Puerto Rico). It is telling that Eduardo Seda Bonilla, an important academic of the time and Elena Padilla's former husband and colleague, actually questioned Padilla's political commitment and the merit of her participation in the controversial 1956 study, *The People of Puerto Rico*. In fact, Seda Bonilla viewed Padilla's participation in the Columbia University–sponsored project as evidence of her abdication of her personal anticolonial principles for the "Weberian hypocrisy of the researcher's ethical [value-free] neutrality."[40] Seda Bonilla was accusing Padilla of being uncritical of or even complicit with the colonial compromise engineered between 1946 and 1952. Along with many other scholars, Seda Bonilla has argued that *The People of Puerto Rico* research obscured the existence of a people and a national historical project because, like other U.S. studies of Puerto Rico, "its 'empiricism' was incapable of grasping the existence of the nationality, of the national project, or of the forms and mutability of imperial domination."[41]

Elena Padilla's use of personal narratives and thematic concerns could hardly be criticized for a rigid empiricism but actually reflects an exception to such a tendency that was perhaps uncommon among the other researchers in the Columbia project. In the work of Elena Padilla, the fluidity of "private" and "public" domains is reflected in the researcher's methodological and thematic concerns that, in turn, become the "raw materials" for a theory building organically from intimate interpersonal connections developed through fieldwork and reflections on the everyday-ness of social life in the "private" realm. As Antonio Lauria-Perricelli notes in his doctoral dissertation, "In her research in Puerto Rico, Elena Padilla, who lived in the home of the *curandera* . . . gives magic, witchcraft and *espiritismo* much greater consideration than her [male] colleagues. Her monograph also depicts a stronger vision of the role of gossip and mistrust in everyday rural proletarian life than does [Sidney] Mintz—a perception facilitated perhaps, by her own identity."[42] Lauria-Perricelli attributes Padilla's ability to focus on the everyday world of belief systems (*espiritismo*, witchcraft) and informal mechanisms of social control (gossip, mistrust) in rural proletariat life to "her own identity."

Yet, paradoxically, and despite the personal and professional connection between Seda Bonilla and Padilla, Seda's criticism of *The People of Puerto Rico* project seems to disregard Padilla's intellectual contribution. In this section I argue that Elena Padilla was overlooked in the subsequent acknowledgment both in the form of praise and criticism directed toward *The People of Puerto Rico* project, because she did not meet the implicit criteria of what an "intellectual" was, as determined both by the white U.S. scholars with whom she worked at Columbia and by the Puerto Rican male academics who were almost exclusively invested in projects focused on nation building and explicit nationalist politics.

Public intellectual life values thought that canvasses matters of public concern, and generally undermines discussions of subjects traditionally associated with the private domain. The gendered nature of public intellectual life largely occurs as a result of the privileging of the public sphere over the private sphere, and the historical association of women with the private sphere.[43] It has been long established that the public/private separation is a rather artificial analytical distinction. The very separation of "private" and "public" privileges normative and dominant views of class, race, and gender that do not always reflect the lived experiences of marginal groups, for whom private and public are rarely as clearly delineated, and for whom a lack of access to "the public" may in fact reconfigure the characteristics of "the private." In the context of this essay, I use the terms "private" and "public" not to designate actual material or ideological spaces that are separate from one another, but to question the very nature and endurance of such separation in the realm of popular and academic discourses.

When participants in public debate focus on the "private," they are often-times marginalized as speakers by the gatekeepers of public thought. But "private" and "public" are powerful categorical distinctions largely because they are coded terms for power domination and subordination. As suggested in Antonio Lauria-Perricelli's dissertation, the curtailing of Elena Padilla's activities signaled her relative powerlessness and the uncomfortable distance between a political male elite who was both white and Puerto Rican in institutions of power and Padilla's uneasy position as de facto spokesperson for Chicago Puerto Ricans and rural peasants in Barceloneta, who by and large remained on the outskirts of dominant political institutions. The sanctions imposed upon these figures pinpoint the coordinates at which public discourse and state power meet. In reference to *The People of Puerto Rico* project, Lauria-Perricelli notes:

> At the time of the research, gender inequality tended to go unremarked, and most practice[s] in the academy, as elsewhere, easily reproduced the underlying relations. . . . At the most superficial level, the early proposals assumed research personnel were "men," and assessed the value of a wife through the extra $500/ year budgeted for married fieldworkers. Throughout the fieldwork, the field team was frequently called "the boys," negating the women involved, and less likely, making them honorary men. . . . Elena Padilla, the only Puerto Rican staff researcher—as distinct from assistant—was the focus of many intersecting contradictions. These were both national and sexual, involving her, one gathers, in a personal struggle as a Puerto Rican woman and intellectual confronting the various gender definitions current in both colony and metropolis. To be sure, the field team's practice concerning gender . . . also included an openness to the intellectual participation of women which paralleled the remarkably open structure of dialogue within the project. Yet it is perhaps significant that neither of the women who authored parts of the project's corpus were willing to discuss their experience.[44]

The term "public intellectual" has historically defined not just the space in which intellectuals carry out their work but also the ideas that get heard in this space and the ways in which the space itself dialectically generates the ideas. Thus, the "private" is regarded as being outside the jurisdiction of credible public thinkers, who not coincidently constitute in themselves a social elite.

Common to descriptions of public intellectual discourse is the need for issues about which intellectuals speak and write not only to be concerned with public life but indeed to be limited to the public realm. This definition of "appropriate" thought ignores the extent to which matters of public policy get defined, by those making the claim, to exclude policy relating to the private sphere and the women who occupy it. In the case of Elena Padilla and Kathleen Wolf, the only recourse has been to remain silent and not discuss their experiences. Incidentally, Kathleen Wolf's paper was not cited by in the introductory theoretical comments, and her work was not even published in the final document.[45]

Feminist scholars have argued that for matters of private significance to have a place in public thought, a broader definition of appropriate public intellectual discourse is required. This is an important recognition of the need to identify alternative sites of intellectual discourse and of women's participation as public thinkers. Identifying such alternative sites also highlights the reliance on elitism in determining "proper" topics of discussion for public thinkers that are premised on privileging the public sphere and denying the place of the private sphere. Nevertheless, despite the validity of such suggestions, it is important to note that to the extent that women focus on the private sphere in articulating discourse in the public domain, they are likely to be denied the status of "public intellectual," as the case of Padilla shows.

Padilla's Puerto Rico research, which began as a Columbia University doctoral dissertation entitled "Nocorá: An Agrarian Reform Sugar Community," in fact theorized a developmental relationship between stages of colonial history and plantation forms.[46] Nevertheless, it became clear that while Sidney Mintz, as well as Eric Wolf, went on to become virtually a "founding father" of Latin American and Caribbean anthropology, Elena Padilla was effectively marginalized to the perpetual role of "research assistant" in The People of Puerto Rico project. Rather than attributing the inequality in career paths to discriminatory racial and gender practices, however, Elena Padilla's "liberal" colleagues did not consider their own privilege as white males even in light of salient colonial configurations that insisted on the power of whiteness in contradistinction to the savagery of the Puerto Rican colonial other.

The power of discourse to produce meaning not only occurs in its articulation but is also generated through the granting of status to certain voices and topics, so that when some voices are privileged over others, dominant knowledge with the potential to engender meaning and influence is created. The conflation of the public domain, regarded as the "true" site of intellectual production, on the one hand, and of the private sphere, viewed as relational and even emotive, on the other, in Padilla's work actually suggests the researcher's development of an eminently hemispheric conception of intellectual life influenced by her experiences in multiple academic margins. It likewise served to explain the fact that Padilla was relegated to a secondary academic path of scholars who refuse to privilege the "public" realm and for whom rejecting the "private" realm meant disconnecting one's research from one's community commitments.[47] But, more importantly, these conceptions of "private" and "public" intellectual realms are proxies for the racial and gender inequalities that are conveniently hidden as possible explanations for why Padilla was not as publicly honored in the field of anthropology as the highly venerated members of her cohort, which included Eric Wolf and Sidney Mintz. Hence, "public" and "private" are not only concepts describing neutral spaces of intellectual production but also the very vocabulary used to undermine configurations of racial and gender inequalities that are central to the production of dominance and "true knowledge."

Conclusion

An argument developed throughout this essay, then, has been that Elena Padilla was subordinated in her scholarship and academic career because her participation in public intellectual life was never considered "political enough" and was confined to the realm of "private" concerns with presumably "less relevance" to academic and national matters. Padilla was in a subordinate position as a Puerto Rican working with mostly American researchers for whom anthropologists needed to be separate from the "exotic-Other-subject" of their study. Likewise, Padilla was marginalized as a woman whose academic and methodological work in the "private sphere" was viewed by her Puerto Rican male colleagues as not sufficiently engaged in the nation-building project of the 1940s and 1950s politics in Puerto Rico and the consolidation of colonial control.

In her critical examination of citizenship, Iris Young has noted that a clear distinction has historically been made between the public realm of citizenship and civic activity, on the one hand, and a private realm of particular identities, roles, affiliations, and interests, on the other.[48] Young challenges the tendency for participatory democracy to rely on an opposition between the public sphere of a general interest and the private sphere of particular interest and affiliation. An important implication of this distinction to Padilla's work in the 1940s and 1950s was that the definition of citizenship as pertaining to the public domain clashed with her inclusion and at times privileging of the "private" domain of Puerto Rican life in Chicago, New York, and rural Puerto Rico. In this sense, Elena Padilla's work recognized what Paula Moya convincingly argued Mendieta's conception of a "Latino *point of discussion* (handwritten annotation in margin)

"public intellectual" missed: "The political imagination of Puerto Ricans is crucially shaped by the dynamics of colonialism, and they are often subjected to a kind of second-class cultural citizenship, but they do not imagine themselves—nor should they—as foreigners in the United States."[49]

By insisting on a definition of citizenship exclusively in the domain of civic society, mainstream scholars avoided and obscured the requirement that all experiences, needs, and perspectives on social events have a voice and are respected. The political ideology and practice of the time persisted in defining some groups as unworthy of equal citizenship status because of supposedly "natural" (and later essentialized "cultural") differences from white male citizens, as the case of *The People of Puerto Rico* project shows. But the internal logics of Puerto Rican academic politics also insisted that female scholars in general, and female scholars whose academic work focused on the lived experiences of people in the "private" realm in particular, were of lesser value for the construction of a citizenship project in which Puerto Ricans either demonstrated their deservingness to be part of the United States (as a "commonwealth") or demonstrated their capacity for self-determination and nation-state building (as the Nationalists posed).

As Edward Said reminds us, struggles of public intellectuals occur in various places, including the struggle against the disappearance of the past. Elena Padilla's interest in documenting the lives of Puerto Rican migrants, commonly ignored in island-based politics or deemed "inauthentic," is a clear attempt to bring forth the everyday consequences of colonial and imperialist U.S. politics and Puerto Rico's academic elitism. The government of Puerto Rico encouraged migration to the United States by obliterating the reality of cruelty, discrimination, and marginality that Puerto Rican migrants faced there and the costly price of rapid industrialization for a rural proletariat. Elena Padilla's work unveiled the misleading optimism of public discourse around Puerto Rican migration and rapid industrialization in the 1940s and 1950s, when the U.S. government's investment in creating a tractable body of cheap labor continued to set the terrain for rewriting colonialism as "benign intervention" and "progress." An insistence in collapsing distinctions between academic disciplines, as well as rigid ideas of "personal versus political" issues would bring U.S. "public intellectuals" closer to Latin American and Caribbean scholars for whom intellectual projects, whether public or private, have always been political and organically driven. These distinctions are not harmless; they have in fact been at the center of discussions that have contributed to the marginalization of women of color, including Elena Padilla, for decades.

In many respects, universities and knowledge production around the world, particularly in the United States, are living through a period of extraordinary turmoil as their mission and purpose are articulated in light of neoliberal, market-driven objectives. This tendency poses significant challenges to contemporary scholars who face an ever shrinking public space in the midst of surveillance and even persecution as they engage their role as public intellectuals in the United States. Elena Padilla's experience navigating academic marginality offers potential strategies that may aid us in drawing on our own individual biographical and political experiences in asserting what a racialized "counter public" might look like around university research.[50] Padilla's conception of urban space serves as metaphor around which to begin to frame what happens to knowledge as it is increasingly treated as another commodity. This essay has aimed to provide a road map, albeit decidedly limited and incomplete, to identifying research themes, methodologies, and epistemologies concerning Puerto Rican public intellectual life; it is by no means exhaustive and indeed will perhaps engage other scholars in broader projects that consider what a documentation of "Puerto Rican public intellectuals" or even "Latino public intellectuals" would mean for present-day Puerto Rican politics in the United States and on the island.

Notes

Some of the themes in this paper were developed in conversation with members of the "Race in the Americas" working group sponsored by the Social Science Research Council. Special thanks are due for the members of that group, particularly Marisol de la Cadena and Marcial Godoy.

1. E.g., Michael Hanchard, "Cultural Politics and Black Public Intellectuals," in *Disciplinarity and Dissent in Cultural Studies,* edited by Cary Nelson and Dilip Parameshwar Gaonkar, pp. 251–264 (New York: Routledge, 1996); *Nepantla: Views from the South* 4, 2 (2003): entire issue; Rutledge M. Dennis, ed., *Research in Race and Ethnic Relations,* vol. 10: *The Black Intellectuals* (Greenwich, Conn.: JAI Press, 1997).

2. E.g., Dennis, *Research in Race and Ethnic Relations.*

3. See Eduardo Mendieta, "What Can Latinas/os Learn from Cornel West? The Latino Postcolonial Intellectual in the Age of the Exhaustion of Public Spheres," *Nepantla: Views from the South* 4, 2 (2003): 213–233"; Edward Said, "The Public Role of Writers and Intellectuals," lecture broadcast on May 20, 2001, Melbourne Town Hall.

4. Russell Jacoby, *The Last Intellectual* (New York: Basic Books, 1987); Richard Posner, *Public Intellectuals: A Study of Decline* (Cambridge, Mass.: Harvard University Press, 2001).

5. Cf. Robert Boynton, "The New Intellectuals," *Atlantic Monthly,* March 1995; Tim Dunlop, "If You Build It, They Will Come: Blogging and the New Citizenship," n.d., http://evatt.labor.net.au/publications/papers/91.html (accessed June 17, 2003); Edward Said, *Representations of the Intellectual (London: Vintage, 1994).*

6. Jane Juffer has questioned the value of emphasizing the centrality of identifying such a "public sphere," arguing that this notion is so general as to provide little insight into the functions of power across different contexts and historical periods. Jane Juffer, "In Search of the Latino Public Sphere: Everywhere and Nowhere," *Nepantla: Views from the South* 4, 2 (2003), p. 263. For the purposes of this essay, I aim to problematize the very designation of a space as "public" or "private," rather than insinuating that a "public sphere" is necessarily ahistorical or devoid of sociopolitical value.

7. Dunlop, "If You Build It."

8. This merits further discussion on the role of other contemporary "public intellectuals," including Arturo Schomburg and Jesús Colón; due to space limitations, such discussion is not undertaken in this essay.

9. An exception to the otherwise celebratory and even uncritical acceptance of Mendieta's propositions that Latinos follow the intellectual model of Cornel West—as opposed to, say, bell hooks or Angela Davis or Toni Morrison, to name a few Black public intellectuals—was Paula Moya's "With Us or Without Us: The Development of a Latino Public Sphere," *Nepantla: Views from the South* 4, 2 (2003): 245–251. Curiously, the two female respondents—Paula Moya and Jane Juffer—were the only ones to also question Mendieta's elision of the specific colonial histories and U.S. imperialist aspirations that contribute to the particular histories of the Latino groups Mendieta would rather lump together under a more amorphous "Latino" label.

10. Mendieta, "What Can Latinas/os Learn?" p. 215.

11. Cf. Hanchard, "Cultural Politics and Black Public Intellectuals; bell hooks, *Talking Back: Thinking Feminist, Thinking Black* (Boston: South End Press, 1989; Robin D. G. Kelley, "'But a Local Phase of a World Problem': Black History's Global Vision, 1883–1950," *Journal of American History* 86, 3 (December 1999): 1045–1072.

12. Jorge Castaneda, *Utopia Unarmed: The Latin American Left after the Cold War* (New York: Random House, 1994), p. 177.

13. See Antonio Lauria-Perricelli, "A Study in Historical and Critical Anthropology: The Making of 'The People of Puerto Rico'" (Ph.D. diss., New School for Social Research, 1989), p. 29. Lauria-Perricelli examines the academic and personal motivations of the researchers who participated in Julian Steward's Puerto Rico project. See Julian Steward, Robert A. Manners, Eric R. Wolf, Elena Padilla Seda, Sidney W. Mintz, and Raymond L. Scheele, *The People of Puerto Rico: A Study in Social Anthropology* (Urbana: University of Illinois Press, 1956). In a personal conversation in 1999, Lauria-Perricelli relayed his frustration about not having found the fieldnotes that Elena Padilla had contributed to the Steward project, which as a graduate student I

had once seen in rather disorganized boxes in the small Anthropology Department library on the top floor of the Schermerhorn Hall at Columbia University. The politics of archival organization and preservation are beyond the scope of this essay. However, it is important to note that examining the legacy of Elena Padilla and other female scholars whose works have gone unrecognized (and unpreserved) for decades is truly a "politics of love and rescue," as Virginia Domínguez described it in "For a Politics of Love and Rescue," *Cultural Anthropology* 15, 3 (2000): 361–393.

14. Steward et al., *People of Puerto Rico*, p. 501.

15. Lauria-Perricelli, "Study in Historical and Critical Anthropology," p. 40.

16. Cf. Said, *Representations of the Intellectual*.

17. Hanchard, "Cultural Politics and Black Public Intellectuals"; Said, *Representations of the Intellectual*.

18. Kelley, "'But a Local Phase of a World Problem,'" pp. 1050–51.

19. Estado Libre Asociado literally means "Free Associated State" and has come to designate the "Commonwealth" status of Puerto Rico. This constitutional status renders Puerto Rico an unincorporated U.S. territory. See also José Trias Monge's *Puerto Rico: The Trials of the Oldest Colony in the World* (New Haven: Yale University Press, 1997).

20. Along with Muna Muñoz Lee, Elena Padilla conducted research and wrote policy briefs for the Welfare Council of Chicago, which were later used to sustain the need for an active Office of Puerto Rico in Chicago that would monitor the recruitment, placement, and treatment of Puerto Rican domestic and foundry workers and other migrants. In correspondence with the Welfare Council of Chicago, Padilla mentions that domestic Puerto Rican workers who had been recruited by the private agency Castle, Barton and Associates and placed in households where they were subjected to mistreatment and cruelty. See Ana Ramos-Zayas, "'La patria es valor y sacrificio': Nationalist Ideologies, Cultural Authenticity, and Community-Building among Puerto Ricans in Chicago" (Ph.D. diss., Columbia University, 1997).

21. See James Clifford and George Marcus, *Writing Culture: The Poetics and Politics of Ethnography* (Berkeley: University of California Press, 1986); Mary Louise Pratt, "Fieldwork in Common Places," in ibid., pp. 27–50.

22. Drawing from a close reading of Weber, Marx, Durkheim, and other European social theorists, the Chicago School aimed to describe the social organization of industrial urbanism by testing and extending theoretical ideas through relentless processes of empirical investigation that encompassed all means of data collection. Elijah Anderson and Douglass Massey, "The Sociology of Race in the U.S.," in *Problems of the Century: Racial Stratification in America,* edited by E. Anderson and D. Massey, pp. 3–11 (New York: Russell Sage Foundation, 2003). While the white men of the Chicago School have been commonly considered the "founding fathers" of U.S. social sciences, Anderson and Massey have demonstrated how this standard foundational account of American sociology's birth needs to be revised. As they argue, the birth of American sociology happened at the University of Pennsylvania in the 1890s; "rather than being led by a group of classically influenced

white men, it was directed by W.E.B. Du Bois, a German-trained African American with a Ph.D. from Harvard. His study of The Philadelphia Negro, anticipated in every way the program of theory and research that later became known as the Chicago School" (3–4). Nevertheless, the Chicago School has historically been given centrality in the expansion of U.S. academic thought and institutional development and has been examined extensively. See, e.g., Martin Bulmer, The Chicago School of Sociology: Institutionalization, Diversity, and the Rise of Sociological Research (Chicago: University of Chicago Press, 1984); Rolf Lindner, The Reportage of Urban Culture: Robert Park and the Chicago School (Cambridge: Cambridge University Press, 1996). In this essay, the Chicago School is alluded to only to the extent that it informs Elena Padilla's work.

23. Anderson and Massey, "Sociology of Race in the U.S."; Bulmer, Chicago School of Sociology.

24. Mary Jo Deegan, Jane Addams and the Men of the Chicago School, 1892–1918 (New Brunswick, N.J.: Transaction Books, 1986).

25. Ibid., pp. 1–4. In Jane Addams and the Men of the Chicago School, the first of a series of three volumes on the role of women in the Chicago School, Mary Jo Deegan singles out Jane Addams as one of the exceptional female sociologists who were in fact recognized as leaders even by the male sociologists. Deegan challenges the patriarchal tradition of the Chicago School of Sociology and argues that Jane Addams, whose involvement as one of the few female sociology students at the turn of the twentieth century at the University of Chicago has been obliterated, should be considered as a founder of American sociology. Addams's leadership in sociology was based on considerably more than her relationship to the now recognized male Chicago School of Sociology. She coordinated and led a massive network of women sociologists who either worked at the "daring" new university or who studied there as graduate students. This first volume, then, establishes Addams as a central figure in sociology. Deegan argues that while the male sociologists of the Chicago School are already recognized as the earliest and most powerful figures in sociology, Jane Addams's work and the women's network that she promoted in her practice of sociology were ultimately considered less powerful and visible. Addams's most lasting influence over the discipline was channeled through these early male colleagues.

26. Elena Padilla, "Puerto Rican Immigration in New York and Chicago: A Study of Comparative Assimilation" (master's thesis, University of Chicago, 1947), p. 47. The thesis is reprinted in part 1 of this volume; all citations are to the reprint.

27. Ibid.

28. Pratt, "Fieldwork in Common Places," p. 32.

29. Eduardo Seda Bonilla, "El Pueblo de Puerto Rico: Dónde está el pueblo?" in The Anthropology of the People of Puerto Rico, edited by R. Duncan, pp. 65–75 (San Juan: Inter American University of Puerto Rico, 1979).

30. Cf. Pratt, "Fieldwork in Common Places," pp. 31–32.

31. Padilla, "Puerto Rican Immigration," p. 47.

32. Ibid., p. 48.

33. Ibid., p. 47.

34. Cf. Pratt, "Fieldwork in Common Places," p. 32.

35. Padilla, "Puerto Rican Immigration," pp. 47–48.

36. Ibid., p. 48.

37. Cf. Dunlop, "If You Build It"; Judith Brett, *Speaking Their Minds: Intellectuals and the Public Culture in Australia,* edited by Robert Dessaix (Sydney: ABC Books, 1998).

38. Pratt, "Fieldwork in Common Places."

39. Padilla, "Puerto Rican Immigration," pp. 48–49.

40. Seda Bonilla, in Lauria-Perricelli, "Study in Historical and Critical Anthropology," p. 11.

41. Lauria-Perricelli, "Study in Historical and Critical Anthropology," p. 10.

42. Ibid., p. 334.

43. Cf. Kathryn Edgeworth, "Women as Public Intellectuals: The Exclusion of the Private in Public Intellectual Life" (paper, Women's Worlds 99: The 7th International Interdisciplinary Congress on Women, Tromso, Norway, June 20–26, 1999).

44. Lauria-Perricelli, "Study in Historical and Critical Anthropology," pp. 339–340.

45. Ibid., p. 339.

46. Elena Padilla, "Nocorá: An Agrarian Reform Sugar Community" (Ph.D. diss., Columbia University, 1951), p. 72.

47. In the case of Black public intellectuals, the assumption has traditionally been that in order to embody the travails of one's community, intellectuals belonging to marginalized ethnic or racial groups must travel some distance from the groups to make their concerns "public," which may place them at a distance from the people when they claim to represent or, at least, identify themselves with. When these intellectuals go home again, their old comrades might look suspiciously at the fancy new car or the new suit acquired in their time away from community struggles over housing, race-related violence, or glass ceilings in professional employment. Hence, Black public intellectuals, like other Black middle-class professionals, have had to provide defenses for their personal success amid high Black unemployment, urban violence, and whatever else has been deemed to be a "Black problem," as if their successful dance with U.S. capitalism and racism required them to explain why they had become neither middle managers, athletes, nor crackheads. Hanchard, "Cultural Politics and Black Public Intellectuals," pp. 257–258.

48. Iris Young, "Polity and Group Difference: A Critique of the Ideal of Universal Citizenship," *Ethics* 99 (January 1989): 250–274.

49. Moya, "With Us or Without Us," p. 246.

50. Jurgen Habermas, *The Structural Transformation of the Public Sphere: An Inquiry into a Category of Bourgeois Society* (Cambridge, Mass.: Polity, 1989); Peter Uwe Hohendahl, "Critical Theory, Public Sphere and Culture: Jurgen Habermas and His Critics," *Public Sphere* (2001): 89–118.

Works Cited

Anderson, Elijah, and Douglass Massey. "The Sociology of Race in the U.S." In *Problems of the Century: Racial Stratification in America,* edited by E. Anderson and D. Massey, pp. 3–11. New York: Russell Sage Foundation, 2003.

Boynton, Robert. "The New Intellectuals." *Atlantic Monthly,* March 1995.

Brett, Judith. *Speaking Their Minds: Intellectuals and the Public Culture in Australia,* edited by Robert Dessaix. Sydney: ABC Books, 1998.

Bulmer, Martin. *The Chicago School of Sociology: Institutionalization, Diversity, and the Rise of Sociological Research.* Chicago: University of Chicago Press, 1984.

Castaneda, Jorge. *Utopia Unarmed: The Latin American Left after the Cold War.* New York: Random House, 1994.

Clifford, James, and George Marcus. *Writing Culture: The Poetics and Politics of Ethnography.* Berkeley: University of California Press, 1986.

Deegan, Mary Jo. *Jane Addams and the Men of the Chicago School, 1892–1918.* New Brunswick, N.J.: Transaction Books, 1986.

Dennis, Rutledge M., ed. *Research in Race and Ethnic Relations.* Vol. 10: *The Black Intellectuals.* Greenwich, Conn.: JAI Press, 1997.

Domínguez, Virginia. "For a Politics of Love and Rescue." *Cultural Anthropology* 15, 3 (2000): 361–393.

Dunlop, Tim. "If You Build It, They Will Come: Blogging and the New Citizenship." N.d. http://evatt. labor.net.au/publications/papers/91.html (accessed June 17, 2003).

Edgeworth, Kathryn. "Women as Public Intellectuals: The Exclusion of the Private in Public Intellectual Life." Paper presented at Women's Worlds 99: The 7th International Interdisciplinary Congress on Women. Tromso, Norway, June 20–26, 1999.

Habermas, Jurgen. *The Structural Transformation of the Public Sphere: An Inquiry into a Category of Bourgeois Society.* Cambridge, Mass.: Polity, 1989.

Hanchard, Michael. "Cultural Politics and Black Public Intellectuals." In *Disciplinarity and Dissent in Cultural Studies,* edited by Cary Nelson and Dilip Parameshwar Gaonkar, pp. 251–264. New York: Routledge, 1996.

Hohendahl, Peter Uwe. "Critical Theory, Public Sphere and Culture: Jurgen Habermas and His Critics." *Public Sphere* (2001): 89–118.

hooks, bell. *Talking Back: Thinking Feminist, Thinking Black.* Boston: South End Press, 1989.

Jacoby, Russell. *The Last Intellectual.* New York: Basic Books, 1987.

Juffer, Jane. "In Search of the Latino Public Sphere: Everywhere and Nowhere." *Nepantla: Views from the South* 4, 2 (2003): 263–268.

Kelley, Robin D. G. "'But a Local Phase of a World Problem': Black History's Global Vision, 1883–1950." *Journal of American History* 86, 3 (December 1999): 1045–1072.

Lauria-Perricelli, Antonio. "A Study in Historical and Critical Anthropology: The

Making of 'The People of Puerto Rico.'" Ph.D. diss., Anthropology, New School for Social Research, 1989.

Lindner, Rolf. *The Reportage of Urban Culture: Robert Park and the Chicago School.* Cambridge: Cambridge University Press, 1996.

Mendieta, Eduardo. "What Can Latinas/os Learn from Cornel West? The Latino Postcolonial Intellectual in the Age of the Exhaustion of Public Spheres." *Nepantla: Views from the South* 4, 2 (2003): 213–233.

Moya, Paula. "With Us or Without Us: The Development of a Latino Public Sphere." *Nepantla: Views from the South* 4, 2 (2003): 245–251.

Padilla, Elena. "Nocorá: An Agrarian Reform Sugar Community." Ph.D. diss., Anthropology, Columbia University, 1951.

———. "Puerto Rican Immigration in New York and Chicago: A Study of Comparative Assimilation." Master's thesis, Anthropology, University of Chicago, 1947.

Posner, Richard. *Public Intellectuals: A Study of Decline.* Cambridge, Mass.: Harvard University Press, 2001.

Pratt, Mary Louise. "Fieldwork in Common Places." In *Writing Culture: The Poetics and Politics of Ethnography,* edited by James Clifford and George Marcus, pp. 27–50. Berkeley: University of California Press, 1986.

Ramos-Zayas, Ana. "'La patria es valor y sacrificio': Nationalist Ideologies, Cultural Authenticity, and Community-Building among Puerto Ricans in Chicago." Ph.D. diss., Anthropology, Columbia University, 1997.

Said, Edward. "The Public Role of Writers and Intellectuals." Lecture broadcast on May 20, 2001, Melbourne Town Hall.

———. *Representations of the Intellectual.* London: Vintage, 1994.

Seda Bonilla, Eduardo. "El Pueblo de Puerto Rico: Dónde está el pueblo?" In *The Anthropology of the People of Puerto Rico,* edited by R. Duncan, pp. 65–75. San Juan: Inter American University of Puerto Rico, 1979.

Steward, Julian, Robert A. Manners, Eric R. Wolf, Elena Padilla Seda, Sidney W. Mintz, and Robert L. Scheele. *The People of Puerto Rico: A Study in Social Anthropology.* Urbana: University of Illinois Press, 1956.

Young, Iris. "Polity and Group Difference: A Critique of the Ideal of Universal Citizenship." *Ethics* 99 (January 1989): 250–274.

CONTRIBUTORS

NICHOLAS DE GENOVA has taught anthropology at Columbia University and Stanford University. In the autumn of 2009, he held the Swiss Chair in Mobility Studies as a visiting professor at the University of Bern. In the spring of 2010, he was a visiting professor in the Institute for Migration and Ethnic Studies at the University of Amsterdam. He is the author of *Working the Boundaries: Race, Space, and "Illegality" in Mexican Chicago* (2005), co-author of *Latino Crossings: Mexicans, Puerto Ricans, and the Politics of Race and Citizenship* (2003), editor of *Racial Transformations: Latinos and Asians Remaking the United States* (2006), and co-editor of *The Deportation Regime: Sovereignty, Space, and the Freedom of Movement* (2010). He is completing a new book, titled *The Spectacle of Terror: Immigration, Race, and the Homeland Security State.*

ZAIRE ZENIT DINZEY-FLORES is an assistant professor in the Department of Latino and Hispanic Caribbean Studies and the Department of Sociology at Rutgers University. She is currently working on a book manuscript that examines the use of gates to prevent crime in Puerto Rico and their consequences for urban community life in private and public housing communities. Her publications include "Temporary Housing, Permanent Communities: Public Housing Policy and Design in Puerto Rico" in the *Journal of Urban History* and "From the Disco to the Projects: Urban Spatial Aesthetics and Policy to the Beat of Reggaeton" in the *Centro Journal.*

ELENA PADILLA is a fellow at the New York Academy of Medicine and was previously a scholar-in-residence at Saint Barnabas Hospital in the Bronx. After receiving her B.A. from the University of Puerto Rico, she was awarded a scholarship for graduate study at the University of Chicago, where she earned an M.A. in anthropology. Upon earning her doctorate from Columbia

University, where she was a co-author of *The People of Puerto Rico* (1956), she pursued advanced studies in anthropology and economic history at the London School of Economics. She is author of several books and articles related to U.S. Puerto Ricans including *Up from Puerto Rico* (1958).

ANA Y. RAMOS-ZAYAS is an associate professor in the Department of Anthropology and the Department of Latino and Hispanic Caribbean Studies at Rutgers University–New Brunswick. She is the author of *National Performances: Class, Race, and Space in Puerto Rican Chicago* (2003) and co-author of *Latino Crossings: Mexicans, Puerto Ricans and the Politics of Race and Citizenship* (2003). She has also published various articles on issues of citizenship, race, and space in relation to U.S. Latinos and Latin American populations. Her current work—*Street Therapists: Race, Affect, and Neoliberal Personhood in Latino Newark*—focuses on contemporary conceptions of "racial democracy," affect, and neoliberalism among Brazilians and Puerto Ricans in Newark, New Jersey, Belo Horizonte, Brazil, and Santurce, Puerto Rico.

MÉRIDA M. RÚA is an associate professor of Latina/o studies and American studies at Williams College. Her research explores the complex ethnoracial dimensions of identity and space and their necessary connections through an analysis of the history and politics of Puerto Rican identity and community life in the city of Chicago. She is completing her first book, *A Grounded Identidad: Places of Memory and Personhood in Chicago's Puerto Rican Neighborhoods*.

ARLENE TORRES is the director of the City University of New York's Latino Faculty Initiative. As a cultural anthropologist who focuses on the study of race and ethnicity, she has conducted research in the Anglophone and Hispanic Caribbean and in the United States. Her current research builds upon the work "Collecting Puerto Ricans" in Kevin Yelvington's *Afro-Atlantic Dialogues: Anthropology in the Diaspora* (2004), which focuses on the racialization of ethnic groups in museum settings. Other published works include volumes 1 and 2 of *Blackness in Latin America and the Caribbean: Social Dynamics and Cultural Transformations* (1998), co-edited with Norman E. Whitten Jr. As a public intellectual, Torres serves as a member of the advisory board and consultant to a national project on race, "Understanding Race and Human Variation: A Public Education Program," supported by the American Anthropological Association, the Ford Foundation, and National Science Foundation.

INDEX

Page numbers in *italics* refer to material in the original master's thesis, *Puerto Rican Immigrants in New York and Chicago* by Elena Padilla.

LATINOS IN CHICAGO AND THE MIDWEST

Pots of Promise: Mexicans and Pottery at Hull-House, 1920–40
  Edited by Cheryl R. Ganz and Margaret Strobel
Moving Beyond Borders: Julian Samora and the Establishment of Latino
  Studies   *Edited by Alberto López Pulido, Barbara Driscoll de Alvarado,
  and Carmen Samora*
¡Marcha! Latino Chicago and the Immigrant Rights Movement
  Edited by Amalia Pallares and Nilda Flores-González
Bringing Aztlán to Chicago: My Life, My Work, My Art
  *José Gamaliel González, edited and with an introduction
  by Marc Zimmerman*
Latino Urban Ethnography and the Work of Elena Padilla
  Edited by Mérida M. Rúa

The University of Illinois Press
is a founding member of the
Association of American University Presses.

Composed in 10/12 Sabon
by Celia Shapland
at the University of Illinois Press
Manufactured by Cushing-Malloy, Inc.

University of Illinois Press
1325 South Oak Street
Champaign, IL 61820-6903
www.press.uillinois.edu